Wildly Affordable Organic

WILDLY AFFORDABLE
ORGANIC

Eat Fabulous Food,
Get Healthy, and Save the Planet—
All on $5 a Day or Less

Linda Watson

Da Capo

LIFE
LONG

A MEMBER OF THE PERSEUS BOOKS GROUP

Editorial production by Lori Hobkirk at the Book Factory.
Designed in 11-point Caslon by Cynthia Young at Sagecraft.

Cataloging-in-Publication data for this book is available from the Library of Congress.

First Da Capo Press edition 2011
ISBN: 978-0-7382-1468-9

Published by Da Capo Press
A Member of the Perseus Books Group
www.dacapopress.com

Da Capo Press books are available at special discounts for bulk purchases in the U.S. by corporations, institutions, and other organizations. For more information, please contact the Special Markets Department at the Perseus Books Group, 2300 Chestnut Street, Suite 200, Philadelphia, PA, 19103, or call (800) 810-4145, ext. 5000, or e-mail special.markets@perseusbooks.com.

Note: This book is intended only as an informative guide for those wishing to know more about health issues. In no way is this book intended to replace, countermand, or conflict with the advice given to you by your own physician. The ultimate decision concerning care should be made between you and your doctor. We strongly recommend you follow his or her advice. Information in this book is general and is offered with no guarantees on the part of the authors or Da Capo Press. The author and publisher disclaim all liability in connection with the use of this book.

To my husband Bruce for his unflagging support and willingness to try anything, and to his mother, Catherine Watson, who showed me that thrift, great food, and warm hospitality go hand in hand in hand.

Contents

18 Breads 151

22 Something from Nothing 191

23 Vegetables and Side Dishes 200

24 Desserts 211

Part V
Resources 229

Part I

Discovering the Wildly Affordable Organic Life

Introduction
Why Cook for Good?

If you've wanted to eat like it matters but felt you couldn't afford it, *Wildly Affordable Organic* is for you. It's easy to think that "organic" or "sustainable" are code words for "too expensive." More people than ever want to eat organic food, and the cost of energy is shooting up like genetically modified corn, but eating green doesn't have to mean eating up all your money. You just need to know what to buy and how to get the most out of it.

Use this book to save money, eat delicious food, and make a difference—helping yourself, your family and community, and your planet. You're on the right path even if you only use this book like any other cookbook: one recipe at a time. You can gain more value by following the tips for streamlining meals, from shopping and cooking to storing food and washing dishes. You can take big steps toward living the *Wildly Affordable Organic* life in only twenty minutes a day by following the starter plan, or you can go super-efficient and thrifty on the full seasonal program—cooking in one or two big sessions that take about five hours a week, plus a little bit of warming up and cooking each day. This is probably less time than you would spend going to a restaurant, ordering food, waiting to be served, and paying every night. You can afford organic, sustainable ingredients because you use every scrap.

Slow global warming with easy, scrumptious meals cooked from scratch? Lose weight, save money, and save the polar bears at the same time? Yes! Although *Wildly Affordable Organic* can't do everything—it won't give you a great singing voice or teach you to tango—it *will* help you harness the power of the plate to make the world better.

Immediate and Lasting Benefits
You see immediate benefits when you live the *Wildly Affordable Organic* life.

Save Money
Each seasonal shopping list in *WAO* shows two sets of prices (page 64). The "green" prices show how much you can save cooking with mostly organic or sustainably and kindly raised

ingredients. The "thrifty" prices show how to save even more by picking ingredients with a focus on cost.

Green meals average less than $5 a day per person, $4.97 if you're counting pennies (and who isn't?).[1] Thrifty meals average only $3.21 a day. Go all green if you can, all thrifty if you must, or create a mix that suits you. You'll still be using the same wildly good recipes, menus, and cooking sessions. Cooking fresh, seasonal food from scratch saves the average family hundreds or thousands of dollars a year on their grocery bills. Families who currently eat out often will see even bigger savings.

Even when including all the ingredients for three meals a day and a snack, *Wildly Affordable Organic* meals cost less than the food-stamp allowance in North Carolina, where I track prices. The government will provide up to $5.49 a day per person to help a family of four with no other means to survive.[2] This book shows you how to not just survive but *thrive* on less than $5 using the green prices. For a family of four, that means having an extra $2.08 a day or $760 a year to splurge.

For a national perspective, look at the USDA's meal plans, which track the cost of eating at home at four levels.[3] The USDA's low-cost plan costs 25 percent more than the *Wildly Affordable Organic* green meals. The USDA's "liberal" plan costs a whopping 90 percent more, which I call downright extravagant. A family of four would save $6,500 a year switching from the USDA extravagant plan to the *WAO* green prices.

Want to go lower? *WAO*'s thrifty prices average only $3.21 a day. Save $2.28 a day compared to the North Carolina food-stamp allowance and $1.57 compared to the UDSA's own thrifty plan, its lowest level. A family of four would save over $9,000 a year switching from the USDA extravagant plan to the *WAO*'s thrifty prices!

What's more, these prices show worst-case scenarios—with no coupons, membership clubs, stocking up on sale items, or homegrown vegetables. The prices even include extra food to supplement the Something from Nothing recipes (page 191). So clip a few coupons, stock up during sales, buy ice cream peaches (page 35), and feed your Stoup (page 198) to rack up even more savings.

What do these numbers mean to you? Although the prices in your community may be a little higher or a little lower, you still save loads of money. That's true even if you already cook most meals at home. See the savings in your grocery bills from week one. Watch for savings in your medical bills too, as eating fresh fruits and vegetables plus plenty of whole grains and beans pays off in improved health. My advisers, readers, and students say that the *Wildly Affordably Organic* life is healthy, realistic, and kid friendly.

Eat Well

Saving money doesn't mean subsisting literally on peanuts. You'll be cooking fresh, seasonal food that's so delicious that you'd want to eat this way even if a budget was the last thing on your mind. From the first time you smell homemade bread baking in the oven or dish up fresh peach ice cream, you'll wonder why you ever ate any other way. Eating with the seasons gives you maximum flavor and built-in variety. Even asparagus, strawberries, and blueberries are affordable when purchased at their peak.

A tasty, satisfying breakfast puts a smile on your face and fuels your day. Wake up to peanut butter on toasted homemade bread, blueberry pancakes with eggs, sweet raisin flatbread, oatmeal, and homemade yogurt.

For maximum family appeal, many lunches and dinners feature healthy versions of dishes familiar from eating out, such as pizza, burritos, spicy Asian noodles, and chili. Enjoy a variety of pasta with homemade sauces, bean stews, and roasted or baked dishes.

Lots of fruit and whole grains make the scrumptious desserts nutritious too. Dig into strawberry shortcake, peach ice cream, blueberry pie, oatmeal-raisin cookies, carrot cake, pudding, and chocolate upside-down cake.

Make a Difference

Cooking efficiently and eating fresh, seasonal food really do let you make the world a better place.

On a personal and family level, you'll create a welcoming home full of the smells and tastes of terrific food—and you'll set the example of healthy eating. *Wildly Affordable Organic* will reduce your "what's for dinner?" stress with dozens of tips and tools, from the seasonal menus and shopping lists to ways to cook ahead and reduce dishwashing. Serving less sugar and fewer processed foods to your family will make them calmer and more focused. And you'll lose weight and feel better by eliminating trans fats, preservatives, and artificial anything from your diet.

Gain confidence by learning to cook on a very low budget to help you through any tough times. Make your kitchen a family space where kids learn the fascinating transformations of cooking and develop skills they will need when they have their own kitchens. You might learn something from them too: it's easier to have a heart-to-heart talk at home than at McBurger.

You'll also help your community. Buying from local farmers throughout the year encourages them to continue growing good food near you. You support your local economy and make your country safer: it's harder for the weather, terrorists, or just bad luck to take down a rich network of many local farms. It's also easier to trace and fix any problems, which will be smaller in scope than for a huge industrial source.

What's more, the whole world benefits when you cut back on your use of fossil fuels by minimizing the transportation of food grown far away and the storage of food grown long ago. Organic and sustainable farming encourages deep root growth, builds carbon in the soil, prevents erosion, and helps plants survive drought. You'll save energy by avoiding processed food and eating mostly plants. This all saves money, so you can afford to eat better dairy and eggs: those from kindly and sustainably raised animals. You also have the option to eat better meat and fish from animals raised the old-fashioned way. Refuse to support the modern cruelty of factory farming.

Less fossil fuel, less pollution, and less waste shrink your carbon footprint and slow global warming. You can literally help the polar bears and slow the rising of the seas by eating melons in August and apples in October. You make the world a happier, safer, kinder place when you live a *Wildly Affordable Organic* life.

Making the Plans Work for You and Your Family

The next part of the book streamlines the steps of feeding your family—from navigating a farmers' market to unlocking the power of your freezer. Learn how to buy and store bulk purchases and use a kitchen scale.

The third part covers the super-efficient menus, shopping lists, and cooking plans by the season. Then, finally this book starts to look like a traditional cookbook, with over a hundred delicious, healthy, and easy recipes.

I usually follow a *Wildly Affordable Organic* seasonal cooking plan, so most weeks I cook a few dishes and get ready on one evening, and then I cook for a few hours the next day. But sometimes it's better to have one big cooking afternoon every week. You can cook in batches throughout the week too. If you keep a few frozen meals on hand, you'll always have something ready if you get sick or need to spend extra time at work or with your family.

You Don't Have to Do It All or All at Once

The beauty of cooking from scratch is that you can go as organic and as local as your budget allows. Start with a big pot of beans every week. Have high-protein pasta with quick homemade tomato sauce instead of going out for fast food. Even if you stop there, you are still way ahead.

Better yet, learn something new every week or so. Try the easy core recipes to make yeast bread, pudding, tomato sauce, and more. Then add variety by trying related recipes that build on your new skills. Even yogurt, blueberry pie, and pizza are simple to make once you learn a few tricks.

Learn how to squeeze the most out of your money at the grocery store or farmers' market. Take a minute to start a Stoup container (page 198) or broth jar (page 191) and you'll quit throwing your food dollars down the drain. Save frustration and money with a simple five-minute check every night.

With *Wildly Affordable Organic*, you can choose how you want to save and then use the extra energy and money to save more. Let's get started!

The Experiment

A Summer on a Very Low Budget

Inspiration: Michael Pollan and the Food Stamp Challenge

I began my experiment in thrifty, delicious eating when the philosophy of food ran smack into the politics of food in the summer of 2007. On the philosophical side, Michael Pollan linked the supermarket's middle aisles to the obesity epidemic, citing research that showed that "the rules of the food game in America are organized in such a way that if you are eating on a budget, the most rational economic strategy is to eat badly—and get fat."[1] On the political side, several politicians and antihunger activists showed what eating badly looked like when they took the "Food Stamp Challenge," living on the average national food-stamp allowance of a dollar a meal. I was particularly irritated by Ohio Congressman Tim Ryan's slap-dash approach, with his aides throwing two-ounce bags of coffee into his cart and the Congressman skipping meals. When airport security seized his stash of peanut butter and jelly, he was looking at thirty-six hours with nothing but cornmeal. He wound up cheating with Dunkin' Donuts, peanuts, and a pork chop, blogging "It is nearly IMPOSSIBLE to make [do] on this amount of money."[2]

Nonsense, I thought. These men must not be cooks. A dollar a meal is tight, but it doesn't mean we have to pick Cheetos over carrots. The goal should not be maximum calories but maximum nutrition. The maximum-calories idea had been around for years: that poor people are often fat because they don't have the money to eat food that would allow them to be thin. But we get fat by eating too many calories. Surely buying better food to move closer to the ideal number of calories and nutrients is both possible and desirable.

I found myself chuffing in the grocery store: "Look, this whole bag of dried beans is only seventy-nine cents a pound . . . and it's not even on sale. That's about eight cents a serving." I was garumphing at the farmers' market too: "Here's a flat of delicious local strawberries for fifteen dollars. That's about fifty cents a serving. Why do people insist that people who don't have much money can only drink soda and eat potato chips?"

7

After nearly a week of these mental calculations, I got bored with the limited answers my growling produced. Sure, some foods were both cheap and nutritious. But could I really get by on a dollar a meal? Could I enjoy it?

That night at dinner, I broached the idea to my husband, Bruce. What if I tried the food-stamp diet for three weeks, eating on $1 a meal like Congressman Ryan? But what if I moved the source of our food around to show the options? We are within walking distance of a Whole Foods and a Food Lion, a regional chain grocery. And we can reach the farmers' market where we usually buy our fruits and vegetables by bus, even if somewhat awkwardly. What if we did week one at the Food Lion, week two at the Whole Foods, and week three at the farmers' market? At the end of that time, we'd know a good deal more about eating on the budget our government allows.

My husband looked only mildly horrified. "You can eat extra if you want," I said. "I'll just cook for both of us to that budget and you can have extras if you want."

"No, I'll do it with you. Might as well see just how hungry we get."

You can see why I love him.

"Well," he added, "At least we'll lose some weight."

Baseline: Where Did We Start?

Bruce and I were already flexitarians. I don't buy or cook meat, but I do eat it socially when the choices are "ribs" or "rude." Bruce eats more meat than I do, sometimes buying organic turkey for sandwiches and eating more meat when we travel or visit.

I bought mostly organic and local food at the North Carolina Farmers' Market, Whole Foods, and local grocery chains. We grew a few vegetables, plus blueberries and figs. A typical menu for a day would be peanut butter on toast for breakfast with juice and then beans for one meal and high-protein pasta for the other meal. This may sound tedious, but with a variety of beans, starches, sauces, and lots of fruits and vegetables, we really had a parade of international dishes. We enjoyed lots of vegetables and fruit as well as ice cream and other sweets. Pizza and egg dishes added variety.

So we started with a pretty thrifty and healthy diet. But significant chunks of it couldn't be supported on a food-stamp diet. I wrote in my journal before we started that "The balsamic vinegar, organic butter, and Ben & Jerry's ice cream are out. And I'll have to stop supporting our excellent local brewers for the duration. I will be losing some weight indeed."

Getting Ready: The Rules

In the last few days before we started the dollar-a-meal experiment, we ate or froze the perishables we had on hand. I studied the supermarket's flyer and drafted a menu for week one. I couldn't know what we could afford until I checked prices at the store, so I set priorities: core nutrition came first—enough protein and carbs to keep us going. Add vegetables and fruit to balance the meals and then bring in nutritious desserts to keep everyone happy.

I studied news reports about the national Food Stamp Challenge and the rules for shopping with food stamps. My goal was to make these weeks a realistic test of what a couple on food stamps might be willing and able to do. Here are the rules that came out of all that thinking:

- Budget is king. Nothing can make us spend more than $1 a meal per person.
- Nutrition is essential. The menus must provide balanced nutrition, including enough protein and five fruits and vegetables each day.
- No cheating with staples. Participants in the national challenge could use unlimited staples from their cupboards. I'll use limited staples plus buy all my oil and one long-term staple every week.
- No crazy cooking. I'll cook from scratch but not go overboard. Homemade ravioli may be inexpensive, but it fails the reality test.
- Get some satisfaction. Meals must be tasty and satisfying enough to let us resist the siren call of chips and packaged cookies.
- Be ourselves. I would only buy food we would ordinarily eat—no trans-fat–filled sausages, no matter what the savings.
- Be honest. Report our actual experiences, good or bad.

Adding a Job to the Mix

Two days before we stared the experiment I got a call from the new boss where I used to work. Doris said the person who had my old job was suddenly gone and no one else knew the computer system. Could I help?

"Let me think about it and talk with Bruce." I didn't want to go back to the job permanently, but this would ward off criticism that my experiment wasn't realistic. I could hear Larry King now: "So, Linda, you say you were able to eat well on a buck a meal. But what about someone with a *real* job?"

If I took my old job back, I would not only be working irregular hours with overtime, but I'd have to squeeze in my regular website-design work. Doing this wouldn't compare to some of the multijob nightmares people on food stamps live with, but it was better than working at home.

I called Doris back. "When do I start?"

First Shopping Trip on a Tight Budget

Our dollar-a-meal experiment would start on my first day at work. I had trouble sleeping the night before, being both excited and worried about the experiment. Would I be able to put together enough food to keep us healthy and satisfied? Would it be good enough that we'd stick with it? I also thought about families who couldn't shrug and say, "Give me the extra-virgin olive oil and a wedge of Parm, please—and a pork chop for my friend."

The Price of Small Quantities

I worked a full eight-hour day, then went grocery shopping on the way home with $42 in an envelope and a sketch of the week's menus.

I started in the center aisles, getting essential beans, rice, and flour. My first surprise came right away. Even the cheapest white rice was 79 cents a pound. I was used to spending ten bucks for fifteen pounds of top-notch Basmati rice at a buying club. Mediocre rice, bought one pound at a time, cost 18 percent more than excellent rice bought in bulk.

I put bread flour and whole wheat flour into the cart along with the least expensive yeast available. Usually I buy a pound of yeast a year, spending $6 to make sixty-four bowls of dough, about 9 cents for a loaf of bread. The three-pack I bought was $1.47, costing 40 cents more for every loaf.

Sugar gave me the bulk shock again. I bought the smallest bag available: two pounds for $1.19. Four pounds cost only $1.97. The smaller bag cost 10 cents more a pound.

And on the surprises went, through beans, pasta, and condiments. I tallied my buys and saw that it was looking good. This is a snap, I thought. I might be able to afford the tea and ice cream at the bottom of the list.

But the dairy department slapped the smugness right out of me. The smallest amount of butter I could buy was a half-pound, or two sticks. Those sticks cost $1.99, compared to $3.79 for a whole pound. Store-brand large eggs were $1.79 a dozen.

Clang! I was over my limit and hadn't even hit the produce section yet. I was tired and hungry after an hour of shopping. I returned food I couldn't afford, reworked the menus, and headed for produce.

Budget Rage

While returning a box of rotini, I heard a young couple having a flirty argument about which type of sauce to buy. "One is enough, Honey," simpered the girl. "Baby, get them both. You know it will make you happy." Happy! Feh. I restrained myself from hurling a garlic press and marveled that I'd become so humorless and bitter in only . . . could it be? . . . an hour and a half of shopping.

I slogged on to produce, stopping to get a smaller, cheaper jar of peanut butter. I'd re-claimed nearly six dollars of my budget, enough for a pound of carrots, cabbage, garlic, and five onions. Again, I felt the pang of not buying in bulk. The pound of carrots cost a dollar, but ten pounds cost only six dollars. Even my usual choice, a five-pound bag of organic carrots, cost only 80 cents a pound. It takes money to save money.

Checking Out an Extra Fee

I checked the last item off my list and went to check out. I asked the cashier if food-stamp recipients had to pay taxes on food.

"Oh, yeah," she said, giving me the suspicious glance that I would get with any inquiries about food stamps. "And we charge a fifty-cent processing fee too."

"A fee? For taking food stamps?"

"That's right. You got your card?"

"No, just cash today," I said. Was charging a fee even legal? (It's not, I learned later. Was this clerk mistaken, trying to discourage customers from food stamps, or pocketing the fees? I'll never know.)

I found I'd been holding my breath while the cashier rang up the last dozen items. Phew! My total was only $41.92 including tax. My stomach rumbled as I rolled the cart out to the car, two hours after I'd entered. Clearly, shopping on a budget was harder than it seemed.

Home at Last

"Where have you been? I was getting worried," said Bruce when I got home. "I already fed the cat."

"Shopping."

"All this time?"

"You have no idea."

"Well, what's for dinner? It's time to feed me."

"It's our last big splash tonight." I put water on to boil and then went upstairs to change while he brought in the groceries. No need to rush any ice cream into the freezer. Then I put the groceries away, organized so that it was clear what could be used in the coming week.

I made our standard low-energy work-night dinner: rotini with bottled sauce and fresh-grated parmesan, frozen peas with vinaigrette, and garlic toast. I had the last two glasses in the last bottle of wine in the house. We split an apple and then polished off the last of a pint of yuppie ice cream—altogether a typical meal, but enriched by a certain nostalgic air. Ah, the last wine! The last ice cream!

While Bruce washed the dishes, I made split pea soup to cook overnight in the slow cooker. Then I set up the bread machine to make French bread, which doesn't use milk. After setting the timer so the bread would be ready when we got up, I staggered upstairs to bed.

The First Day Is the Worst

I had trouble sleeping again. Had I added enough water to the pea soup? Did the timer for the bread machine indicate when the machine would start or stop?

Finally, at about 2:30 in the morning, I crept down to the kitchen. Delicious smells wafted up the stairs to meet me. The soup looked fine and the bread was rising nicely, so it would be ready in just an hour or so. Still, better cold bread for breakfast than raw dough.

When the alarm went off at seven, I trotted happily back to the kitchen, looking forward to toast made with homemade bread. First thing: coffee. The store-brand grounds were chunkier than the drip-filter grind I was used to, but it smelled okay. While the coffee perked, I went to check on the bread.

Where was it? I looked across the kitchen through the domed glass lid of the machine, expecting to see a crusty dome of bread underneath. I lifted the lid and looked inside. *Quelle horreur!* The bread—she was flat! I twisted the cylindrical bread pan to release it and then tamped out the bread. Just at that moment, Bruce came in the kitchen.

"What's that?" he asked, seeing me hold a cylinder of bread that was eight inches wide but only two inches tall, not the good foot-long loaf that I'd expected.

"Our bread."

"We're already doomed!"

No Extra Food to Make Up for Cooking Mistakes

"Have some orange juice and I'll make toast."

I poured myself a cup of coffee. Thin and bitter, it had an oily sheen on top. Cheap office coffee—the stuff I'd avoided for years.

I went to work on the dense, hard-crusted bread. Using a serrated knife, I sliced two pieces of bread for toast. There was no way the half-loaf that remained would provide three days of toast and a sandwich meal.

When the toaster went off, I poured another cup of coffee and spread peanut butter on the toast. The peanut butter began to melt and ooze off the bread. We *are* already doomed, I thought, bringing the plates into the dining room.

The toast and bread tasted good, though, even if it was messier than with name-brand peanut butter. But I rediscovered why I always had orange juice with peanut butter toast: coffee and peanut butter taste terrible together. Because Bruce barely had enough OJ for the week, trading coffee for juice wasn't an option. I washed down the toast with water. Better, but not the Breakfast of Champions.

And how was the juice? "Drinkable," Bruce said. It was not tropical like the pineapple-orange-banana mix he usually had, but it would do. I smiled, glad he was being such a trooper about the experiment.

I drank my third cup of coffee while dishing out soup for lunch and refrigerating the rest. I'd planned for us to have a half-slice of bread with the soup for lunch, but there wasn't enough. I showed Bruce where his lunch was and dashed off to work.

Paying for Cheap Coffee

I drank hot water at work instead of my usual tea. By 10:00 I could feel that ache in my bones that a caffeine addict feels when deprived of her usual dose. What was that about? I'd had three full cups of coffee at home.

At lunch I began eating my tasty if monotonous meal. Split pea soup doesn't need a ham bone—just a few carrots and onions. (Although now I know that tahini and spices make it better.) As other staffers came in with their lunches, I gave myself a pep talk to keep up my resistance to the cheese blintzes and other goodies left over from a weekend fundraiser. Congressman Ryan might have snarfed down airport peanuts, but I would be stronger.

By three o'clock I had a blinding headache. No wonder: new budget, new/old job, and not enough caffeine. I fought the nausea, aware of the irony of not wanting to throw up because I didn't want to waste any food. This would turn out to be the low point in the experiment.

Tasty Cabbage and High Hopes

Dinner was the first bright spot in our diet experiment. My original menu had called for high-protein rotini with tomato sauce and whatever had been the cheapest dark-green vegetable at the store. But even a small bag of frozen spinach had been too costly. What to do with cabbage? I simplified a recipe for braised cabbage, which turned out to be surprisingly rich and sweet. The noodles and sauce were tasty, although corn oil is no replacement for olive oil. We split a banana for dessert and felt lucky to have it.

After dinner I froze the remaining split pea soup into three double-serving packages for use later in the week and started a pound of pinto beans in the slow cooker. My headache was gone. I felt full of hope about the rest of the week.

"Honey, We've Got to Talk"

That dinner turned out to be the first of many good meals that week. I figured out how to make bread with the new type of yeast. We had what would become the basis for the Cook for Good menus: bean stews, fresh fruit and vegetables, and dessert every day.

On the last night of week one, when we were enjoying Ginger-Glazed Carrot Cake (page 223), Bruce said the words dreaded in marriages everywhere: "Honey, we've got to talk."

Oh no, I thought. He's had too many carrots, too much cabbage and onions. He's going tell me he wants a woman who will give him cheesecake!

"I hadn't wanted to mention this, but . . ." Oh no! " . . . I'm feeling really good. The food's been great, of course. This cake is fantastic. But I'm also sleeping less and more alert. I'm in a better mood. And I've even lost a couple of pounds without feeling hungry."

"You're right," I said. "I'm feeling better too—brighter, more energetic. I've lost a couple of pounds too. And have you noticed the trash?"

"Yes, we barely filled half a trash bag this week."

"I didn't realize how much packaging we were throwing out. Even doing this for just a few weeks, we'll make a difference."

"That's what I want to talk about," he said. "I don't think this should be a short experiment. This is how I want to live: on real food cooked from scratch. If our food can be this good for a dollar, what can it be like for a little more?"

The Results: Saving Money Leads to Other Savings

We revised the experiment and tried variations for three more months. First, I raised the budget to $1.53 a meal, the actual amount of food stamps then allotted in North Carolina for a couple with no other money to spend on food. I don't think I've ever felt as rich as I did at the start of the second week, when I took my extra 53 cents a meal to the farmers' market and loaded up on peaches, tomatoes, and peppers.

Because food stamps are allocated monthly, I managed our budget on a monthly rather than a weekly basis. This made "bulk" purchases like a pound of butter or a bottle of mustard sensible again. The one-week limit of the original challenge forces participants to buy the smallest and most expensive sizes available.

After that first terrible day, we never felt hungry or deprived. After the first week, I switched from bad-tasting cheap coffee to pretty good cheap tea, which tastes fine with peanut butter. I learned which yeast to buy and began developing no-knead bread recipes that don't require a bread machine or kneading. I learned where to scrimp and where to splurge. I scoured old cookbooks and interviewed older cooks, looking for easy, thrifty recipes made from basic ingredients. And I kept refining my cooking style to make the best use of everything: food, time, energy, and other resources. The lively food scene on the Internet inspired some discoveries. Others were rediscoveries of techniques that pioneer and Depression-era cooks used. Bruce agreed to be my official Taster, keeping me from saving money at the expense of flavor.

We weren't stingy, either. I took cookies to book club, cupcakes to friends who'd had a death in the family, invited friends over for dinner, and brought a dish to community suppers.

Best of all, the food was delicious: spicy beans and rice, fragrant tomato sauce on pasta, burritos, homemade pizza, bread, and yogurt. Fruit and plenty of vegetables. Dessert, made from scratch, every day: strawberry shortcake, peach ice cream, chocolate cookies, and more.

I shopped for a month at chain supermarkets and the state farmers' market, improved the list, and did it again. Then I took my improved and tested list to Whole Foods and the Durham Farmers' Market, buying organic and sustainably raised ingredients. Even this "yuppie" diet was less than two dollars a meal.

Finally, we took all we'd learned and did another week on a dollar a meal, back at our thrifty store but with a summer of learning. What a difference! Terrific food and no stress—that's when I knew I had to share what I'd learned. After three years of refinement, the result is *Wildly Affordable Organic*.

A Way of Life, Not Just an Experiment

The results of these experiments were so good that they permanently changed the way we cook and eat. Except for a few splurges and tests for new recipes, we follow the *Wildly Affordable Organic* seasonal menus. I pay the "green" prices shown in the seasonal shopping lists to get mostly organic, kindly raised, and local food. I feel more connected with my community and the seasons. I've reached my ideal weight and am full of energy.

After years of working in politics, voting with my fork seems direct and effective. We still need laws to ensure that people, animals, and the planet are treated right, but knowing that our shopping habits are not funding brutal factory farms or pesticides that harm workers and the environment feels good. We support farmers who enhance their land and are buying time for scientists and governments to cope with global warming.

Easy to Do, Hard to Figure Out

Cooking on a tight budget was hard at first. It takes a lot of planning or experience. Cooking from scratch takes time and so does cleaning up. Some nights I stayed up well past bedtime waiting for the bread to cool because I had started baking it too late. I ruined several loaves of bread and many batches of yogurt.

But I got the hang of it and you can too. I was raised in a canned-soup and bakery-bread household where we always had plenty to eat. Cooking from scratch with the seasons and making the best use of every bite was new to me. If this is new territory for you too, then please use this book as a guide to help you get it right the first time.

Part II

Streamlining Life
in the Kitchen

2

Planning Strategies
Using Basic Ingredients

Stock your kitchen the way you pack your suitcase: with a mix-and-match set of the best pieces available. Scrimp or splurge on core ingredients and use them in everything (page 21). Go as organic as your budget allows for protein, oil, and grain, but going upscale on sugar, cocoa, or hot sauce won't make a big difference in your level of enjoyment. Although prepared food that is 100 percent organic is often expensive, food cooked from scratch using mostly organic ingredients is wildly affordable.

Take bread, for example. Invest in organic flour and oil, but use conventional yeast and salt. Not only will your bread be closer to your organic goal, but that organic flour also ups the organic level for your pancakes, pizza, and gravy.

When you cook from a small palette, you'll see similarities between recipes. Bread dough and pizza dough are nearly the same, but you can't tell that from buying a plastic-wrapped loaf or heating up a frozen disk. Start making these connections and watch your cooking skills improve.

Enjoy the savings of buying in larger sizes while still using up your supplies while they are fresh. Save money buying larger bags of flour instead of buying mixes or processed food. When you bake from scratch, you have no trouble using a can of baking powder during its year of prime rising ability. However, your baking powder may become dusty and tired if you make biscuits or cakes from scratch only a few times a year. Then, when your scratch-made cake fails, you may wrongly conclude that mixes give better results.

Maybe you are trying to up your locavore score. Unless you live near the Ragu plant in Owenboro, Kentucky, it may be hard to claim bottled tomato sauce as local. But it's easy to give your sauce a local accent using onions and herbs grown nearby. Use local tomatoes in season too.

Dried spices exhale a little flavor every day. Prepared spice mixes can be convenient, but they reduce the turnover on your core spices. Don't buy pumpkin-pie spice that you then use once a year until it tastes like dust. Instead, buy cinnamon and nutmeg to use in cookies, egg dishes, and chilies all year round. Let your cumin work for you in Mexican, Cuban, and Indian dishes.

In the end, what you don't buy is most important. My grocery list never includes guar gum, polysorbate 60, or disodium guanylate. They aren't tempting impulse purchases, either. Buy basic ingredients and cook from scratch to keep your family safe from additives, preservatives, and other chemicals that mask the lack of quality in processed food.

Buy Mostly Certified Organic

Buy certified organic ingredients when you can afford to and when doing so makes sense. You'll be making the best choice for your family, the workers who grow the food, and the environment. But some ingredients aren't available in a certified organic form, and some are so expensive that they put your food budget through the roof. And honey, unfortunately, is so often not what it claims—sometimes it's not even honey at all—that I recommend local and trusted over organic (page 24).

Many small farmers at farmers' markets use sustainable practices and organic techniques but can't afford to be certified. Visit your market's website to check out vendors in advance and talk with farmers at the market. Avoid falling for false claims by looking for farmers who are members of their local agricultural associations and who participate in farm tours.

The Scrimp or Splurge Twenty

During my experimental summer, I cut corners on everything in my quest to make dollar meals. Some of my thrifty choices were disasters, but some were surprisingly unnoticeable. I've saved money ever since. Here's how you can too.

Check for updates to specific recommendations at CookforGood.com/wao.

Olive Oil vs. Vinegar

Of all the cheap ingredients I tried, olive oil surprised me most. Food writers edge into erotic territory with their longing for an extra-virgin olive oil with a floral fragrance, good cling, and a fresh bite. But store-brand, virgin olive oil does the job. Watch for sales and store your extra bottles in a cool, dark place. I now use either Newman's Own Organics or store-brand organic olive oil for everything, even pesto.

Save your money to get good vinegar. Apple-cider vinegar is the most affordable acceptable vinegar. The cheaper white vinegar doesn't have enough flavor for a dressing. Cheap balsamic is worse than no balsamic.

Splurge by getting a good red-wine or balsamic vinegar for dressing salads and drizzling over vegetables. I use Whole Foods' 365 Organic Balsamic Vinegar of Modena.

Sugar vs. Flour

White sugar tastes like white sugar and has no nutritional value beyond calories, so it's one of the last ingredients I would choose to upgrade. Look for 100 percent beet sugar if you want to avoid sugar that has been processed using bone char or "natural charcoal" made

TABLE 2.1

Scrimp or Splurge

SCRIMP	SPLURGE
olive oil	red-wine or balsamic vinegar
sugar	flour
rice	eggs
dried beans	milk, butter, and cheese
pasta	peanut butter
onions	potatoes
fruit you peel (bananas & peaches)	fruit you can't peel (strawberries & apples)
maple syrup	honey
dried herbs and spices	garlic
tea	coffee

from cow bones. The prices and availability of organic and unbleached sugar get better all the time, so if you can't find beet sugar, look for cane sugar made without bone char or animal products,[1] such as Florida Crystals Natural Cane Sugar. Organic sugar cannot be made with bone char, but it costs several times as much as plain sugar.

Flour, however, provides taste, nutrition, and the gluten needed to support rising bread dough. Good flour elevates your baked goods for a minimal investment.

For the best bread, use fresh flour with at least four grams of protein per quarter cup. The food labels are rough measures, and the level of protein varies by season, field, and farming practice. But the four-gram rule will help you avoid flour known to be low in the protein-rich gluten that creates the structure that lets the bread rise.

That's why flour is one of the few products that I recommend buying from well-known companies. For my personal use I usually buy King Arthur brand flour or the Whole Foods store brand. Rose Levy Beranbaum, author of *The Bread Bible*, recommends using King Arthur, Gold Metal, or Pillsbury flour.[2]

If I could buy only one bag of flour, it would be King Arthur's White Whole Wheat, which has the nutrition of whole wheat but a lighter character that makes it work well in desserts as well as bread. When money is tight, get organic whole wheat flour instead of the organic white whole wheat flour.

Next, I'd buy a good all-purpose flour. Its lower protein content and lack of bran makes pizza dough easier to stretch and makes breads and desserts lighter.

Avoid self-rising flour since you may want to have just plain flour. It's easy to add leavenings but impossible to take them out.

Rice vs. Eggs

Even inexpensive long-grain rice cooks up fine. For the best flavor, get basmati rice if you can. Pick brown rice over white. With more fiber and nutrients, brown rice helps you feel full longer and stay healthy. For example, eating brown rice twice a week lowers your risk of getting Type 2 diabetes by 10 percent, while eating white rice increases your risk.[3]

Get organic eggs or ones from pastured chickens. Organic eggs give great value for your food dollar. They come from hens who can go outside, eat organic feed, and have not been treated with antibiotics. Shun eggs raised in brutal factory farms to minimize your risk of salmonella.[4]

I prefer eggs from local, pastured chickens who roam around outside and eat whatever bugs or leafy things that they can get in addition to whatever wholesome feed the farmer gives them. If these aren't available, get eggs from suppliers who raise free-range chickens on organic, vegetarian feed. You'll get more nutrition, more flavor, and your baked goods will rise higher and be more tender. You'll also be making a difference by voting with your wallet for considerate treatment of chickens.

See for yourself: crack a cheap grocery-store egg and the best organic or pastured egg you can find into the same bowl. Notice how the yolk of the organic egg is larger and has a deeper yellow, almost orange color.

Dried Beans vs. Milk, Butter, and Cheese

Beans are essentially peeled: popped out of their pods before being dried. As with onions and bananas, you never eat the part that was sprayed. Beans last a long time, so look for savings from buying in bulk. With low prices and rapid turnover, ethnic markets offer fresh, fast-cooking beans. Explore a world way beyond kidney beans at a Hispanic or Indian grocery.

However, dried beans are one of the most affordable sources of organic protein, so upgrade when you can.

Organic dairy products are easier to find and less expensive than ever. If you can't find or afford organic, look for milk, butter, and cheese from cows not dosed with Recombinant Bovine Growth Hormone (rBGH), also known as Bovine somatotropin (BST). This hormone makes cows produce more, but hormone-laced milk increases cancer risks and is banned in Europe.[5] Makes you ask why we are feeding school kids milk that is illegal in Europe, doesn't it? The other side of this coin is that imported European dairy products are not tainted with rBGH.

As with eggs, choosing milk products that are better for you is also a vote for better treatment for animals.

> ### *Organic Pasta Alternative*
> Use If you prefer organic or egg-free pasta, get a good whole wheat one such as Whole Food's 365 Everyday Value Organic Whole Wheat Fusilli. It's toothsome and costs less than Barilla Plus, but it has only 5.25 grams of protein in a ¾-cup serving.
>
> To make up the protein difference without raising your budget, serve the less expensive 365 pasta with an extra ½-cup serving of beans, ¼ cup of wheat germ, two tablespoons of peanut butter, or six ounces of milk during days when you have pasta. I'll keep looking for good organic alternatives.
>
> Check for updates at CookforGood.com/wao.

Pasta vs. Peanut Butter

The cheapest pasta is no bargain. But pasta is a great nutritional value once you look beyond the all-white-flour varieties. My favorite high-protein pasta, Barilla Plus, is a terrific source of high-quality protein with slightly more flavor than regular pasta. Barilla Plus has the texture and taste of good-quality white pasta, not the gummy or limp texture and cardboard taste of many high-nutrient pastas. I recommend a ¾-cup serving size, which provides 12.75 grams of protein plus lots of ALA Omega-3 fatty acids (brain food) and fiber.

Unfortunately, Barilla Plus is not organic and the company told me it has no plans for an organic line. As of this writing, I have not found an acceptable organic high-protein pasta.

Cheap peanut butter is often diluted with hydrogenated oils and trans fats that melt right off your toast and provide no protein. Sugar and salt help mask the taste. Splurge on organic peanut butter that contains only peanuts, plus salt if desired. Just stir it well once and keep it refrigerated. Even on the thrifty plan, get a national-brand spread like Jif or Skippy. Make sure a two-tablespoon serving has no trans fats and at least seven grams of protein.

Onions vs. Potatoes

Onions naturally repel pests, so farmers don't need to spray them as much as bug magnets like peaches. When you peel them, you get rid of the most toxic layer. That's why onions are tops in the Environmental Working Group's (EWG) Clean 15 in its Shoppers' Guide to Pesticides. But it's not all about you, says Beyond Pesticides in its guide, "Eating with a Clean Conscience."[6] Just because pesticides are blown, washed, or peeled off before you eat them, that doesn't mean they aren't hurting workers or the environment. Sometimes organic onions cost little more or even less than industrial ones, so you may be able to upgrade and save.

Splurge on organic potatoes so you can eat the peels. EWG ranks unpeeled potatoes as number eleven in their Dirty Dozen list. Peeling removes some toxins but throws away much of the spud's taste, nutritional value, and fiber. You'll save time too. Organic potatoes don't cost much more than industrial ones.

Fruit You Peel vs. Fruit You Don't

When you scrimp on fruit, start with the varieties you peel. Bananas are the least expensive, easiest fruit to serve year round. Take advantage of frequent store specials on bananas to stretch your food dollar. Fair-trade bananas are a good step up if you can't afford organic. In the summer, melons and peaches are delicious bargains. EWG gives peaches with their peels on the number-two spot in their Dirty Dozen, but peeling is an easy way to reduce residues.[7]

Strawberries and unpeeled apples are numbers three and four in the Dirty Dozen. A Washington State University study showed that organic strawberries taste better and have higher levels of antioxidants and vitamin C.[8] What's more, strawberries become wildly affordable when you get a discount for buying in quantity. And when eating apples, be careful: the dip around the stem traps pesticides.

Maple Syrup vs. Honey

It's hard to believe you can scrimp on real maple syrup, but the less expensive, darker syrup (US Grade B or Canadian Amber) is more flavorful and costs about 25 percent less than lighter grades. Avoid high-fructose "pancake syrup." When finances are really tight, boil equal parts of brown sugar and water and then stir in enough real maple syrup to add maple fragrance and flavor. Start with ¾ cup water, ¾ cup brown sugar, and ¼ cup dark maple syrup.

Honey's complex taste and power to keep baked goods moist and fresh make it a *Wildly Affordable Organic* staple. Ironically, getting organic honey is difficult. A fascinating *Seattle PI* investigative report says that American honey is probably not organic.[9] Honeybees forage two or more miles from their hives and there are no U.S. organic standards for honey. Canada, however, does have standards for organic honey but acknowledges that "owing to the long distances that foraging bees may travel, it is not possible to limit foraging activities to organic floral sources."[10]

Worse, cheap honey often isn't honey at all. Another article in the *Seattle PI* series on "honey laundering" reveals that cheap, imported honey may contain sugar water, corn syrup, and even dangerous pesticides or antibiotics.[11] Countries with known honey problems and high tariffs ship their honey to other countries before it comes to the United States, to mask the country of origin.

So get good honey from a local beekeeper you trust. Some groceries and co-ops sell local honey in the bulk aisle. If you can't find local honey, look for honey from Florida, which became the first state to require pure honey in 2009.[12] Florida prohibits adding chemicals or adulterants to honey and has inspectors and labs to enforce the law. If you can't find good local or Florida honey, look for reputable suppliers from the United States, Canada, or South America.

Dried Herbs and Spices vs. Garlic

Nearly every cookbook author says to use only fresh herbs and spices. They compare dried basil to sawdust and tell you to throw out every jar that is more than a few months old. There's no doubt fresh is best, but dried oregano, basil, and dill do add flavor and character. A jar of dried herbs lasts a year and costs about the same as a fresh pack of herbs that goes bad in a week. Use only fresh herbs for pesto, but don't be ashamed to put a few pinches of dried herbs in your tomato sauce and stews. Dried chipotle adds a rich, smoky flavor to many dishes, but on a very tight budget, substitute cayenne.

Garlic is another story. Cheap garlic often comes from China. The weak flavor and small clove size means lots of peeling. Save time peeling and get the most flavor by splurging on fresh, firm garlic with relatively big cloves. Look for garlic at your farmers' market and stores frequented by passionate cooks. These stores often have the best quality and price for ginger too.

Tea vs. Coffee

Brew tea from family-size bags for a terrific beverage bargain. Although cheap store brands may be weaker than national brands, all the tea I tried tasted good. It's even good after being refrigerated and reheated. Stretch tea even further by brewing bags twice. I tried this after seeing a high-end tea fancier on TV talking about the eight or so flavor stages he got out of one spoonful of leaves. Watch for sales to get national brands at store-brand prices. Family-size tea bags, which hold enough tea to brew three cups, are usually less expensive and have less packaging than individual tea bags. Finding organic tea in bigger bags is difficult, but tea is still a bargain in individual bags. Tea that comes in tightly wrapped boxes lasts a long time, so stock up. The loose tea I've found is expensive.

Decent coffee is too expensive to be on a *Wildly Affordable Organic* shopping list. I include coffee here because so many people consider it essential. Two main types of coffee beans are available. High-quality Arabica beans cost twice as much or more than Robusta beans, which are what you'll get and regret in a discount bag. Even good beans are fragile, holding flavorful oils that go bad when stored or heated too long. Don't even think about double-brewing the grounds.

If you adore coffee, find a way to afford the real thing, even if not very often. Brewed at home, it's an affordable indulgence.

3

Feed Your Freezer

Making good use of even a small freezer saves time and money. Feed your freezer to even out seasonal prices and to keep the food you cook in bulk.

Get good prices buying fruits and vegetables in season. Get better prices by buying in bulk. At the farmers' market, you can save 50 cents or more by getting two quarts of produce instead of one. Eat some right away and freeze the rest.

For example, I freeze strawberries made up for shortcake every spring and peach ice cream base every summer for thrifty, healthy desserts in the winter. This adds even more variety and savings than you'll see in the *Wildly Affordable Organic* shopping lists and menus, which are limited to a month's worth of food at a time. But try it yourself if you have extra money during the warm months for wildly, wildly affordable and delicious winter meals.

Beans freeze particularly well, either just cooked plain or in a sauce. Bread freezes well too, so bake two loaves and freeze one for later in the week.

Planned-Overs, Not Leftovers

How many times have you heard someone say, "I don't eat leftovers"? This is usually said in the same tone of voice one might use to say, "I don't eat monkey chow" or "I don't eat nuclear waste."

Why is that? Many dishes actually get better after a day or two in the fridge, after the flavors have had a chance to mingle. A stew on day two is a better stew. The dough for pizza and whisk breads develops a tasty tang over time. It's odd that people will pay top dollar for aged beef, but they won't accept a doggy bag so they can enjoy it when it's aged one more day.

And what, really, is a leftover? If you make a layer cake one day and eat a slice the next, are you eating leftovers? No. Are frozen dinners in the grocery store leftovers? Of course not! Something is left over only when it's accidentally not used. With *Wildly Affordable Organic,* you cook ahead. Make a big pot of chili using two pounds of dried beans. That's enough for about twenty-four servings. Eat some that day and refrigerate the rest. Eat some the next day or not, but make sure to freeze what you aren't going to eat right away in meal- or serving-size containers. Voilà—it's not leftovers! It's a homemade frozen dinner!

Show Your Freezer the Seasons

Whether you have a small freezer in a small refrigerator or a big chest freezer, make the best use of your space.

Freeze Fruits and Vegetables at Their Seasonal Peaks

Pick produce you'd love to have at a different time of the year but would be too expensive or not as good out of season. Use the tips below to freeze solid and then package in freezer-weight bags or freezer-safe containers. Use a straw to suck extra air out of bags, minimizing the risk of freezer burn.

- **Blueberries.** Spread clean berries on a rimmed cookie sheet one berry deep and freeze overnight.
- **Strawberries.** Remove tops and any bad spots from strawberries. Crush or puree about half in a blender or food processor with the blade attachment. Slice rest and stir in with crushed strawberries. Taste and add sugar as needed, starting with a half cup sugar for every two pounds of strawberries.
- **Fruit ice cream base.** Make base according to recipe directions (pages 216–217) up to adding the vanilla or almond extract. Freeze for up to a year. Thaw in the refrigerator overnight and then continue with the recipe.
- **Peppers.** Cut each pepper in half and cut out the stem, seeds, and white parts. Remove the pesky extra seeds inside of the pepper by dipping pepper halves into a bowl of water. The seeds rinse away and float to the bottom, so the same bowl of water is good for a big box of peppers. Spread pepper pieces in a single layer on a cookie sheet. Freeze for several hours until solid. Use a spatula to loosen peppers from the sheet, then package and freeze.
- **Pesto.** Put in muffin pans. If space or money is tight, freeze just the basil and oil, then add nuts, garlic, and cheese after thawing. After pesto freezes solid, dip pan bottoms in warm water, pop the "muffins" out, then package and freeze.

Keep Your Freezer Full to Manage Heat and Your Budget

As the January bills roll in and you are looking for a rest after the busy holidays, you'll be able to take advantage of your thrift and foresight. You fed the freezer all summer and fall. In the winter, eat what you've got and make room for baked goods. Bake extra bread and desserts and enjoy the oven's heat. Use the frozen baked goods during the hottest days of summer, when you'll need room again for produce.

Freeze Food You've Made in Bulk

- Save money and your health by replacing fast-food dinners with homemade food from your freezer. Pair bean stews loaded with vegetables with rice or bread to make a complete meal.
- Eat and replace frozen meals regularly so that you have about a week's worth on hand for emergencies or busy times (page 30).
- Freeze bean broth the same way you freeze pesto.
- Freeze plain cooked beans that you won't use right away.
- Save room for at least one loaf of bread so you can bake two at once, saving time and energy.
- Cookies freeze well and resist the Midnight Snacker better than if they are at room temperature.

Freeze Core Kitchen Staples

- Freeze butter you won't be using right away in a freezer bag dedicated to butter. I usually freeze three sticks out of every pound purchased.
- Make room for an ice cube tray for freezing yogurt bought for yogurt starter. Pop frozen cubes out and store in a freezer bag or container.
- Use the same ice cube tray to freeze citrus juice and zest. For example, if a recipe calls for one tablespoon of lemon juice, zest the lemon before cutting it by grating off the thin yellow part of the skin but not the bitter white pith. Put the zest into a cell of the tray. Cut the lemon in half, juice it, and put the extra juice on top of the zest. Freeze and then pop the cube into a bag you keep for lemon juice and zest.
- Freeze bread scraps to make bread crumbs. Never throw away homemade bread, not even the heels.
- Freeze raw wheat germ, which can go rancid in just a few weeks at room temperature. Rancid wheat germ smells bad, tastes bad, and is bad for your health. Open and sniff wheat germ when you first buy it to make sure it's fresh.

Freeze Stoup

Okay, stoup really *is* leftovers. Stoup, which is short for "stew-soup," is actually the most leftover of leftovers, but it is also a free lunch and a good use of what you already have (page 198).

Freeze the Cylinder of Your Ice Cream Maker as Needed

The cylinder of my ice cream maker performs best when frozen a day or two in advance. If you're tight on space, thaw your Stoup container to make room.

If You Have Room and Money Left,
Freeze Great Buys and Whole Grain Flour

Stores often use cheese and butter as loss leaders to bring in customers. Stock up if you can. If you still have room and find it on sale, freeze whole wheat flour so the wheat germ in it doesn't go bad. Otherwise, refrigerate whole wheat flour that you won't use within a month.

Freeze Your Own Good Food, Not the Supermarket's

- Don't waste space on anything that's too old to eat or that you won't eat.
- Don't freeze things that the store can store for you, unless you've got the room and it's a big sale. Do you need ten pounds of frozen peas? Ten cans of orange juice? Will you use all that whole wheat flour before it goes rancid?
- Don't freeze expensive, premade food. If you already have it, eat up the toaster waffles, manufactured frozen dinners, and factory rolls. Actually, check the rolls for trans fats first; you might be better off throwing them out. Use the freezer space for your own delicious, fresh creations.
- Don't freeze things that don't freeze well. Freezing ruins the texture of raw potatoes and leafy or watery vegetables such as lettuce or cucumbers. Cream, sour cream, mayonnaise, and cream cheese also suffer from being frozen.
- Don't refreeze something that's already been frozen, such as cooked Stoup.

Freeze for Quality Results

Cool food quickly and in stages to reduce the risk of spoilage, moving it from room temperature to refrigerated to frozen. Putting hot food directly in the refrigerator can raise the temperature enough in the refrigerator that it may put other foods at risk. Freezing cooled food quickly minimizes damage to its structure, which keeps it from being mushy when thawed.

- Cool small quantities on your counter and larger ones in an ice bath or outside during cold weather. Make an ice bath by filling your sink or a big container with water and ice. However, be careful: putting hot glass or pottery dishes into very cold water could cause them to break.
- Package food in freezer-safe material. Use freezer-quality canning jars, plastic bags, and storage containers for liquids. Wrap solids in heavy aluminum foil.
- Air leads to freezer burn. Squeeze air out of freezer bags or suck it out with a straw. Use the straw only for larger or heavier food that won't zip down your lungs and bend the straw before inhaling. I learned this tip the hard way with bread crumbs.
- Think thin: lay your freezer bags of food out on a cookie sheet so the cold can get to the center as soon as possible. Once they are frozen hard, you can stack them.

Find and Use What You've Frozen

Now that you know what and when to freeze, make sure you find and use what you've frozen.

Clean and Organize Your Freezer

Get a notebook and pen. Sketch a plan for how to use the sections of the freezer. Some sections will grow or shrink as the seasons change. Consider having a shelf or area for:

- beans, bean stews, and rice
- complete meals, such as lasagna and your emergency-meal stash
- vegetables and pasta sauces
- fruit, fruit ice cream base, and the cylinder for your ice cream maker
- baked goods and desserts
- bags of butter, lemon juice and zest, yogurt starter, and wheat germ
- stoup container
- a flat space for freezing new additions

Now open the door, take food out in sections, and decide whether to keep, toss, or thaw for eating in the next day or two. Toss anything with trans fats, freezer burn, or that you are never going to eat. If you have a lot of UFOs (unidentified frozen objects), put them in a Mission: Identification area so you can thaw the UFOs and eat what's edible over the next few weeks.

Keep It Organized

- Label each package with the contents plus the date (month and year).
- List it in your freezer inventory. The inventory lets you check what's in the freezer without actually digging around in it while the cold air rushes out.
- As you take food out of the freezer, update your inventory list.

Prepare for Busy Times

Want to breeze through the holidays as if you had a personal chef? Swap kitchen work for time spent planning your daughter's wedding or getting ready for that big case? Here's how to plan ahead to give yourself a day off from cooking every week or smooth out your budget by enjoying food purchased when prices were low.

Make a Freezer Calendar

- Grab a blank calendar. Check CookforGood.com/wao for a free calendar you can customize and print.
- Mark special occasions when you'd like to serve favorite foods. I freeze strawberries for strawberry shortcake on Valentine's Day and for when my in-laws visit in late summer.

- Highlight busy periods. I like a break during the December holidays and the spring planting season.
- Flag months when your budget will be the tightest and food most expensive. For most people, that's late winter and early spring.
- As you shop or cook ahead, note on your calendar when you will eat what you've saved.

Say you cook a big pot of Red Bean Chili in September, when peppers are crisp and plentiful. Freeze a few bags of chili and then note on your calendar when you will eat them. Cover your special occasions first and then fill in for your busiest times. Use the calendar's back as your freezer list.

Don't forget breakfast. Blueberry pancakes freeze well.

Plan and Practice for Emergencies

Keep some meals off the calendar to tide you through an illness or unexpected event, good or bad. Having your own frozen fast food on hand is a lot better than having your family bring you a Bodacious Bucket o' Fried Dough when you have a migraine.

Keep these meals in a special area of the freezer, such as a box labeled "Safety Meals." Grab food out of this area when you need a break and add to it when you have extra. Do some rehearsal dinners before an emergency hits so other family members know the system.

4

Shopping Strategies

Get a Better Deal in the Next Aisle

Until I started seriously seeking bargains for my dollar-a-meal experiment, I never thought about comparison shopping within a grocery store. Now I know that a single ingredient may be in two or three places in the same store at vastly different prices.

Even medium-size grocery stores these days stock ingredients for international dishes. You won't find bargains for items that are presented as glamorously foreign. But depending on the ethnic mix of your neighborhood, you may find ingredients for the good home cooking of other lands—and often with the best prices in the store.

For example, the grocery store where I do my thrifty price checks has two Mexican food sections: one for authentic Hispanic food and one for people who want the Taco Bell experience at home. The Hispanic section has real bargains as well as more interesting and authentic ingredients. Table 4.1 shows how prices compare to those in the baking aisle.

And the "imitation" vanilla in the Hispanic section is actually a mix of imitation and real vanilla.

Dried beans and grains are also all over the store—in the dried and canned bean aisle, in the Hispanic section, and in the new Indian (South Asian) section. The Indian section has the best price on chickpeas, which come in two-pound bags.

It will take some time to search for bargains and compare prices in your store. But once you find the pattern, you'll save big week after week without clipping coupons or going from store to store.

Watch the Unit Price, not Package Price

Spotting good deals can be hard, but most stores post the cost per item plus its unit cost. The unit prices should help you find the best values.

Don't fall for the "bigger is better" myth. Often the middle size costs the least per serving. Stores count on thrifty shoppers grabbing the big size without checking for a big price. For example, you'll often pay less for several medium jars of peanut butter than one

TABLE 4.1
Baking Aisle/Hispanic Aisle

INGREDIENT	BAKING AISLE	HISPANIC AISLE	SAVINGS
cinnamon	$1.29 for 1 oz.	$1.49 for 2 oz.	42%
cumin	$3.89 for 0.8 oz.	$2.99 for 7 oz.	90%
sesame seeds	$3.43 for 1 oz.	$0.59 for 1.5 oz.	89%
real vanilla	$5.95 for 2 oz.	$3.59 for 2 oz.	40%
imitation vanilla	$2.21 for 2 oz.	$1.99 for 8.4 oz.	79%

big jar with the same amount. And although I usually buy 28-ounce cans of tomatoes, sometimes the 14.5-ounce cans are a better deal.

Notice how the small-can/big-can comparison is harder now that the small can isn't exactly half the size of the bigger one? Finding different sizes in even multiples is rare these days.

Even worse, the unit costs are often mixed, so you need a calculator and patience to make the best choice. I nearly gave up trying to figure out the best deal for olive oil the other day. Sure, the shelf labels for all had "unit costs"—but the units mixed metric and imperial units and liquid and dry measurements: ounces, cups, liters, and even pounds!

Are stores and manufacturers trying to trick you into spending more? Or is it a case of uncoordinated labeling? I'd bet the answer is "some of each." Whatever the reason, take your calculator to the store and watch unit costs, especially for expensive items like olive oil and cheese.

Paying More for Less Packaging
If you have room to spare in your food budget, do the planet a favor and pay a little more to get the sizes with the least packaging.

The Great Grated-Cheese Myth
Do you think pregrated cheese is a luxury that thrifty shoppers should always avoid? Is it a sign of laziness or decadence? Some people think so, given the response to a *Washington Post* article about the shopping strategies of a woman on food stamps.[1] She dared to buy pregrated cheese. Readers posted harsh comments, telling her to learn to use a grater.

I think of those mean-spirited comments when gathering thrifty prices. How many people miss the best prices because they think convenience always costs more? Blocks of Cheddar are usually $4 a pound and feature bright orange stickers saying "best deal!" But shredded cheese is often a loss leader. Name-brand shredded cheese can cost 40 cents a pound less than store-brand block cheese. Shredded organic cheese also often costs less than block cheese.

Smaller packages of preshredded cheese let you buy close to the amount you need. You'll save water and time by not scrubbing a grater. And some of the mixes are useful. When you can't afford organic Parmesan, look for organic Italian mixes.

Powdered Milk: Not So Thrifty Anymore

Powdered milk was on my first shopping list for the Cook for Good experiment. But when I did the math, I was astonished to find that fresh milk was actually a much better buy. How could that be, given the expense of packaging, transporting, and refrigerating fresh milk . . . not to mention its habit of going bad after a few weeks?

My Taster the engineer pointed out that turning liquid milk to powder takes energy. As energy costs rise, so does the cost of powdered milk.

It's a shame because powdered milk now tastes nearly the same as fresh once it's been mixed and chilled. Using powdered milk instead of fresh in yeast breads saves you the scalding step. Still, if your goal is to save money, head to the dairy case.

Shop with the Seasons at the Farmers' Market

Tomato-laden vines and fruit-heavy trees mean bargains for you at your farmers' market. You'll be getting great prices, just-picked freshness, and peak taste. You'll also be saving energy by reducing or eliminating the refrigeration, freezing, and transportation needed to get food from the farm to your plate.

If you aren't already cooking with the seasons, your farmers' market is the easiest place to start. What's in season? No research needed. If your local farmers have it, it's in season.

Turn a Chore into a Treat

Go to the farmers' market for the sheer pleasure of it all too. Enjoy the colorful tables loaded with ripe tomatoes, juicy blackberries, fuzzy peaches, and glossy peppers in all shapes and colors. Do a little people watching: babies in strollers, kids proudly carrying flowers, fit and fetching people on both sides of the stands. I usually can't stop smiling as I gather the makings for gazpacho, cobbler, and pesto with green beans. People are friendly, ready to swap cooking tips or simple pleasantries.

I used to dread grocery shopping. Now I look forward to the lively crowd at the market each Saturday. Festivals like "Tomatopalooza" add to the fun: I tasted six different types of tomatoes plus everything from white gazpacho to tomato jam while watching a clown juggle tomatoes. Yes, going to the farmers' market takes more time than getting produce when I'm already at the grocery store for other items. But doing so changes the entire nature of the event from a chore to a field trip or a visit with friends. Wouldn't you rather have thirty delightful minutes instead of twenty efficient but mundane ones? I would!

Bring Your Own Bags and Return Packaging

Shopping at the farmers' market is a great way to reduce, reuse, and recycle. Farmers will appreciate it because packaging is a big expense for them.

Bring your own shopping bags to the farmers' market if you can. I've seen everything from willow baskets to logo-covered cloth bags to paper supermarket bags. Bring smaller plastic or paper bags for produce sold by weight, and use bigger bags to carry your purchases. Bring back clean, reusable packaging, including egg cartons, baskets, or plastic shell packs for fruit, as well as cardboard boxes for flats of berries or large quantities of peppers.

Find Great Deals at the Farmers' Market

Ripe Ice Cream Peaches

Ask your fruit vendor for "ice cream peaches" to get fruit so ripe the tropical scent will waft through your car on the way home and the skins practically slide off. They won't be the prettiest peaches and will often have bruises. The supply will be limited, so go early in the day to get a good box.

Use these very ripe peaches for ice cream, cobbler, or pancakes within a day or two. Or just peel, cut, and freeze some to be eaten plain later in the week.

Sometimes you get terrific bargains, like the box I got for $4 that had forty peaches in it. Only eleven had any bruises at all. I made two big cobblers, two batches of ice cream, and a batch of tomato-peach salsa from that one box. The *Wildly Affordable Organic* price calculations use a more typical price, with a half bushel with forty-eight prime peaches for $5.

Ugly Tomatoes and Canning Tomatoes

A gorgeous tomato is indeed a thing of beauty, but if you are making sauce, salsa, or even tomato sandwiches, you don't need to pay for that ideal. Look for signs offering "ugly tomatoes" with interesting shapes and sometimes tan scars caused by leaning against a vine. Ugly tomatoes are usually in top shape except for their appearance. "Canning tomatoes" cost less because, like ice cream peaches, they are usually very ripe and have bruises or bad spots.

Conventionally grown ugly tomatoes cost 99 cents a pound here in July 2010; beauties cost 25 cents more. Canning tomatoes cost only $8 or $9 for a twenty-five-pound box, which is only 35 cents a pound.

Smooth, Stem-Free Blueberries

When you buy berries, look for plump ones with few stems still attached. These berries were picked ripe. To clean, spread them out a few handfuls at a time on a light-colored plate and pick through them as you would dried beans. Remove any stems or withered berries and then rinse.

Score with Seasonal Specials at the Supermarket

Grocers keep an eye on the calendar, looking for ways to bring in shoppers. One time-honored way is to offer loss leaders tied to a holiday. Putting cranberry sauce on sale in April won't bring in much traffic, but doing so in November appeals to millions of cooks planning Thanksgiving feasts.

The *Wildly Affordable Organic* shopping lists vary by season for both these reasons. We want to celebrate the holidays. We also want to take advantage of products on sale because of the holidays. Summer has several big grilling holidays, so finding sales on ketchup, mustard, and mayonnaise is easy. Use these on your bean burgers or in potato salad, deviled eggs, or slaw. Get enough ketchup to adorn your burgers now and your oven fries in the winter.

During the cold months we celebrate several baking holidays, starting with Thanksgiving. Stock up on yeast that has an expiration date far in the future and keep it fresh in your refrigerator or freezer. Flour and sugar will also be on sale in November and December.

In the spring, chocolate goes on sale around Valentine's Day and Mothers' Day. Eggs are abundant and sold at a loss around Easter.

The Weather Makes a Difference,
Even Under Fluorescent Lights

I felt pretty foolish when I noticed the jump in prices for potatoes and apples during the summer. Even though I've been cooking with the seasons for years now, I somehow thought they were always available at the same quality and price.

But at the height of summer, the cost of fruits and vegetables harvested in the fall soars. Organic apples and potatoes were available only by the pound, not in big bags. The apples went from 44 to 83 cents a serving. Potatoes leapt from 37 cents to 85 cents a serving.

In the fall, the price of canned tomatoes drops after the summer harvest.

Don't Ship Cold Air

When you shop using a *Wildly Affordable Organic* shopping list, you waltz right by the frozen-food section and barely pause in the cooler section. Your produce probably comes from a farm stand, where it doesn't need refrigeration between the field and your home.

By shopping this way you greatly reduce the energy used to store and transport your food. For example, 17 percent more energy is needed to freeze and package a pound of corn than to put it in a can.[2] Frozen corn requires energy every day to keep it frozen too. It travels in freezer trucks and waits in freezers in warehouses, the store, and your home.

You'll also use less packaging. Take rice, for example. Sometimes I buy big bags of basmati rice in a burlap bag. Other times I use a flimsy plastic bag to buy rice in bulk and then reuse the bag at the farmers' market. But when you buy precooked frozen rice at the store, you're also buying a single-use, freezer-safe container for each cooking unit of rice. Cooking increases the weight and size of the rice, increasing the energy used in transportation and storage.

Don't Ship Water

One of the fastest ways to trim your food budget is to drink water and home-brewed tea instead of bottled or canned drinks of any kind. It's a healthy way to reduce your carbon footprint.

Make $77 an Hour Boiling Water

Last summer, I slunk into the supermarket and bought products for a booth at the Women on the Move forum. My goal was to show how expensive and inconvenient buying bottled or canned drinks is.

The twelve-pack of bottled "iced" tea cost $6.93. Each bottle held 16.9 fluid ounces of tea. I found that I could make the same amount of tea using a national brand of tea bags for 54 cents. **That's a savings of $6.39 for boiling a little water.** Even a slow person can brew a pot of tea in five minutes. Repeat that twelve times and you've saved $77 boiling water.

Brewing tea also helps you save the planet. That twelve-pack of tea weighs a whopping fourteen pounds, eight ounces. Six tea bags, however, including their share of a twenty-four-bag box, weigh just under eight ounces. Picking tea bags over bottled tea for just one twelve-pack means you didn't haul fourteen pounds of water and plastic off the shelf, into your cart, up onto the register, out to the car or bus, and then into your home. Precious oil wasn't used to make the plastic bottles, transport them, or send them to the recycler or landfill either.

Save More with Water, Maybe Even Your Teeth

The difference is even more striking with water. I bought a twelve-pack of twelve-ounce bottles of water for $4.58. The same amount of water from the tap would cost only one-third of one cent. **Drinking tap water is the next best thing to free.**

Buying bottled water where tap water tastes or smells bad makes sense. But here in Raleigh, companies bottle our city tap water[3] and sell it back for an enormous markup to the people who live here. Bottled water is often filtered, which may not be good for your teeth. The Center for Disease Control says,

> If you mainly drink bottled water with no or low fluoride and you are not getting enough fluoride from other sources, you may get more cavities than you would if fluoridated tap water were your main water source.[4]

Even Diet Drinks Lead to Weight Gain and Diabetes

Pick healthy water and tea over soft drinks to lose weight and lower your risk of diabetes.[5] According to a study done by the Harvard School of Public Health, soft drinks made with high-fructose corn syrup or sugar are downright bad for you. Walter C. Willett, a researcher who helped conduct the study, writes, "The message is: Anyone who cares about their health or the health of their family would not consume these beverages. Parents who care about their children's health should not keep them at home." The Boston University School of Medicine did a study that shows even diet sodas lead to weight gain and increase your risk of heart disease and diabetes.[6]

Making the Most of Home-Brewed Tea and Tap Water

- Drink unsweetened, home-brewed tea for antioxidants without additives.
- Flavor tea with lemon balm, lemon, or mint if you want.
- Brighten a whole tea pitcher with one bag of herbal tea. I brew our standard house tea using three family-size bags of Lipton's Iced Tea blend and one single-serving bag of Celestial Seasonings' Mandarin Orange Spice tea.
- Encourage teens to drink tap water away from home by letting them pick a stylish, reusable bottle. In fact, everyone in your family should have a reusable water bottle. Make sure the bottles are not made with bisphenol-A, an ingredient in plastic that our bodies absorb and use like extra estrogen. Canada and several US states ban BPA in plastics used to line food cans and make baby bottles as well water bottles.[7] Why wait for the FDA to finish its study before banning it from your home?
- On a trip where you can't take your reusable water bottle, buy one bottle of water per person and then refill it with tap water.

Buy Big, Pay Little

The Power of Mini-Bulk

You don't have to indulge in excess at a warehouse store to save money buying in bulk. The popular size of a product often costs less than the smallest size, so going up a size or two can mean big savings.

I remember my despair in the dairy aisle during my first week of living on a dollar a meal. I couldn't imagine two people eating a whole pound of butter in one week, but buying the smallest size, two sticks of butter, cost nearly as much as a whole pound. A dozen eggs was a much better buy than just six, but it was more than we needed.

When I was able to buy for one month at a time, the worst of these problems went away. But even so, I found myself choosing the smallest container of oatmeal or cayenne when a larger one would have cost just a few pennies more. Because the *Wildly Affordable Organic* shopping lists assume a month's worth of grocery money, even now they recommend buying one ounce of cayenne for $2.86 instead of 7.25 ounces for $3.14. But if you have the extra 28 cents one month, get the bigger container so you won't have to buy it again for at least seven months, saving over $12.

What to Buy in Mini-Bulk and What to Avoid

Look for multipound bags of rice and beans. Get carrots in five- or ten-pound bags. Go for bigger containers of oatmeal, spices you use regularly, and vanilla. Even buying tomatoes in 28-ounce cans instead of 14.5-ounce ones will tend to save you money and reduce packaging.

It makes less sense to get bigger sizes of items that you buy only twice a year in the small sizes, such as corn starch. Baking powder starts to lose its oomph after about three months. Avoid stocking up on food that may spoil, including oils, whole-grain flour, and produce that you don't plan to freeze or preserve.

Storing Your Bargains Safely Without Spending a Fortune

It's a kitchen nightmare that has happened to me only once, but how well I remember. I saw movement in the flour canister where all should be still: pantry moths! I threw out the flour and checked items near it. Infected! On and on until I found the Mother Lode of Moths. I threw out nearly all our flour, sugar, and grains, and I spent hours scrubbing the pantry.

This spring, as I started to put a fresh bag of organic flour from a reputable market into a canister, I noticed a dead moth in it. Who knew what live moths or eggs also lurked in the bag? The store told me to take the buggy flour outside and throw it away. They gave me a refund with only the receipt as proof of purchase. But it was a close call.

Now if I have freezer space and time, I freeze new bags of flour and sugar for a week before unleashing them into the pantry. That way, if there are moths, they will be killed before they can spread. At the very least, I put the flour and sugar bags in plastic bags and twist the tops closed, then I check for invaders before using.

I use a wide range of containers with tight seals. Some of my favorites are freebies: repurposed cashew cans and plastic bottles that held brown rice or couscous. But don't ruin food with bad containers that smell like pickles, are too flimsy to keep out bugs or mice, or were never intended to hold food.

Grow Savings in Your Garden

Cut your grocery bills to well under $5 a day when you grow your own fruit and vegetables. The size and diversity of a home garden make it easy to go organic. Enjoy the freshest possible food and varieties selected for delight, not shipping. Don't let tales of $64 tomatoes frighten you off. Gardening is well worth the time and money invested if you start with good choices.

Grow What Thrives

I read somewhere that it's easiest to grow leaves, then seeds, and finally fruits. This makes sense because the less a plant has to produce to provide food, the less sun, water, and nutrients it needs.

Leaf crops, such as lettuce, spinach, chard, kale, and Asian cabbage are a snap to grow, as are leafy herbs such as basil and parsley. Radishes grow quickly and can be planted early, working well as markers for slower-growing plants.

With more sun, you can grow beans of all sorts, sugar snap peas, cucumbers, summer squash, okra, garlic, and peppers.

The most demanding of resources and most in demand by pests are tomatoes, melons, and stone fruit, such as peaches and cherries.

Look for seeds that do well in your region. Experiment with exotic or heirloom seeds. I've had luck with seeds from Baker Creek Heirloom Seeds, Southern Exposure Seed Exchange, and Seeds of Change.

Grow What's Hard to Find or Expensive to Buy

Finding organic green beans in grocery stores or at farmers' markets is difficult. It turns out that if you grow big fields of them, the flea beetles come to feast. This is not much of a problem in a home garden, however.

But the real problem is that green beans take a lot of picking if you are trying to gather basketfuls to sell. Picking a few handfuls for dinner at home is downright pleasant, especially if you grow varieties that climb up trellises. Plant marigolds around your beans to repel Mexican bean beetles, and plant catnip to discourage flea beetles and encourage your kitties.

Plant Once, Harvest for Years

Some years the only food I gathered from the garden came from plants that have been there for years. Even during my busiest times, I count on a getting a sprig of rosemary, snip of chives, and as much lemon balm as I need. My blueberry bushes and fig trees produce lots of fruit most years without ever being sprayed or given special treatment. My neighbor Marge taught me the trick: harvest fruit just after dawn before the birds can get to fruit that ripened overnight.

Let Your Garden Go to Pots

Even if you don't have space for a garden, grow basil and chives in pots. Lettuce and other greens look lovely with a few pansies mixed in. One friend grows a big garden in containers, including tomatoes. Grow containers of attractive, edible plants even if you have a strict neighborhood association or only an eighth-floor window.

5

Cooking Strategies

You Can Make It at Home!

My mother-in-law tells a story about buying a big bunch of apples at the grocery store. She mentioned to the cashier that she was going to make applesauce. The teenage clerk looked at her with big-eyed wonder, saying, "You can *make* applesauce? I thought it only came in jars!"

I'd laugh at that story and then load up my grocery cart with jars of pasta sauce and salad dressing; boxes of pancake mix, pie crust, and cookies; cans of beans and soup; and a tub of ice cream. Sure, I'd think, Martha Stewart or Julia Child might make this stuff at home, but regular people don't have the time or know-how.

But when I started the Cook for Good experiment, I learned how easy it is to make nearly anything at home. Make salad dressing in five minutes. Taste it, count the savings, and vow never to buy the bottled stuff again. Think about whatever packaged food disappoints you the most with its stale, chemical taste, questionable ingredients, or high cost. Then make your own version.

A few foods are worth the effort at home only if you are cooking as a hobby. I eat ravioli and stuffed Indian breads in restaurants and skip snacks like Pizzeria Pretzel Combos altogether. But it wasn't a big leap from making a pie crust to making crackers or from gravy to cheese sauce. As I write this, my first-ever batch of peach jam rests on the kitchen counter.

Even if you don't cook from scratch all the time, knowing that you can gives you a sense of power and freedom. Make your recipes as organic as you can afford, ingredient by ingredient. With *Wildly Affordable Organic*, you'll see how easy making bread, pizza, yogurt, pie crust, and ice cream can be.

Take Five

Take five minutes every night to think about what you will eat and drink the next day. Then soak beans, brew tea, or put something frozen into the fridge to defrost overnight. Pack lunch to save the time, hassle, and expense of going out.

No more frantic microwave defrosting, calling out for pizza, or banging your head on the fridge in despair after a long day. Develop the Good Night Food habit of thinking ahead each night for what you will eat tomorrow. Invest a minute tonight and reap the time-savings tomorrow.

Cook Clean

Rinsing and Peeling Vegetables

If you are new to cooking, read this section to learn how to clean and store food. Experienced cooks should skim it for assumptions in the recipe section.

- Peel produce that comes in its own wrapper, such as corn, garlic, and mature onions.
- Peel apples, carrots, and potatoes only if the recipe calls for peeling or if that is your preference. Peeling takes time and removes nutrients and fiber, so I avoid it when possible when using organic produce. For industrially raised produce, peeling removes some of the pesticides and other chemicals used during growing. If the slightly bitter taste of carrot peels bothers you when eating carrot sticks, peel carrots before cutting and cook peels in stews or Stoup.
- Peeling peaches starts at the market. Always ask for free-stone peaches. Cling peaches cling to their pits. Once at home, put a few peaches at a time into a pot of boiling water, boil for thirty seconds, and then put immediately into a big bowl of ice water for another thirty seconds or so. Cut off any bad spots, slide off skin, and cut in half or quarters so fruit falls away from the pit.
- Soak and rinse leafy greens, such as lettuce, chard, kale, and collards. You may need two or three changes of water to get rid of bugs and dirt trapped in the leaf folds. Spin lettuce dry or roll gently in a tea towel. For robust greens, just shake off extra water and proceed with the recipe.
- Rinse all other produce, including the outside of melons and winter squash.
- Core and remove seeds from apples and peppers. Seed melons and winter squash, scraping out the soft stringy center.
- To chop chard, collards, or kale, stack leaves up on your cutting board so stems line up, then make a V-shaped cut to separate stems from leaves. Make multiple stacks if you are cooking a lot of greens. Cut off bottom edges off stems and chop the rest into ¼-inch pieces. Cut leaves into ribbons about ¼ inch wide and 2 inches long.

To be extra safe, spritz smooth-skinned produce with a diluted vinegar mix. Mix one part white vinegar to three parts water in a spray bottle, the kind used to mist plants. Lightly cover the produce with the vinegar mix and then rinse with running water. You'll kill off 98 percent of the bacteria. Scrubbing with a brush and rinsing gets 85 percent of the bacteria, while just rinsing gets 80 percent. Don't waste money on expensive food washes.[1]

Chop, Dice, or Mince?

This cooking lingo is about the size of the pieces after you cut something. Chop is bigger than dice, which is bigger than mince, which has pieces that are about as small as you can make them.

Giving Garlic Time to Breathe

Recipes in this book often start with peeling and mincing garlic, then setting it aside. Exposing raw garlic to air starts an enzyme reaction that helps garlic boost our natural levels of hydrogen sulfide, which may help ward off cancer and heart disease.[2]

Storing Basil and Making Basil Ribbons

Store basil for a week or more with this trick from one of my students. Put basil in a plastic bag, use a straw to suck air out of the bag, and then quickly seal or twist bag shut.

To make basil ribbons, rinse leaves and roll lengthwise like a cigar. Cut across roll with a sharp knife, turning leaves into thin strips. Use for garnish. The French call this technique *chiffonade*, which sounds fancy until you realize "chiffon" means "rag." Let's call them ribbons instead.

Hot Tap Water Is Bad for You

Never cook with or drink hot tap water. It may contain lead from the water heater or plumbing.[3] Instead, heat cold water up in an electric kettle, a microwave, or on the stove.

Take Care of Your Hands

When cutting hot peppers such as jalapeños, wear gloves or use a plastic sandwich bag to hold the peppers, especially if you wear contact lenses. The chemical heat of peppers clings to skin even after repeated washings and may irritate your skin or eyes.

After handling raw onions or garlic, wash your hands, rub them on your kitchen faucet, and wash again. Somehow the stainless steel neutralizes the odors.

All Hail the Kitchen Scale

The kitchen or food scale gets my vote for the most ignored and most useful kitchen appliance. More Americans should join Europeans in adopting this essential kitchen tool. In *The Cake Bible*, Rose Levy Beranbaum says, "There's no doubt about it; weighing is faster, easier, and more accurate than measuring."[4]

Favorite Features

I use an OXO Good Grips food scale with a pull-out display. It has many useful features:

- Weighs in pounds and ounces or in grams.
- Resets to zero, so you can weigh food in whatever container you like and also weigh several ingredients in the same container. To get a scale that will reset to zero, look for one with a "tare" feature.

- Displays weights using big numbers. If you are cooking by candlelight, just touch a button to light the display.
- The display pulls out away from the scale, so you can see it even if you are using a big bowl or plate.

Benefits of Using a Scale

Saves you time while cooking

Just put your mixing bowl on the scale, set the scale to zero, and then pour in the ingredients until you have enough. Measuring 4 ½ cups of flour is one step instead of 5 (dip and level 4 cups plus one half cup). Some flours I pour right from the bag. For the next ingredient, just set the scale back to zero and you're ready to measure again.

Ups the odds that your baked goods will turn out right

Good measuring is a key to good cooking, especially for baked goods. Successful baking relies on using the right proportions of ingredients so that the chemical changes occur as intended. But measuring dry ingredients with measuring cups is amazingly inaccurate. As *Cook's Illustrated* reports, "We've found that when measuring dry ingredients using a 'dip and sweep' method, different cooks can be off by as much as 10 percent—a variance that, in baking, can mean the difference between a dense cake or a fluffy, tender crumb."[5]

I weigh rather than measure dry ingredients that are bigger than a tablespoon. If you'll do the same, we'll be using the same amounts. Some people note that weighing ingredients won't help you match the writer's intention for a recipe given in cups. That's true, but if you note how well the recipe came out and what adjustments would make it better, you will soon be able to match your own intention with the recipe. For instance, you'll find that the note "try twenty more grams of flour" is a more useful message than the one that just says "soggy."

Saves dishwashing time

Most of my measuring cups are not dishwasher safe, so there would always be a stack to wash after a big baking session. Sometimes I'd wash them midrecipe, say when I needed a quarter cup of both cocoa and powdered sugar. Now that I use a scale, I mostly measure right from the container into the mixing bowl, reducing the need for measuring cups. I pour honey from the jar, saving cleanup and waste (although I do miss licking the honey spoon). For flour and sugar, I keep old measuring cups right in the canisters so I don't need to use a fresh cup for dipping. Some ingredients I pour right from the bag, and others I dip out with a spoon that goes right into the dishwasher. All told, having a scale means washing a lot fewer measuring cups.

Practically eliminates the risk that you'll run out of ingredients unexpectedly

Say you are following the *Wildly Affordable Organic* summer shopping list and menu, so you expect to use fifteen pounds of all-purpose flour. Let's also say you are one of the people who packs a cup of flour more than most people when you measure, so it contains 10 percent more flour than it should. You'll be scooping out sixteen pounds of flour where by weight you'd be getting fifteen pounds (and other people will be scooping less than fourteen pounds). At the end of the month, you'll be more than five cups short. It takes four cups of all-purpose flour to make two loaves of bread, so this could be a real problem.

Makes it easy to cook with bulk food purchase

I buy beans from the bulk bins and big bags of other staples such as brown sugar. Having a scale makes it easy to follow recipes that call for a pound of this or eight ounces of that. I've even found a local dairy that makes butter, but they sell it in tubs instead of sticks. I use the scale to weigh out the equivalent of a tablespoon or a stick.

You Bought It, So Cook It

Americans throw away about a third of the perfectly good food they buy. In the *Wildly Affordable Organic* kitchen, we not only don't throw away good food, we find new categories of good food.

Do You Have Trashy Habits?

Keep an eye on food you throw away. Look for patterns. Do you buy a gallon of milk because it's cheaper than two half-gallons but throw most of it away because it spoils before you can use it? Consider buying a smaller size that is more expensive per purchased serving but actually cheaper per serving eaten. My bad habit is to buy fresh okra, which I love but my Taster loathes. I always think I'll cook it just for me, but in fact I rarely cook food that only one of us will eat.

One Bad Spot Don't Spoil the Whole Apple, Girl

Was it M. F. K. Fisher who raved about French restaurants that threw away any produce that was not perfect? One tiny spot on the tomato and bon voyage into the garbage. Even perfect tomatoes are skinned and seeded before being used in many recipes today. Not in my house! Don't risk eating spoiled food, but do respect and enjoy the whole tomato, perfectly good half of a spotted green bean, or the majority of the corn on a cob where the insects took a few bites at the tip.

Flat Is Where You Make It

At a cooking class, a chef showed us how he makes a flat surface on a potato so it holds still while being cut. He sliced off the curves so the potato was rectangular: flat on four long sides. However, you can get the same effect without waste by simply cutting the potato in half. The center becomes the flat side. Let the potato skin add taste and nutrition to your meals. Use this tip for carrots, onions, and eggplant.

Don't Skip the Seeds

At another cooking class, I watched a chef quarter young zucchini lengthwise and then cut away the centers where the seeds form. You'll want to do this when you find a big, tough squash lurking under the leaves in your garden. But when seeds are barely formed, eat them. Buy small zucchini, yellow squash, and cucumbers so you can eat as much of them as possible.

Strain Your Melons

Before you cut open a melon, set up a big strainer over a bowl. Scoop the seeds and pulp from the inside of the melon cavity into the strainer. Use a spoon to press down on the seedy mass and then let it drain while you cut up the melon. You'll get enough juice to flavor a pitcher of iced tea.

6

Dining Strategies

Control Portions to Control Your Budget and Your Health

Why Portion Control Matters

Controlling the amount we eat is most often talked about in terms of achieving and maintaining a healthy weight. Clearly, many of us eat more than we should. According to the Centers for Disease Control and Prevention, obesity rates have doubled between 1984 and 2004. Now, 68 percent of American adults are overweight or obese.[1]

Being overweight means more than finding that your jeans are getting too snug. Excess weight increases your risk of getting heart disease, cancer, and diabetes. The Organisation for Economic Co-Operation and Development (OECD) urges governments to fight fat. The OECD sees the obesity epidemic getting relentlessly worse, with one in three children overweight worldwide, health care costs for an obese person being 25 percent higher than for someone of normal weight, and severely obese people living eight to ten fewer years.[2] I hope *Wildly Affordable Organic* will help reverse this trend, even if governments are slow to act.

Eating just the right amount of food is also key to making the best use of your food dollars. What good does it do you to save 15 percent by taking advantage of a store sale or a bulk buy at the farmers' market if you eat 22 percent more than you really wanted or needed . . . in part because you picked the wrong plate?!

Easy Ways to Eat the Right Amount
- Use a small plate. Dr. Brian Wansink and others at Cornell University have conducted research showing that just using a ten-inch plate instead of a twelve-inch one leads people to eat 22 percent fewer calories per meal. That could add up to losing eighteen pounds a year.[3]
- Make cupcakes. Most layer-cake recipes produce a two-layer cake or twenty-four cupcakes. Only a surgeon with excellent self-control could cut a layer cake into

twenty-four servings, but with cupcakes, even young family members can serve themselves the right portion. Make corn bread in muffin pans too.

- When you cook in bulk, freeze in serving sizes. I freeze beans and stews in one- or two-meal amounts and label them as such. Freeze pesto or spicy enchilada sauce in muffin pans; a "muffin" of sauce serves two. Ice cream not eaten right away goes into single-serving containers for easy softening and serving.

What Portion Control Doesn't Do

The smallest plate won't make an empty cupboard full. In 2008, according to Feeding America, 14.6 percent of Americans were sometimes "food insecure"—meaning that they don't know where their next meal is coming from—and 5.6 percent of families had a high rate of food insecurity.[4]

However, taking easy steps to help your family eat the right amount of food now can boost your health and your savings. You'll be more ready to enjoy good times, get through hard times, and help others along the way.

Make It Delicious at First Sight

I remember a vividly bland dinner that two roommates cooked for my vegetarian girl-friend and me: macaroni and cheese, white bread, corn, and lemon Jell-O. It was so boring it was funny.

Make your meals delicious at first sight. Think orange carrots with black beans, green salad with tan chickpeas, and green beans with lasagna. Toss a few radish slices in your salad or sprinkle basil ribbons on nearly anything. Mix bite-size food with larger pieces, such as beans on rice with carrot sticks.

However, you don't have to compete with Bubba's All-You-Can-Eat Buffet Extravaganza. According to Dr. Brian Wansink of Cornell University, people eat more when there are more options available.[5] A little repetition can keep your waistline and spending in check.

The most useful chapter in Anthony Bourdain's hilarious *Kitchen Confidential* is "How to Cook Like a Pro." His rant on garnish ends with:

> Good food is very often, even *most* often, simple food. Some of the best cuisine in the world—whole roasted fish, Tuscan-style for instance—is a matter of three or four ingredients. Just make sure they're *good* ingredients, *fresh* ingredients, and then *garnish* them. How hard is that?[6]

That chapter changed my cooking style. Garnish is now a family joke, funny in part because it *does* make such a difference. Take Noodles in Spicy Peanut Sauce (page 175). A minute spent cutting vegetables into attractive shapes and a sprinkling of basil ribbons (or *chiffonaded* basil, as Bourdain would say) turns it into a company dish.

Many *Wildly Affordable Organic* recipes make good one-pot meals. Sometimes when I'm really busy or tired, I plop a big ladleful of bean stew over a bowl of rice and call it dinner. But I'd rather move the meal up from fueling toward dining by slicing carrot or green-pepper sticks, setting out cherry tomatoes, or, yes, adding garnish. It ups the value of your meal without much cost.

Start meals by pleasing your eyes with contrasts in color, shape, and texture. Follow through with differences in temperature and tastes: sweet with savory, calm with spicy. Use a tender mint tip, a few long chive leaves, or a tablespoon of finely chopped tomato to add contrast and flavor. A swirl of yogurt adds cool interest and a little protein to hot curries or chili.

Cleaning Strategies

Wash Reusable Grocery Bags

Remember just a few years ago, when only the most earnest environmentalists brought their own bags to the grocery store? Now some stores pay you to bring your own bags. It's a great example of green behavior becoming commonplace. According to Allen Hershkowitz, a senior scientist for the National Resources Defense Council, one reusable bag can replace three hundred to seven hundred disposable bags. It matters: throw-away bags are the most common form of litter in the world.[1]

Researchers at the University of Arizona conducted a study showing that bags can become contaminated with dangerous bacteria.[2] Dr. Charles Gerba says the contamination happens when raw food leaks onto a bag, allowing bacteria to grow that can contaminate food the next time you use the bag. I asked Dr. Gerba whether meat was the only problem. He told me that most of the risk comes from meat, but he still recommends washing bags, especially if you put them on the floor. So:

- Wash reusable bags by hand or by machine occasionally. Even without bleach, washing reduces any E. coli and salmonella below detectable levels.
- Don't use your food bags for nonfood purposes such as carrying dirty gym clothes.

Keep a Clean Counter

I admire the Buddhist practice of cleaning counters before and after cooking. It's a way to focus on cooking rather than the distractions of the rest of your life. Although I don't clean twice for every cooking session, the following habits keep me from wasting food:

- Start cooking with a counter that is clean enough to eat from. If food slips onto the counter, you don't have to throw it away.

- Keep your cutting board back a few inches from the edge of the counter. If food slips toward you, it doesn't wind up on the floor.
- Peel slippery or awkward food, such as cucumbers or potatoes, over a clean bowl, not over the sink.
- Use small plates or saucers as spoon rests. They're likely to be even cleaner than your countertop. Pop them into the dishwasher when you're done. During a big cooking session, I often use two spoon plates: one dry and one wet.
- If you're cooking sweet and savory dishes in the same big cooking session, use one cutting board and set of measuring spoons for sweet items and another for savory. For example, cut apples on your blue cutting board and garlic on your white one.

Cook from Sweet to Savory and from Dry to Wet

Oddly enough, cooking more can help you wash fewer dishes if you cook in the right order. Start with sweet and dry ingredients and move toward savory and wet. For example, I've made all of the following dishes in a single afternoon and washed only my food processor at the end:

- Baking mix
- Pie crust
- Grated cheese
- Pesto
- Crackers

In fact, the crackers got a flavor boost by following the pesto. Instead of being simply Cheddar crackers, they became Pesto Cheddar crackers.

Stop Washing Dedicated Tools

- Keep your flour sifter in an airtight container or freezer bag between sifting sessions. Unless you are sifting something that will flavor future recipes, such as cocoa, there's no need to wash your sifter more than once a year. I often sift onto a piece of waxed paper. When I'm done, I shake off the waxed paper and tuck it into the storage bag with the sifter. One piece of waxed paper usually lasts for six months and makes it easy to move sifted ingredients from the counter to the bowl.
- Keep your rolling pin in two plastic bags, kept tight in the middle with a rubber band. I don't like to get my wooden rolling pin wet any more than I have to. The plastic keeps any traces of flour from being beacons of welcome to any creepy crawlies.

- Tuck right-size measuring cups into canisters for sugar, flour, pasta, beans, rice, and other grains. I have cup measures in my flour containers, a ¾-cup measure in my rotini, and a half-cup measure in my sugar. I use them as scoops when weighing ingredients too. Bonus: the cups serve as handy guides for portion control, saving money and calories.

Use, Reuse, and Recycle

In the *Wildly Affordable Organic* kitchen, nearly all food gets eaten. What little packaging there is gets reused.

Nearly everything else winds up in the compost pile. If you have a garden or live in a community that recycles food, let the stems, cores, skins, and seeds that you don't want to eat nourish a garden. Add eggshells for calcium, but milk and meat products should go into the garbage. Tuck in your compost with shredded newspapers.

Use plastic bags several times before recycling them. Brush up on your community's recycling policies. Strive to waste less, not recycle more.

Part III

The Wildly Affordable
Organic Plans

8

Get Ready for *Wild* Savings

No matter what season it is, you can start your *Wildly Affordable Organic* adventure. Be most efficient by using the tips below to put your kitchen in order and make the best use of what you have. If you can't wait, plunge right in with the Twenty-Minutes-a-Day plan (page 58) or a single tempting recipe. It's up to you!

Check Your Equipment and Supplies

You don't need much equipment for the core recipes in this book. I developed the Whisk recipes so you can make homemade bread, buns, and pizza without a bread machine, stand mixer, or kneading. On the road I cook many of these recipes in hotel rooms with just a rice cooker, knife, and a few other essentials.

However, the right tools will pay for themselves quickly if they encourage you to cook at home. Here's what I use on a regular basis, in order of importance:

Essentials

- Pot with lid to use on a stove, or an electric rice cooker
- Sharp knife
- Cutting board
- Strainer for rinsing rice, beans, and vegetables
- Can opener
- Big heat-resistant spoon
- Measuring cups and spoons
- Cleaning supplies (detergent, sponge, and dish towel)
- Place setting for everyone (plate, bowl, knife, fork, spoons, and cup)

Useful

- Small, medium, and large pots with lids
- Oven-proof skillet
- Food scale that measures ounces and grams and has a "tare" function
- Food processor
- Slow cooker
- Instant-read thermometer
- Heating pad and heat-proof container for making yogurt
- Ice cube tray for freezing yogurt starter and lemon juice
- Stoup container
- Rolling pin (or use a tall, flat-sided bottle)
- Pastry blender if you don't have a food processor
- Jar for salad dressing
- Hand-crank ice cream maker with freezer cylinder (such as Donvier)
- Cooler for meals away and for transporting food from the store and market in hot weather
- Parchment paper, freezer-weight bags, and heavy-duty aluminum foil
- A straw for sucking air out of bags

Favorite Frills

- Bread stone
- Extra measuring cups and spoons
- Flour sifter
- Cake keeper
- Citrus press
- Tea pot
- Electric kettle for heating water
- Electric wok
- Biscuit cutter
- Ice cream scoop for ice cream and for making muffins or cupcakes
- Electric labeler
- Bread machine for kneading dough

Bargain Kitchenware

If you need equipment right away, start by checking restaurant supply stores. Otherwise, keep an eye out for good buys at yard sales or drop hints around the holidays. Get high-quality, sturdy equipment, use it all your life, and pass it down to your grandchildren. I love the feeling of family I get when putting up peach jam in my grandfather's canning jars or making cakes in my mother-in-law's pans.

Put Your Kitchen in Order

Check all the food in your cupboards and refrigerator. Throw out anything that is too old, spoiled, or contains trans fats. Wipe down shelves and make your kitchen clean and inviting.

- Inventory your freezer and start a freezer list (page 30).
- List good food that you want to use up, such as meat or prepared meals or sauces.
- Note on the grocery list what ingredients you already have.
- Note on the equipment list any equipment or other products you need.

Decide Where to Shop

Locate nearby farmers' markets. If you have more than one market in your area, try to find out which one will be best for your needs. In Raleigh, for example, the State Farmers' Market is very large and inexpensive, but smaller markets have more organic and sustainably grown food.

Review your local supermarkets and groceries. Don't overlook Whole Foods, Trader Joe's, or other stores known for gourmet food. They often have high turnover in core ingredients, which means fresh food at competitive prices. Look for good values in the bulk aisles and on organic produce.

Visit ethnic stores to look for great buys on products used in that region's cooking. You may not find many organic ingredients, but you'll often get great prices and selection.

If you can't find good flour locally or have trouble getting heavy groceries home, order from the King Arthur Flour Company by mail. Get together with baking friends to place an order big enough to get discounts or free shipping. For more recommendations about reliable mail-order sources, visit CookforGood.com/wao.

9

Go *Wild* in Twenty Minutes a Day
The Starter Plan

Use this starter plan to ease into the *Wildly Affordable Organic* life. It will help smooth the transition for your family as well. The amount of wonderful, healthy food you can make in just twenty active minutes a day will amaze you. You'll pick up skills and confidence to do more of the program when you have time.

You'll be cooking about two-thirds of your food from scratch with the twenty-minute plan. Fill in the blanks by cooking your own favorites, eating with friends or family, or going out. See the month-long, seasonal menus when you want to cook more (page 64). For more examples and information about using the Twenty-Minutes-a-Day plan to start the *Wildly Affordable Organic* Challenge, visit cookforgood.com/wao.

Cook It Forward

You'll enjoy quite a bit of homemade food the first week, but this plan starts to shine in the second or third week, as you can see from the sample menus that follow. By then you've stocked up on cooked beans and pasta sauce, so some homemade meals will come from your freezer.

Two pounds of dried beans yield about twenty servings of cooked beans. For the most variety, make two recipes from them and keep some plain to use in salad. Make just one recipe if you'd rather save time. Eat some beans this week and freeze the rest after they've cooled. The first week you have one type of beans to eat. The next week make another type of beans and have two types to choose from. A family of four will get five meals from two pounds of most beans and six meals from kidney beans. If you keep it up, you'll be able to eat a different type of bean three or four times a week, all from cooking one pot a week.

A double batch of tomato sauce serves twelve. Serve it twice during the week you make it and freeze the rest for the end of the next week. A recipe of Southern Summer Pesto serves eighteen, so freeze some to use on weeks when you make peanut sauce or for the winter.

The cooking plan calls for making Baked Pears with Cinnamon Yogurt Sauce every week on the day you bake bread. For more variety, consider serving melon for dessert. Or spend an extra ten minutes to make ice cream. You would still average twenty minutes a day that week if you made just one bean recipe, perhaps a double batch of hummus.

The example menus are based on a family of four. If you are cooking for fewer people, you can serve homemade bread more often. If you are cooking for one, consider baking just one loaf of bread a week or baking two loaves but freezing one. You could also cook one pound of beans at a time and then skip a week occasionally.

Cooking Plan:
Twenty Minutes x Seven Days

Day 1. Make Chocolate Pudding (page 212) or Vanilla Pudding (page 212). Prepare fruit as a topping or side dish. Make Vinaigrette (page 201) for tomorrow.

Day 2. Make double recipes of Noodles Cooked in Very Little Water, any tomato sauce (pages 171 through 174), and Green Beans (page 204) or steamed broccoli. Save pasta broth in a jar for rice tomorrow. Sort and soak two pounds of dried beans in a slow cooker. If you don't have a slow cooker, soak beans in a large pot and spend just a few more minutes tomorrow getting the beans to a simmer.

Day 3. Cook beans and make two quick bean dishes, such as Bean and Tomato Stew (page 134) with Red Bean Chili, Cuban Black Beans (page 140) with Black Bean Chili (page 143), or Hummus (page 142) with Bean and Tomato Stew (page 134). (These pairs of recipes have overlapping steps, which shorten the total time.) Make double recipes of Rice (page 203) and one vegetable: Glazed Carrots (page 204), Green Salad (page 200), or Grilled Summer Squash Two Ways (page 207).

Day 4. Make Good Whisk Bread dough and let rise, then refrigerate overnight (page 153). Bag up five days of walnut and raisin snacks and two days of bell pepper sticks.

Day 5. Bake bread along with sweet potatoes and pears for Baked Pears with Cinnamon Yogurt Sauce (page 220). Make enough cinnamon yogurt sauce to serve with the pears tonight and with sweet potatoes for breakfast. Make a main-dish bean salad using the Vinaigrette you made on the first day, either Bean Salad with Fresh Corn, Peppers, and Tomatoes (page 136) or Bean and Green Salad (page 200).

Day 6. Make Noodles in Spicy Peanut Sauce with Seasonal Vegetables (page 175), Southern Summer Pesto (page 177), or Parsley Pesto (page 178). Bag up two days of carrot sticks.

Day 7. Make Ginger-Glazed Carrot Cake (page 223), Chocolate Pumpkin Snack Cake (page 221), or Chocolate Upside-Down Cake (page 222).

Sample Menu for Week One:
Twenty Minutes x Seven Days

Day 1
Dinner: warm Chocolate Pudding with banana slices

Day 2
Dinner: high-protein pasta with Tomato Sauce with Bell Peppers and Onions, warm Green Beans with Vinaigrette, chilled Chocolate Pudding with banana slices

Day 3
Dinner: Cuban Black Beans with Rice and Grilled Summer Squash Two Ways

Day 4
Dinner: high-protein pasta with Tomato Sauce with Bell Peppers and Onions, chilled Marinated Green Beans

Day 5
Lunch: bell pepper sticks
Snack: walnuts and raisins

Dinner: Bean Salad with Fresh Corn, Peppers, and Tomatoes with black beans and Grilled Summer Squash Two Ways, Baked Pears with Cinnamon Yogurt Sauce

Day 6
Breakfast: baked sweet potatoes with Cinnamon Yogurt Sauce
Lunch: Good Whisk Bread, perhaps for a sandwich
Snack: bell pepper sticks
Dinner: Noodles in Spicy Peanut Sauce with Seasonal Vegetables

Day 7
Breakfast: Good Whisk Bread toast with peanut butter
Snack: carrot sticks
Dinner: Black Bean Chili with Rice, Vinaigrette (on salad mix), Ginger-Glazed Carrot Cake

---

Only pudding for dinner?!

No, the Starter Plan isn't meant to provide 100 percent of your food. Balance the meals with your own favorite recipes, healthy prepared food, or eating out. See the momentum build: by week three, you'll be cooking most of your food from scratch!

Sample Menu for Week Two:
Twenty Minutes x Seven Days

Day 1
Breakfast: Good Whisk Bread toast with peanut butter
Lunch: carrot sticks
Snack: walnuts and raisins
Dinner: warm Vanilla Pudding with blueberries

Day 2
Breakfast: Good Whisk Bread toast with peanut butter
Snack: walnuts and raisins
Dinner: high-protein pasta with Tomato Sauce with Summer Squash, hot steamed broccoli with Vinaigrette, Ginger-Glazed Carrot Cake

Day 3
Snack: walnuts and raisins
Dinner: Bean and Tomato Stew with kidney beans, Rice, Green Salad with Vinaigrette, chilled Vanilla Pudding with blueberries

Day 4
Snack: walnuts and raisins
Dinner: high-protein pasta with Tomato Sauce with Summer Squash, chilled marinated broccoli, Ginger-Glazed Carrot Cake

Day 5
Lunch: bell pepper sticks
Snack: walnuts and raisins
Dinner: Green and Bean Salad with kidney beans, Good Whisk Bread, Green Salad with Vinaigrette, Baked Pears with Cinnamon Yogurt Sauce

Day 6
Breakfast: baked sweet potatoes with Cinnamon Yogurt Sauce
Lunch: Cuban Black Beans, Good Whisk Bread
Snack: bell pepper sticks
Dinner: Southern Summer Pesto with Green Beans

Day 7
Breakfast: Good Whisk Bread toast with peanut butter
Lunch: high-protein pasta with Tomato Sauce with Bell Peppers and Onions
Snack: carrot sticks
Dinner: Red Bean Chili, Rice, Vinaigrette (on salad mix), Chocolate Upside-Down Cake

Sample Menu for Week Three:
Twenty Minutes x Seven Days

Day 1
Breakfast: Good Whisk Bread toast with peanut butter
Lunch: Southern Summer Pesto with Green Beans, carrot sticks
Snack: walnuts and raisins
Dinner: Black Bean Chili, warm Vanilla Pudding with peaches

Day 2
Breakfast: Good Whisk Bread toast with peanut butter
Snack: walnuts and raisins
Dinner: high-protein pasta with Persian Tomato Sauce, hot Green Beans with Vinaigrette, Chocolate Upside-Down Cake

Day 3
Snack: walnuts and raisins
Dinner: Hummus (on pita bread, save Rice for tomorrow), Glazed Carrots, chilled Vanilla Pudding with peaches

Day 4
Lunch: Red Bean Chili with Rice
Snack: walnuts and raisins
Dinner: high-protein pasta with Persian Tomato Sauce, chilled Marinated Green Beans

Day 5
Lunch: bell pepper sticks
Snack: walnuts and raisins
Dinner: Bean Salad with Fresh Corn, Peppers, and Tomatoes with chickpeas, Good Whisk Bread, Glazed Carrots, Baked Pears with Cinnamon Yogurt Sauce

Day 6
Breakfast: baked sweet potatoes with Cinnamon Yogurt Sauce
Lunch: Red Bean Chili, Good Whisk Bread
Snack: bell pepper sticks
Dinner: Noodles in Spicy Peanut Sauce with Seasonal Vegetables

Day 7
Breakfast: Good Whisk Bread toast with peanut butter
Lunch: high-protein pasta with Tomato Sauce with Summer Squash
Snack: carrot sticks
Dinner: Bean and Tomato Stew with chickpeas, Rice, Vinaigrette (on salad mix), Chocolate Pumpkin Snack Cake

Sample Pattern for Week C,
Which Follows Weeks A and B

Day 1

Breakfast: Good Whisk Bread toast with peanut butter

Snack: walnuts and raisins

Lunch: high-protein pasta with pesto sauce (if you are making peanut sauce on day six), carrot sticks

Dinner: bean dish from Week A, warm pudding with fruit

Day 2

Breakfast: Good Whisk Bread toast with peanut butter

Snack: walnuts and raisins

Dinner: high-protein pasta with tomato sauce from week C, hot green vegetable, cake from Week B

Day 3

Snack: walnuts and raisins

Dinner: first bean dish from Week C, Rice, salad or yellow vegetable, chilled pudding with fruit

Day 4

Snack: walnuts and raisins

Lunch: kidney bean dish from previous week (optional)

Dinner: high-protein pasta with tomato sauce from Week C, cold green vegetable, cake from Week B if recipe served twelve

Day 5

Lunch: bell pepper sticks

Snack: walnuts and raisins

Dinner: main-dish salad with beans from Week C, Good Whisk Bread, salad or yellow vegetable, Baked Pears with Cinnamon Yogurt Sauce

Day 6

Breakfast: baked sweet potatoes with Cinnamon Yogurt Sauce

Lunch: bean dish from Week B, Good Whisk Bread

Snack: bell pepper sticks

Dinner: high-protein pasta with pesto or peanut sauce and vegetables

Day 7

Breakfast: Good Whisk Bread toast with peanut butter

Lunch: tomato sauce from week B

Snack: carrot sticks

Dinner: second bean dish from Week C, Rice, Vinaigrette (on salad mix), cake

10

Seasonal Menus, Shopping Lists, and Cooking Plans

The four menus in the following chapters show you how to cook seasonally and affordably year round. Bring luck to your new year with Hoppin' John and the winter menu. Switch to the spring menu when local asparagus and strawberries appear at your farmers' market. Use the summer menu when summer fruit, peppers, and vine-ripened tomatoes abound. After the first frost, settle in with the fall menu.

The efficient cooking plans show you how to turn the ingredients you bought using the shopping lists into delicious meals with much less effort and time than if you made them one meal at a time.

The winter cooking plan is the foundation for all the cooking plans. Use it all winter and for other weeks that don't call for quiche, ice cream, lasagna, or bean burgers and buns. The summer plan gets most of your cooking out of the way with one big session every month. The spring plan includes ice cream and Magic Quiche with Asparagus. The fall holiday plan shows you how to make a feast with lasagna.

The shopping lists—with both "green" and "thrifty" prices—show everything you need to buy to make all the meals on the menus, using real-world sizes. Some items, like green beans in the winter and sugar, show only thrifty prices because the green versions were either too expensive or simply unavailable.

The "% left" column in the shopping lists shows how much you'll have left at the end of the longest months. Use it to see whether you can have an extra cup of tea (you can!) or what ingredients are available for your own recipes. Use it to see how often you'll have to buy ingredients. For example, with 79 percent of the baking soda left at the end of a winter month, you won't be buying it again for several months. With just 5 percent of the peanut butter left, though, you might want to stock up if you spot a sale.

Sometimes rounding the prices up or down to show whole cents makes the total price per day show a penny or two more or less than the sum of the prices for each meal. So the green winter menu shows that black beans cost $0.12 a serving, but the underlying calculations use $0.1170 a serving for accuracy.

Go Organic for $5 a Day

Enjoy food made from mostly organic, sustainably and kindly raised ingredients using these shopping lists and menus. Your costs may be a little higher or lower depending on where you live and shop, but nearly everyone can afford to make a difference by choosing food that is healthy for them and the planet.

Save even more money by using coupons, shopping at membership clubs, stocking up during sales, freezing summer produce to eat in the winter, or growing a garden. The shopping lists include extra food so you'll have plenty to eat even if your Stoup container is only half-full and you don't cook your jack-o'-lantern.

Make the Calendar Work for Your Life

Every menu shows four weeks of meals, starting with Sunday. Getting into the rhythm of the cooking sessions and menus is easiest if you start with the menu for Sunday night, usually with pizza hot out of the oven. However, you can make changes to fit your schedule. Maybe what I serve on Sunday you'd rather have on Saturday or Wednesday.

For example, if you'd rather have pizza on Friday, just mix up the dough on Thursday night. It takes only a few minutes. You might be able to go shopping on Thursdays and do your main cooking on Friday. If you can't go to the farmers' market every week, time your biggest cooking sessions for after you've stocked up on fresh produce.

You Don't Have to Do All of This Every Week

If you are eating just one pizza a week, then you need to mix pizza dough only every other week. It keeps fine in the refrigerator. You will probably have cooked all six kinds of beans for the month by the third cooking session, so you won't need to make beans in week four. If you have room in your freezer, make double batches of pizza and pasta sauce.

Cooking for One or Two

Because a key concept is cooking in batches and then freezing, cooking for one or two is a snap using these menus and cooking plans. Many singles find that cooking in batches lets them eat quality food without scaling down recipes or spending a lot of time in the kitchen. Try these tricks to keep bulk cooking manageable for smaller families or kitchens:

- Freeze in smaller units.
- Cook one pound of beans at a time instead of two.
- Use smaller cans of tomatoes (14.5 ounce instead of 28 ounce).
- Make one batch of bread or pizza dough, cook some the next day and the rest over the next two weeks (or one week if you use the Whisk Sandwich Bread, which has milk in it).
- Bake two loaves of bread at a time. Cut both loaves in half and freeze three halves for later.

Fit Your Household

Scale the plans up or down if you aren't cooking for four people. I cook for two, so I freeze more food and cook less often. Larger families, however, can double recipes. The active cooking times will go up a little, but as my generous and sociable mother-in-law says, "It's no harder to cook for ten people than to cook for two."

Celebrate Holidays

Each seasonal menu plans special meals around that season's holidays. Have something sweet on Valentine's Day, something grilled on Independence Day, and feast on Thanksgiving. When planning your own month, check your calendar for birthdays, anniversaries, and other special days. Just adding a little fruit to the main dinner or having a favorite dessert that day can make it festive.

Eat All Month,
Not Just the First Twenty-Eight Days

Rookie project managers get caught thinking that months are four weeks long. Even February is longer than that every four years. Thirteen four-week months fit into a year, which can be hard on the budget.

The *Wildly Affordable Organic* menus cover four weeks of menus plus three extra days at the end of the month. Use the food shown for these days for longer months, to share with friends or family, or just as a backup in case you drop a pizza or put too much hot pepper in the chili.

Start with a Good Breakfast

My favorite breakfast is peanut butter on toast with hot tea. It's the recommended breakfast for any day that doesn't mention another option. PB on toast is easy, quick, and provides enough protein, carbohydrates, and fiber to help you stay active and alert until lunch. My Whisk Breads make particularly good toast.

Drink Tea or Tap Water

At breakfast this plan assumes six cups of home-brewed tea will be split among a family of four. Unlike coffee, tea tastes great with peanut butter. And inexpensive tea is often quite good, while inexpensive coffee is often very bad (see Scrimp or Splurge Twenty, page 20). Make it even better by adding a few sprigs of fresh mint or lemon balm if you have it. Drink tap water the rest of the time.

Splurge on fruit juice, coffee, beer, or wine when you have extra money, but make it a treat rather than just something to wash down a meal. Drinking away your money and health with sugary drinks or alcoholic beverages is easy to do, which is just one reason why I say don't ship water (page 37).

Thrive with Good Nutrition

The USDA dietary guidelines strongly influence the *Wildly Affordable Organic* menus.[1] Every day includes lots of whole grains, veggies, and at least two servings of fruit. Fats are kept low, with mostly mono- or polyunsaturated fats used, and no trans fats. Protein ranges from fifty-five to sixty-five grams a day.

However, for calcium the menus are more in line with the World Health Organization recommendations.[2] I became concerned about eating too much dairy after reading *The China Study*. In it Cornell nutrition researcher Dr. T. Colin Campbell points out that "those countries that use the most cow's milk and its products also have the highest fracture rates and the worst bone health."[3] Of course, as with any diet, you need to get exercise and sunlight or vitamin D to put the calcium you eat to work. If you want to, add a multivitamin, a glass of milk, or a glass of calcium-fortified orange juice every day.

Jill Nussinow, registered dietitian and author of *The Veggie Queen: Vegetables Get the Royal Treatment*, wrote this about *Wildly Affordable Organic*:

> You will definitely be moving people toward a much healthier way of eating and living. I like how you are providing ways for people to cut down on sugar, salt, and fat while eating "real" food.

Get Enough to Eat

Each "serving" is sized for a moderately active adult who has a lean body mass of around 150 pounds. Of course, some family members will eat more than others. In this way, your track-star teenaged son will get more protein and other nutrients than your elderly in-law or your spouse with the desk job. If you are a diabetic or have other special dietary needs, please consult a nutritionist or physician.

Get Enough Protein But Not Too Much

How much protein does the average adult need? Nutritionist Jane Brody answered that question for me on her *New York Times* blog: "The amount of protein you need each day is a function of your lean body mass (not your weight if you are overweight). You can calculate your need by multiplying your ideal weight in pounds by 0.36 to get grams of protein needed daily by an adult who is not pregnant or nursing."[4]

So that would be thirty-six grams of protein a day if your ideal weight is 100 pounds, fifty-four grams if it's 150, and seventy-two grams if it's 200 pounds. Ironically, too much protein can actually lead to osteoporosis and other problems. You don't need to eat a Triple-Patty MacWhopper twice a day (or ever) to get your protein. But many veg-leaning cookbooks take too casual an approach to getting enough. True, even apples contain protein, but in developing the *Wildly Affordable Organic* menus, I tuned the menus to provide fifty-five to sixty-five grams a day.

11

Winter

Plan a special meal for Valentine's Day, such as Sunday in Week 3. Dice a red apple in the salad and top off your meal with warm Chocolate Upside-Down Cake.

Winter Menus ($green / $thrifty)

Winter Menu Week One

Breakfast every day unless mentioned otherwise ($0.46 / $0.29): two slices of toasted Good Whisk Bread, peanut butter, and tea

Sunday ($6.35 / $3.36)
Breakfast ($0.60 / $0.38): Sweet Raisin Flatbread toast with peanut butter, tea
Lunch ($2.32 / $1.33): Hoppin' John, Tasty Tahini Greens, Corn Bread (one piece), apple
Snack ($0.27 / $0.16): Oatmeal-Raisin Cookies
Dinner ($3.16 / $1.49): Pizza with Kale, Garlic, and Onions (two slices); Green Salad with Vinaigrette; orange

Monday ($5.41 / $3.22)
Lunch ($2.32 / $1.33): Hoppin' John, Tasty Tahini Greens, Corn Bread (one piece), banana
Snack ($0.27 / $0.16): Oatmeal-Raisin Cookies
Dinner ($2.36 / $1.44): Potato Peanut Curry, steamed broccoli with lemon juice, orange, Chocolate Pudding

Winter Menu Week One (*cont.*)

Tuesday ($4.37 / $2.61)

Lunch ($1.51 / $0.79): Pizza with Kale, Garlic, and Onions (one slice); carrot, banana

Snack ($0.27 / $0.16): Oatmeal-Raisin Cookies

Dinner ($2.13 / $1.39): Bean Burritos, Green Salad with Vinaigrette, Vanilla Yogurt, orange

Wednesday ($4.53 / $2.92)

Lunch ($1.25 / $1.00): Bean Burritos, carrot, apple

Snack ($0.27 / $0.16): Oatmeal-Raisin Cookies

Dinner ($2.54 / $1.48): pasta with Parsley Pesto, Glazed Carrots, orange

Thursday ($6.19 / $3.52)

Breakfast ($0.37 / $0.25): Oatmeal with peanut butter, tea

Lunch ($2.42 / $1.60): rotini with Tomato Sauce with Bell Peppers and Onions, broccoli, orange

Snack ($0.27 / $0.16): Oatmeal-Raisin Cookies

Dinner ($3.13 / $1.52): Green Eggs Scramble, baked sweet potato, banana

Friday ($4.99 / $3.05)

Breakfast ($0.60 / $0.38): Sweet Raisin Flatbread toast with peanut butter, tea

Lunch ($2.02 / $1.16): pasta with Parsley Pesto, carrot

Snack ($0.40 / $0.25): Vanilla Yogurt, banana

Dinner ($1.97 / $1.26): Bean and Tomato Stew with black beans, Rice, Green Salad with Vinaigrette, orange, Oatmeal-Raisin Cookies

Saturday ($4.21 / $3.04)

Lunch ($1.07 / $0.77): Stoup with black beans, apple

Snack ($0.40 / $0.25): Vanilla Yogurt, banana

Dinner ($2.27 / $1.72): rotini with Tomato Sauce with Bell Peppers and Onions, onions sautéed in butter, orange, Chocolate Pudding

Winter Menu Week Two

Breakfast every day unless mentioned otherwise ($0.49 / $0.30):
two slices of toasted Whisk Sandwich Bread, peanut butter, and tea

Sunday ($5.06 / $2.97)
Breakfast ($0.70 / $0.41): Sweet Raisin Flatbread toast, egg, tea
Lunch ($1.70 / $1.18): Red Bean Chili, Rice, orange
Snack ($0.35 / $0.16): Ginger-Glazed Carrot Cake
Dinner ($2.31 / $1.21): Pizza with Bell Peppers and Onions (two slices), Green Salad with Vinaigrette, apple

Monday ($5.22 / $3.32)
Lunch ($1.66 / $1.20): Red Bean Chili, Rice, carrot, banana
Snack ($0.35 / $0.16): Ginger-Glazed Carrot Cake
Dinner ($2.73 / $1.66): rotini with Tomato Sauce with Robust Greens and Onions, slice Cheddar, broccoli with Vinaigrette, orange

Tuesday ($3.81 / $2.30)
Lunch ($1.14 / $0.69): Pizza with Bell Peppers and Onions (one slice), carrot, apple
Snack ($0.29 / $0.18): Vanilla Yogurt
Dinner ($1.89 / $1.14): Spicy Black-Eyed Peas, Rice, Tasty Tahini Greens, orange, Chocolate Pudding

Wednesday ($4.11 / $2.59)
Lunch ($1.42 / $0.86): Spicy Black-Eyed Peas, Rice, Tasty Tahini Greens, banana
Snack ($0.29 / $0.18): Vanilla Yogurt
Dinner ($1.91 / $1.25): Noodles in Spicy Peanut Sauce with Winter Vegetables, orange

Thursday ($5.67 / $3.40)
Breakfast ($0.85 / $0.70): Bean Burritos, tea
Lunch ($2.08 / $1.40): rotini with Tomato Sauce with Robust Greens and Onions, broccoli, orange
Snack ($0.35 / $0.16): Ginger-Glazed Carrot Cake
Dinner ($2.39 / $1.13): Potato Pudding, Tasty Tahini Greens, banana

Friday ($4.86 / $3.03)
Breakfast ($0.60 / $0.38): Sweet Raisin Flatbread toast with peanut butter, tea
Lunch ($1.91 / $1.25): Noodles in Spicy Peanut Sauce with Winter Vegetables, orange
Snack ($0.27 / $0.16): Oatmeal-Raisin Cookies
Dinner ($2.08 / $1.24): Cuban Black Beans, side-dish serving of Potato Pudding, carrot, banana, Vanilla Yogurt

Saturday ($4.36 / $3.00)
Lunch ($0.79 / $0.60): Cuban Black Beans, Rice, carrot
Snack ($0.82 / $0.67): Vanilla Yogurt, banana
Dinner ($2.28 / $1.44): rotini with Tomato Sauce with Robust Greens and Onions, slice Cheddar, Green Salad with Vinaigrette, Chocolate Pudding

Winter Menu Week Three

Breakfast every day unless mentioned otherwise ($0.46 / $0.29): two slices of toasted Good Whisk Bread, peanut butter, and tea

Sunday ($5.36 / $2.81)
Breakfast ($0.70 / $0.41): Sweet Raisin Flatbread toast, egg, tea
Lunch ($1.03 / $0.64): Babe's Split Pea Soup, Corn Bread (two pieces), banana
Snack ($0.27 / $0.16): Oatmeal-Raisin Cookies
Dinner ($3.36 / $1.60): Pizza with Kale, Garlic, and Onions; Green Salad with Vinaigrette; orange; Chocolate Upside-Down Cake

Monday ($4.46 / $2.90)
Lunch ($1.47 / $1.10): Bean Burritos, Corn Bread (one piece), carrot, orange
Snack ($0.27 / $0.16): Oatmeal-Raisin Cookies
Dinner ($2.26 / $1.36): Potato Peanut Curry, steamed broccoli with lemon juice, banana, Vanilla Pudding

Tuesday ($4.25 / $2.28)
Lunch ($1.00 / $0.62): Babe's Split Pea Soup, Corn Bread (one piece), orange
Snack ($0.27 / $0.16): Oatmeal-Raisin Cookies
Dinner ($2.52 / $1.22): Pizza with Kale, Garlic, and Onions (one slice); broccoli; banana; Vanilla Pudding

Wednesday ($4.01 / $2.74)
Lunch ($1.47 / $1.10): Bean Burritos, carrot, Corn Bread (one piece), orange
Snack ($0.27 / $0.16): Oatmeal-Raisin Cookies

Dinner ($1.81 / $1.20): Noodles in Spicy Peanut Sauce with Winter Vegetables, banana

Thursday ($6.12 / $3.51)
Lunch ($2.89 / $1.76): rotini with Tomato Sauce with Bell Peppers and Onions, slice Cheddar, broccoli, orange
Snack ($0.27 / $0.16): Oatmeal-Raisin Cookies
Dinner ($2.49 / $1.31): Swiss Chard Frittata, Oven Fries, apple

Friday ($5.48 / $3.59)
Breakfast ($0.60 / $0.38): Sweet Raisin Flatbread toast with peanut butter, tea
Lunch ($1.91 / $1.25): Noodles in Spicy Peanut Sauce with Winter Vegetables, orange
Snack ($0.94 / $0.46): walnuts and raisins
Dinner ($2.03 / $1.49): Chickpea Stew on Couscous, Oatmeal-Raisin Cookies

Saturday ($4.43 / $2.83)
Breakfast ($0.37 / $0.25): Oatmeal with peanut butter, tea
Lunch ($1.19 / $0.79): Stoup with split peas, Corn Bread (one piece), banana
Snack ($0.41 / $0.28): apple
Dinner ($2.45 / $1.52): rotini with Tomato Sauce with Bell Peppers and Onions, slice Cheddar, Green Salad with Vinaigrette, Chocolate Upside-Down Cake

Winter Menu Week Four

Breakfast every day unless mentioned otherwise ($0.49 / $0.30):
two slices of toasted Whisk Sandwich Bread, peanut butter, and tea

Sunday ($5.43 / $3.39)
Breakfast ($0.60 / $0.38): Sweet Raisin
  Flatbread toast with peanut butter, tea
Lunch ($2.26 / $1.64): Chickpea Stew on
  Couscous, orange
Snack ($0.26 / $0.16): Cocoa Cookies
Dinner ($2.31 / $1.21): Pizza with Bell
  Peppers and Onions (two slices), Green
  Salad with Vinaigrette, apple

Monday ($5.40 / $3.40)
Lunch ($2.45 / $1.51): rotini with Tomato
  Sauce with Robust Greens and Onions,
  slice Cheddar, broccoli, banana
Snack ($0.35 / $0.16): Ginger-Glazed
  Carrot Cake
Dinner ($2.12 / $1.43): Red Bean Chili,
  Corn Bread (two pieces), carrot, orange,
  Chocolate Pudding

Tuesday ($4.68 / $2.78)
Lunch ($1.77 / $0.89): Pizza with Bell
  Peppers and Onions (one slice),
  broccoli, banana
Snack ($0.35 / $0.16): Ginger-Glazed
  Carrot Cake
Dinner ($2.08 / $1.43): Red Bean Chili,
  Corn Bread (two pieces), carrot, apple,
  Vanilla Yogurt

Wednesday ($5.79 / $3.71)
Breakfast ($0.46 / $0.35): Oatmeal with
  tahini, tea
Lunch ($2.45 / $1.51): rotini with Tomato
  Sauce with Robust Greens and Onions,
  broccoli, banana

Snack ($0.35 / $0.16): Ginger-Glazed
  Carrot Cake
Dinner ($2.54 / $1.68): Roasted Winter
  Vegetables, Hummus, apple

Thursday ($5.83 / $3.61)
Lunch ($2.63 / $1.70): Roasted Winter
  Vegetables, Hummus, orange
Snack ($0.26 / $0.16): Cocoa Cookies
Dinner ($2.45 / $1.46): pasta with Parsley
  Pesto, Glazed Carrots, apple

Friday ($5.83 / $3.54)
Breakfast ($0.60 / $0.38): Sweet Raisin
  Flatbread toast with peanut butter, tea
Lunch ($2.43 / $1.44): pasta with Parsley
  Pesto, carrot, apple
Snack ($0.29 / $0.18): Vanilla Yogurt
Dinner ($2.51 / $1.54): Red Bean Chili,
  Green Salad with Vinaigrette, Corn
  Bread (one piece), orange, Cocoa
  Cookies

Saturday ($4.01 / $2.76)
Lunch ($1.13 / $0.78): Stoup with black
  beans, Corn Bread (one piece), banana
Snack ($0.50 / $0.30): orange
Dinner ($1.90 / $1.38): rotini with
  Tomato Sauce with Robust Greens and
  Onions, slice Cheddar, onions sautéed
  with butter, Chocolate Pudding

Winter Menu: Extra Days

Day one
Breakfast: two slices of toasted Good Whisk Bread, peanut butter, tea, apple
Lunch: rotini with Tomato Sauce with Bell Peppers and Onions, onions sautéed with butter
Snack: walnuts and raisins
Dinner: Red Bean Chili, Tasty Tahini Greens, Rice, carrot, orange

Day two
Lunch: Stoup, Corn Bread (two pieces)
Snack: raisins
Dinner: Chickpea Stew on Couscous, Green Salad with Vinaigrette, slice of remaining cheese (Cheddar or mozzarella), banana

Day three
Breakfast: Oatmeal, yogurt, tea
Lunch: Babe's Split Pea Soup, Corn Bread (two pieces), carrot
Snack: raisins
Dinner: Stoup, Good Whisk Bread (two slices), slice of remaining cheese (Cheddar or mozzarella), apple, Oatmeal-Raisin Cookie (one)

TABLE 11.1

Winter Shopping List

(All Food for One Month Using the Winter Menu)

GOT IT?	ITEM	CATEGORY	AMOUNT	GREEN PRICE	THRIFTY PRICE	% LEFT AT END OF MONTH
____	baking powder	baking	10 oz.		$1.16	77%
____	baking soda	baking	8 oz.		$0.46	79%
	brown sugar	baking	2 lbs.		$0.79/lb.	34%
____	cocoa	baking	8 oz.		$2.58	29%
____	cornmeal	baking	2 lbs.	$0.99/lb. bulk	$1.25/2 lb.	20%
____	cornstarch	baking	1 lb.		$0.99	57%
____	flour, all-purpose	baking	two 5-lb. bags	$4.69 ea.	$1.99 ea.	24%
____	flour, white whole wheat	baking	two 5-lb. bags	$8.99 ea.	$4.39 ea.	11%
____	sugar	baking	5 lbs.		$3.33	20%
____	walnuts	baking	1 lb.	$10.99/lb. bulk	$4.49	0%
____	yeast, rapid-rise	baking	4 three-packs		$1.00 ea.	8%
____	oats	cereal	3 lbs. or 42 oz.	$3.57/lb. bulk	$2.45	15% or 3%
____	wheat germ	cereal	1 lb.		$2.69	25%
____	tea	coffee & tea	three 80-bag boxes/individual bags or two 24-bag boxes/ family-size bags	$3.99 ea.	$1.72	23% or 14%
____	butter	dairy	3 lbs.	$4.69 ea.	$1.88 ea.	26%
____	cheese, cheddar	dairy	five 8-oz. packages	$4.99 ea.	$1.67 ea.	0%
____	cheese, mozzarella	dairy	five 8-oz. packages	$4.29 ea.	$1.67 ea.	0%
____	cheese, parmesan	dairy	five 5-oz. or five 6-oz. packages	$3.99 ea.	$1.67 ea.	0%
____	eggs, large	dairy	four dozen	$3.50 dozen	$1.85 dozen	2%
____	milk, fresh 2%	dairy	four gallons	$4.89 ea.	$2.86 ea.	14%
____	yogurt for starter	dairy	two 6-oz. containers	$0.75 ea.	$0.50	0%
____	raisins	fruit	4 lbs. or three 24-oz. boxes	$2.99/lb. bulk	$3.29 ea.	6% or 17%

(continues)

Winter Shopping List (cont.)

GOT IT?	ITEM	CATEGORY	AMOUNT	GREEN PRICE	THRIFTY PRICE	% LEFT AT END OF MONTH
____	beans, black	grains	2 lbs.	$1.69/lb. bulk	$1.17/lb.	0%
____	beans, black-eyed peas	grains	1 lb.	$1.99/lb. bulk	$1.18/lb.	0%
____	beans, chickpea	grains	2 lbs.	$1.89/lb. bulk	$2.69/2 lbs.	0%
____	beans, kidney	grains	2 lbs.	$1.99/lb. bulk	$1.53/lb.	0%
____	beans, pinto	grains	2 lbs.	$1.99/lb. bulk	$2.29/2 lbs.	0%
____	beans, split peas	grains	2 lbs.	$1.79/lb. bulk	$0.90/lb.	0%
____	couscous	grains	31.7-oz. box or two 10-oz. boxes	$7.99	$2.05 ea.	39% or 4%
____	rice, long-grain brown	grains	4 lbs. bulk or two 2-lb. bags	$1.49/lb. bulk	$2.39 ea.	5%
____	burritos, 10-inch flour	grocery	two 10-count packages	$1.99/package		0%
____	honey	grocery	1 lb.	$3.99/lb. bulk	$5.49	3% or 35%
____	lemon juice (thrifty list)	grocery	15 oz.	X	$1.99	51%
____	peanut butter	grocery	eight 18-oz. jars	$2.99 ea.	$2.00 ea.	3%
____	rotini pasta	grocery	fourteen 14.5-oz. boxes		$2.15 ea.	0%
____	tomatoes, crushed	grocery	twelve 28-oz. cans	$1.99 ea.	$1.69 ea.	0%
____	tomatoes, diced	grocery	eleven 28-oz. cans	$1.89 ea.	$1.69 ea.	0%
____	vinegar, apple cider	grocery	16 oz.	$3.39	$1.23	63%
____	soy sauce	int'l	10 oz.	$2.69	$1.49	20%
____	tahini	int'l	15 or 16 oz.	$7.69	$5.99	29% or 24%
____	corn or canola oil	oil	16 oz. or 48 oz.	$4.69	$2.25	6% or 69%
____	olive oil	oil	four 16.9-oz. (½ liter) bottles or one 51-oz. bottle	$6.49 ea.	$10.93	18% or –1%*
____	apples	produce	seven 3-lb. bags or four 6-lb. bags	$3.69/bag	$5.00/bag	11% or 22%
____	bananas	produce	40 lbs.	$0.79/lb.	$0.50/lb.	0%

* Use butter or corn oil in place of 1 ½ tablespoons of olive oil.

Winter Shopping List *(cont.)*

GOT IT?	ITEM	CATEGORY	AMOUNT	GREEN PRICE	THRIFTY PRICE	% LEFT AT END OF MONTH
_____	bell peppers, green	produce	14	$2.49 ea.	$1.39 ea.	0%
_____	broccoli	produce	9 lbs. or 7 bunches	$3.49/lb.	$1.99/bunch	2% or 6%
_____	cabbage, green	produce	3 lbs.	$1.69/lb.	$0.59/lb.	7%
_____	carrots	produce	three 5-lb. bags	$3.99 ea.	$3.99 ea.	19%
_____	chard or mustard	produce	1 lb.	$3.00	$1.29	40%
_____	collards or kale	produce	8 bundles or 5 lbs.	$1.75 ea.	$0.99/lb.	7% or 1%
_____	garlic	produce	8 heads	$0.59 ea.	$0.79 ea.	5%
_____	ginger	produce	10 oz.	$7.99/lb.	$3.99/lb.	0%
_____	lemons (green list)	produce	6	$0.69 ea.	X	2%
_____	lettuce	produce	4 lbs. or 2 large heads	$4.00/lb.	$1.79/head	20%
_____	onions, green	produce	two 4-oz. bunches	$1.00 ea.	$0.50 ea.	13%
_____	onions, yellow or white	produce	five 3-lb. bags	$2.49 ea.	$2.99 ea.	12%
_____	oranges	produce	40 lbs. or five 8-lb. bags	$1.25/lb.	$5.99 ea.	0%
_____	parsley	produce	three 4-oz. bunches	$1.69 ea.	$0.99 ea.	25%
_____	potatoes, all-purpose	produce	two 5-lb. bags	$3.99 ea.	$1.78 ea.	20%
_____	potatoes, sweet	produce	6 lbs.	$1.35/lb.	$0.59/lb.	0%
_____	bay leaves	spices	⅛ oz. or 0.12 oz.	$1.16/oz. bulk	$0.69	81%
_____	cayenne	spices	1 oz.	$0.50/oz. bulk	$2.86	52%
_____	chipotle	spices	1 ¾ oz. or 2 oz.	$5.69	$4.87	41% or 48%
_____	cinnamon	spices	1 oz. or 2 oz.	$0.56/oz. bulk	$1.49	0% or 50%
_____	cumin	spices	2 oz. or 7 oz.	$1.12/oz. bulk	$2.29	3% or 72%
_____	oregano	spices	½ oz.	$0.50/oz. bulk	$0.59	33%
_____	salt	spices	26 oz.		$0.47	37%
_____	vanilla	spices	4 oz.	$8.69	$1.50	30%
_____	nutmeg	spices, optional	1 oz.	$2.25/oz. bulk	$2.09	92%
_____	turmeric	spices, optional	1 oz. or 0.95 oz.	$0.91/oz. bulk	$3.72	92%

Winter Cooking Plan

This is the essential *Wildly Affordable Organic* cooking plan. Use it all winter and during weeks throughout the year that don't call for dishes such as ice cream, lasagna, or bean burgers.

Each week, do the first cooking session in the afternoon or evening of one day and the second session the next day. That gives time a chance to work for you on the yogurt, beans, and bread. During the later weeks of the month you may cook less if you've been able to shop and cook ahead. For example, it's always more efficient to cook all the black beans you need for the month at once, if you have the budget and freezer room to do so.

Cooking Session One:
Core Cooking Plan with Pudding

 Time: 1 hour and 15 minutes

In this session you'll mix dough for two loaves of bread and two large pizzas, start making two kinds of beans, and make pudding and yogurt.

1. Mix dough for pizza and let rise for at least an hour (page 185).
2. Make Yogurt (page 127). If making Whisk Sandwich Bread, scald milk for yogurt and bread at the same time. When milk boils, measure out the amount needed for bread.
3. Mix dough for Good Whisk Bread (page 153) or Whisk Sandwich Bread (page 155) and let rise for at least an hour.
4. Make Chocolate Pudding (page 212) or Vanilla Pudding (page 212) using the pot used for yogurt.
5. While the pudding cooks, clean and soak two types of beans (page 132). Put beans that cook fastest into slow cooker, if using.
6. Wash the dishes.
7. Have some warm pudding! Refrigerate the rest.
8. When milk for yogurt cools to about 110°F, finish making yogurt. Refrigerate bread dough and pizza dough.

Cooking Session Two:
Core Cooking Plan with Pizza

 Time: 3 hours and 30 minutes

In this session you'll make two loaves of bread, pizza, a dessert, two pasta sauces, and several recipes using two types of beans.

1. First thing in the morning, refrigerate yogurt and put away nest (see page 128). Continue cooking when ready.

2. Take bread dough out of refrigerator and set bowl on counter to warm.

3. Start beans (page 133). Add other ingredients at this time if the recipes call for it.

4. If you will be using fresh water for beans in a slow cooker, bring it to a boil. Drain beans, add hot water and salt, and turn slow cooker on high.

5. If you will be using a pot on the stove, drain beans if desired and then cover with fresh water. Add salt and bring to a boil. Turn heat down until water just barely boils.

6. Divide bread dough, shape, and let rise again. Put bread stone or heavy cookie sheet in oven.

7. Preheat the oven for dessert. If baked potatoes or winter squash is on the menu this week, clean, wrap in foil, and bake in the oven corners or on another rack while you bake the dessert and bread.

8. Make cookies or cake.

9. While the dessert bakes, prepare the rest of the bean recipes. Cook onions and bell peppers in one big pot and divide them up for recipes. Use that same pot later to make tomato and pizza sauce.

10. Bake bread and take a little break. Have a fresh cookie or cupcake if you'd like.

While bread bakes, make a tomato sauce for pasta. Then use the same saucepan to make pizza sauce.

11. Make another kind of pasta sauce.

12. Take bread out of oven and cool on wire racks. Check to see if any baking vegetables are done. If so, take them out to cool. If not, let them cook more while you heat the oven for the pizza.

13. Turn up oven temperature for pizza. Make pizza, Green Salad (page 200), and Vinaigrette (page 201).

14. Have hot pizza and salad.

15. Refrigerate or put up the food when it is cool.

16. The next day, freeze food as needed, including any beans needed for Stoup at the end of the week.

12

Spring

Celebrate spring holidays with Magic Quiche with Asparagus or Strawberry Shortcake. Make Friday-night popcorn a family tradition.

Spring Menus

Spring Menu Week One

Breakfast every day unless mentioned otherwise ($0.46 / $0.28): two slices of toasted Good Whisk Bread, peanut butter, and tea

Sunday ($5.13 / $3.18)
Breakfast ($0.67 / $0.46): Sweet Raisin Flatbread toast with peanut butter, tea
Lunch ($1.27 / $0.76): Cuban Black Beans, Rice, carrot, banana
Snack ($0.69 / $0.39): walnuts
Dinner ($2.50 / $1.58): Pizza with Mustard Greens and Spring Onions (two slices), Green Salad with Vinaigrette, Strawberry Ice Cream

Monday ($5.86 / $3.92)
Lunch ($1.66 / $1.12): Cuban Black Beans, Rice, carrot, Chocolate Pudding
Snack ($0.41 / $0.39): apple
Dinner ($3.33 / $2.13): pasta with Parsley Pesto, Skillet Asparagus, Strawberry Ice Cream

Tuesday ($4.79 / $3.03)
Lunch ($1.93 / $1.03): Pizza with Mustard Greens and Spring Onions (one piece), broccoli, banana

Snack ($0.27 / $0.17): Oatmeal-Raisin
Cookies
Dinner ($2.13 / $1.56): Bean Burritos,
Green Salad with Vinaigrette, orange,
Vanilla Yogurt

Wednesday ($5.11 / $3.45)
Lunch ($1.96 / $1.45): Bean Burritos,
sugar snap peas, orange
Snack ($0.27 / $0.17): Oatmeal-Raisin
Cookies
Dinner ($2.43 / $1.56): Potato Peanut
Curry, Rice, broccoli, Vanilla Yogurt,
strawberries

Thursday ($5.21 / $3.02)
Lunch ($1.46 / $1.28): rotini with Tomato
Sauce with Spring Onions, carrot,
strawberries
Snack ($0.27 / $0.17): Oatmeal-Raisin
Cookies
Dinner ($3.02 / $1.29): Green Eggs
Scramble, microwaved or baked sweet
potato, banana

Friday ($4.81 / $3.79)
Breakfast ($0.30 / $0.26): Oatmeal with
peanut butter, tea
Lunch ($1.90 / $1.33): pasta with Parsley
Pesto, carrot
Snack ($0.51 / $0.33): strawberries
Dinner ($2.10 / $1.87): Bean and Tomato
Stew with black beans, Rice, Green
Salad with Vinaigrette, apple, Bright
Popcorn

Saturday ($3.95 / $3.09)
Lunch ($1.35 / $0.99): Stoup with black
beans, Garlic Toast, banana
Snack ($0.36 / $0.29): Bright Popcorn
Dinner ($1.76 / $1.53): rotini with
Tomato Sauce with Spring Onions,
sugar snap peas, Chocolate Pudding

Spring Menu Week Two

Breakfast every day unless mentioned otherwise ($0.48 / $0.29):
two slices of toasted Whisk Sandwich Bread, peanut butter, and tea

Sunday ($6.29 / $3.61)
Breakfast ($0.67 / $0.46): Sweet Raisin
Flatbread toast with peanut butter, tea
Lunch ($2.18 / $1.30): Red Bean Chili,
Rice, orange, Vanilla Yogurt
Snack ($0.69 / $0.39): walnuts
Dinner ($2.75 / $1.47): Magic Quiche
with Asparagus, baked potato, broccoli,
Strawberry Shortcake

Monday ($5.70 / $3.78)
Lunch ($1.76 / $1.16): Red Bean Chili,
Rice, carrot, banana
Snack ($0.41 / $0.39): apple
Dinner ($3.05 / $1.95): rotini with
Tomato Sauce with Robust Greens and
Onions, Skillet Asparagus, Strawberry
Shortcake

Spring Menu Week Two (cont.)

Tuesday ($5.01 / $3.00)

Lunch ($2.37 / $1.36): Magic Quiche with Asparagus, sugar snap peas, baked potato, orange

Snack ($0.27 / $0.15): Vanilla Yogurt

Dinner ($1.89 / $1.20): Spicy Black-Eyed Peas, Rice, Tasty Tahini Greens, Strawberry Shortcake

Wednesday ($4.47 / $2.81)

Lunch ($1.10 / $0.69): Spicy Black-Eyed Peas, Rice, Tasty Tahini Greens

Snack ($0.90 / $0.52): Vanilla Pudding, strawberries

Dinner ($1.98 / $1.32): Noodles in Spicy Peanut Sauce with Spring Vegetables, orange

Thursday ($5.64 / $3.88)

Breakfast ($0.93 / $0.78): Bean Burritos, tea

Lunch ($1.97 / $1.46): rotini with Tomato Sauce with Robust Greens and Onions, broccoli, apple

Snack ($0.27 / $0.17): Oatmeal-Raisin Cookies

Dinner ($2.47 / $1.47): Swiss Chard Frittata, Roasted Spring Vegetables, banana

Friday ($5.06 / $3.48)

Breakfast ($0.30 / $0.26): Oatmeal with peanut butter, tea

Lunch ($1.98 / $1.32): Noodles in Spicy Peanut Sauce with Spring Vegetables, orange

Snack ($0.27 / $0.17): Oatmeal-Raisin Cookies

Dinner ($2.51 / $1.74): Hoppin' John, Roasted Spring Vegetables, banana, Bright Popcorn

Saturday ($5.33 / $3.53)

Lunch ($1.79 / $1.10): Hoppin' John, carrot, banana

Snack ($0.36 / $0.29): Bright Popcorn

Dinner ($2.73 / $1.86): rotini with Tomato Sauce with Robust Greens and Onions, sugar snap peas, strawberries, Vanilla Pudding

Spring Menu Week Three

Breakfast every day unless mentioned otherwise ($0.46 / $0.28):
two slices of toasted Good Whisk Bread, peanut butter, and tea

Sunday ($5.87 / $3.56)

Breakfast ($0.67 / $0.46): Sweet Raisin
Flatbread toast with peanut butter, tea

Lunch ($2.01 / $1.13): Lentil Stew with
Spring Onions, Corn Bread (two
pieces), Skillet Asparagus, banana

Snack ($0.69 / $0.39): walnuts

Dinner ($2.50 / $1.58): Pizza with
Mustard Greens and Spring Onions
(two slices), Green Salad with
Vinaigrette, Strawberry Ice Cream

Monday ($4.81 / $3.04)

Lunch ($1.55 / $1.03): Bean Burritos with
Cheddar, carrot

Snack ($0.60 / $0.30): orange

Dinner ($2.20 / $1.44): Potato Peanut
Curry, Rice, broccoli, Strawberry Ice
Cream

Tuesday ($4.70 / $2.76)

Lunch ($2.01 / $1.28): Pizza with
Mustard Greens and Spring Onions
(one slice), broccoli, walnuts, apple

Snack ($0.78 / $0.48): Vanilla Yogurt with
strawberries

Dinner ($1.45 / $0.73): Lentil Soup with
Spring Onions, Corn Bread (two
pieces), Tasty Tahini Greens, Chocolate
Upside-Down Cake

Wednesday ($4.87 / $3.28)

Lunch ($1.36 / $0.85): Red Bean Chili,
carrot, Corn Bread (one piece)

Snack ($0.78 / $0.48): Vanilla Yogurt with
strawberries

Dinner ($2.27 / $1.67): Noodles in Spicy
Peanut Sauce with Spring Vegetables,
sugar snap peas, banana

Thursday ($5.84 / $3.56)

Lunch ($2.56 / $1.69): rotini with Tomato
Sauce with Spring Onions, broccoli,
strawberries

Snack ($0.27 / $0.17): Oatmeal-Raisin
Cookies

Dinner ($2.56 / $1.43): Egg and Spring-
Onion Burritos, Skillet Asparagus,
apple

Friday ($4.80 / $3.56)

Breakfast ($0.30 / $0.26): Oatmeal with
peanut butter, tea

Lunch ($1.79 / $1.40): Noodles in Spicy
Peanut Sauce with Spring Vegetables,
apple

Snack ($0.27 / $0.17): Oatmeal-Raisin
Cookies

Dinner ($2.44 / $1.73): Chickpea Stew on
Couscous, raisins, Bright Popcorn

Saturday ($4.32 / $3.30)

Lunch ($1.36 / $0.96): Stoup with lentils,
Garlic Toast, banana

Snack ($0.36 / $0.29): Bright Popcorn

Dinner ($2.13 / $1.77): rotini with
Tomato Sauce with Spring Onions,
sugar snap peas, strawberries, Chocolate
Upside-Down Cake

Spring Menu Week Four

Breakfast every day unless mentioned otherwise ($0.48 / $0.29):
two slices of toasted Whisk Sandwich Bread, peanut butter, and tea

Sunday ($6.15 / $4.11)
Breakfast ($0.67 / $0.46): Sweet Raisin Flatbread toast with peanut butter, tea
Lunch ($2.24 / $1.61): Chickpea Stew on Couscous, apple
Snack ($0.40 / $0.25): banana
Dinner ($2.84 / $1.79): Pizza with Bell Peppers and Onions (two slices), Green Salad with Vinaigrette, Strawberry Shortcake

Monday ($5.39 / $3.70)
Lunch ($2.22 / $1.59): rotini with Tomato Sauce with Robust Greens and Onions, slice Cheddar, sugar snap peas, banana
Snack ($0.41 / $0.39): apple
Dinner ($2.28 / $1.43): Red Bean Chili Casserole with Corn Bread Topping, carrot, Strawberry Shortcake

Tuesday ($5.38 / $3.20)
Lunch ($1.72 / $1.11): Pizza with Bell Peppers and Onions (one slice), sugar snap peas, banana
Snack ($0.27 / $0.15): Vanilla Yogurt
Dinner ($2.90 / $1.65): Red Bean Chili Casserole with Corn Bread Topping, carrot, slice Cheddar, Strawberry Shortcake

Wednesday ($4.75 / $3.15)
Lunch ($2.42 / $1.49): rotini with Tomato Sauce with Robust Greens and Onions, broccoli, banana

Snack ($0.25 / $0.14): Cocoa Cookies
Dinner ($1.60 / $1.23): Roasted Spring Vegetables, Hummus, strawberries

Thursday ($4.85 / $3.30)
Lunch ($1.69 / $1.20): Roasted Spring Vegetables, Hummus, orange
Snack ($0.25 / $0.14): Cocoa Cookies
Dinner ($2.43 / $1.68): pasta with Parsley Pesto, Glazed Carrots, strawberries

Friday ($4.94 / $3.43)
Breakfast ($0.30 / $0.26): Oatmeal with peanut butter, tea
Lunch ($2.31 / $1.71): pasta with Parsley Pesto, carrot
Snack ($0.78 / $0.48): Vanilla Yogurt with strawberries
Dinner ($1.55 / $0.98): Lentil Stew with Spring Onions, Garlic Flatbread, orange, Bright Popcorn

Saturday ($5.26 / $3.47)
Lunch ($1.74 / $1.11): Red Bean Chili, Garlic Flatbread, banana
Snack ($0.36 / $0.29): Bright Popcorn
Dinner ($2.68 / $1.78): rotini with Tomato Sauce with Robust Greens and Onions, slice Cheddar, sugar snap peas, orange, Cocoa Cookies

Spring Menu: Extra Days

Day one
Breakfast: Whisk Sandwich Bread toast, peanut butter, tea
Lunch: rotini with mixed sauces, Whisk Sandwich Bread, apple
Snack: Oatmeal-Raisin Cookies, milk
Dinner: Bean and Tomato Stew with chickpeas, banana

Day two
Breakfast: Whisk Sandwich Bread toast, peanut butter, tea
Lunch: Stoup, Garlic Flatbread, apple, Oatmeal-Raisin Cookies
Snack: Bright Popcorn
Dinner: remaining Hoppin' John and split peas, Couscous, remaining cheese, raisins

Day three
Breakfast: Oatmeal, egg, Yogurt
Lunch: Lentil Stew with Spring Onions, Tasty Tahini Greens,
Snack: walnuts and raisins
Dinner: black beans in Enchilada Sauce with onions, Couscous, remaining apple and raisins, Bright Popcorn

TABLE 12.1

Spring Shopping List

(All Food for One Month Using the Spring Menu)

GOT IT?	ITEM	CATEGORY	AMOUNT	GREEN PRICE	THRIFTY PRICE	% LEFT AT END OF MONTH
____	baking powder	baking	10 oz.		$1.49	83%
____	baking soda	baking	8 oz.		$0.46	90%
____	brown sugar	baking	2 lbs.		$0.68	44%
____	cocoa	baking	8 oz.		$2.79	62%
____	cornmeal	baking	1 or 2 lbs.	$0.99/lb. bulk	$1.25/2 lbs.	20% or 60%
____	cornstarch	baking	1 lb.		$1.30	79%
____	flour, all-purpose	baking	two 5-lb. bags	$4.69 ea.	$1.99 ea.	7%
____	flour, white whole wheat	baking	two 5-lb. bags	$8.99 ea.	$4.99 ea.	27%
____	sugar	baking	5 lbs.		$2.77	29%
____	walnuts	baking	2 lbs.	$10.99/lb. bulk	$6.24/lb.	25%
____	yeast, rapid rise	baking	4 oz.		$5.49	38%
____	oats	cereal	3 lbs. or 42 oz.	$1.19/lb. bulk	$2.99	15% or 3%
____	wheat germ	cereal	1 lb.		$2.69	14%
____	tea	coffee and tea	three 80-bag boxes of individual bags or two 24-bag boxes of family-size bags	$3.99 ea.	$1.49 ea.	23% or 14%
____	butter	dairy	2 lbs.	$4.69 ea.	$1.99 ea.	24%
____	cheese, cheddar	dairy	five 8-oz. packages or 3 lbs.	$4.99 ea.	$3.50	0%
____	cheese, mozzarella	dairy	1 lb. plus 8 oz.	$7.99 plus $4.99	$3.50 plus $2.00	0%
____	cheese, parmesan	dairy	three 6-oz. packages	$3.99 ea.	$2.00 ea.	0%
____	eggs, large	dairy	three dozen	$3.99/dozen	$1.32/dozen	0%
____	milk, fresh 2%	dairy	three gallons	$4.89 ea.	$2.89 ea.	1%
____	milk, fresh whole	dairy	half gallon	$3.29	$2.29	38%
____	whipping cream	dairy	two 8-oz. cartons	$1.99	$1.59	0%
____	yogurt for starter	dairy	three 6-oz. containers	$0.99 ea.	$0.50 ea.	25%
____	raisins	fruit	3 lbs. or two 24-oz. boxes	$2.99/lb. bulk	$3.95 ea.	8%
____	beans, black	grains	2 lbs.	$1.69/lb. bulk	$1.17/lb.	0%

Spring Shopping List (cont.)

GOT IT?	ITEM	CATEGORY	AMOUNT	GREEN PRICE	THRIFTY PRICE	% LEFT AT END OF MONTH
____	beans, black-eyed peas	grains	2 lbs.	$1.99/lb. bulk	$1.18/lb.	0%
____	beans, chickpea	grains	2 lbs.	$1.89/lb. bulk	$2.69/2 lbs.	0%
____	beans, kidney	grains	2 lbs.	$1.99/lbs. bulk	$1.53/lb.	0%
____	beans, lentils	grains	2 lbs.	$1.79/lb. bulk	$0.90/lb.	20%
____	beans, pinto	grains	2 lbs.	$1.99/lb. bulk	$2.39/2 lbs.	20%
____	couscous	grains	31.7-oz. box or three 10-oz. boxes	$7.99	$2.05 ea.	19% or 15%
____	rice, long-grain brown	grains	5 lbs. or one 3-lb. bag plus one 2-lb. bag	$1.49/lb. bulk	$3.99 plus $2.39	0%
____	burritos, 10-inch flour	grocery	two 10-count packages		$1.99 ea.	0%
____	honey	grocery	1 lb. or one 24-oz. jar	$3.99/lb. bulk	$5.29	7% or 38%
____	lemon juice (thrifty list)	grocery	15 oz.	X	$1.99	73%
____	peanut butter	grocery	nine 18-oz. jars or four 40-oz. jars	$2.99 ea.	$4.99 ea.	5% or 4%
____	popcorn	grocery	2 lbs.	$1.99/lb. bulk	$2.99/2 lbs.	0%
____	rotini pasta	grocery	thirteen 14.5-oz. boxes		$2.15 ea.	0%
____	tomatoes, crushed	grocery	ten 28-oz. cans	$1.99 ea.	$1.69 ea.	4%
____	tomatoes, diced	grocery	eleven 28-oz. cans	$1.89 ea.	$1.69 ea.	0%
____	vinegar, apple cider	grocery	16 oz.	$3.39	$1.23	63%
____	hot sauce	grocery, optional	12.3 oz.		$0.73	93%
____	soy sauce	int'l	10 oz.	$2.69	$1.49	20%
____	tahini	int'l	16 oz. or 15 oz.	$2.69	$6.29	50% or 47%
____	corn oil	oil	16 oz. or 48 oz.	$4.69	$2.25	70% or 90%
____	olive oil	oil	four 16.9-oz. (½ liter) bottles or four 17-oz. bottles*	$4.69 ea.	$2.25 ea.	–2%
____	apples	produce	five 3-lb. bags	$3.69 ea.	$3.49 ea.	0%
____	asparagus	produce	3 lbs.	$5.99/lb.	$2.99/lb.	10%
____	bananas	produce	34 lbs.	$0.79/lb.	$0.50/lb.	0%
____	bell peppers, green	produce	8	$2.99 ea.	$0.99 ea.	6%

* Use butter or corn oil in place of 2 tablespoons olive oil.

(continues)

Spring Shopping List *(cont.)*

GOT IT?	ITEM	CATEGORY	AMOUNT	GREEN PRICE	THRIFTY PRICE	% LEFT AT END OF MONTH
____	broccoli	produce	7 lbs.	$3.49/lb.	$1.49/lb.	8%
____	cabbage, green	produce	2 lbs.	$1.49/lb.	$0.49/lb.	20%
____	carrots	produce	five 2-lb. bags or two 5-lb. bags	$1.69 ea.	$3.49 ea.	2%
____	garlic	produce	8 heads	$0.59 ea.	$0.79 ea.	0%
____	ginger	produce	8 oz.	$7.99/lb.	$3.99/lb.	20%
____	green beans	produce	8 oz.		$1.99/lb.	0%
____	greens, Swiss chard	produce	1 lb.	$2.99/lb.	$1.39/lb.	70%
____	greens, kale or collards	produce	4 lbs.	$2.99/lb.	$1.39/lb.	14%
____	lemons (green list)	produce	4	$0.69 ea.	X	20%
____	lettuce	produce	two large heads or 2 lbs.	$2.00 ea.	$2.00/lb.	36% or 20%
____	onions, green	produce	eight 4-oz. bunches	$1.29 ea.	$0.50 ea.	10%
____	onions, yellow or white	produce	three 3-lb. bags	$2.69 ea.	$3.79 ea.	13%
____	oranges	produce	four 4-lb. bags or two 8-lb. bags	$5.99 ea.	$5.99 ea.	0%
____	parsley	produce	three 4-oz. bunches	$1.69 ea.	$0.99 ea.	25%
____	potatoes, all-purpose	produce	two 5-lb. bags	$3.99 ea.	$2.88 ea.	0%
____	potatoes, sweet	produce	2 lbs.	$1.99/lb.	$0.69/lb.	0%
____	strawberries	produce	three 5-lb. baskets or three 3½-qt. baskets	$14.00 ea.	$10 ea.	1% or 9%
____	sugar snap peas	produce	5 qts.	$4.99 ea.	$4.00 ea.	12%
____	bay leaves	spices	⅛ oz. or 0.12-oz.	$1.16/oz. bulk	$0.69	81%
____	cayenne	spices	1 oz.	$0.50/oz. bulk	$2.86	64%
____	chipotle	spices	2 oz.		$4.87	37%
____	cinnamon	spices	1 oz. or 2 oz.	$0.72/oz. bulk	$1.49	55% or 78%
____	cumin	spices	3 oz. or 7 oz.	$1.12/oz. bulk	$2.99	2% or 58%
____	oregano	spices	½ oz.	$0.50/oz. bulk	$0.59	40%
____	salt	spices	26 oz.		$0.47	52%
____	turmeric	spices	1 oz.	$2.00/oz. bulk	$3.72	33%
____	vanilla	spices	4 oz. or 8.4 oz.	$9.69	$1.99	49% or 75%
____	nutmeg	spices, optional	1 oz.	$2.09/oz. bulk	$2.14	94%

Spring Cooking Plan

These cooking plans put a twist on the basic cooking plan. Use the first cooking session during weeks when the menu shows ice cream instead of pudding. Use the second cooking session during weeks with Magic Quiche with Asparagus. Otherwise, follow the basic plan in the Winter section (page 69).

Do the first cooking session in the afternoon or evening of one day and the second session the next day. That gives time a chance to work for you on the yogurt, beans, and bread.

Cooking Session One:
Strawberry Ice Cream

 Time: 1 hour and 30 minutes

In this session, you'll mix dough for two loaves of bread and two large pizzas, start making two kinds of beans, and make ice cream and yogurt.

1. Mix dough for pizza and let rise for at least an hour (page 185).
2. Make Strawberry Ice Cream (page 216).
3. Make Yogurt (page 127). If making Whisk Sandwich Bread, scald milk for yogurt and bread at the same time. When milk boils, measure out the amount needed for bread.
4. Mix dough for Good Whisk Bread (page 153) or Whisk Sandwich Bread (page 155) and let rise for at least an hour.
5. Clean and soak two types of beans (page 132). Put beans that cook fastest into slow cooker, if using.
6. Wash the dishes.
7. Have some ice cream! Freeze the rest.
8. When milk for yogurt cools to about 110°F, finish making yogurt. Refrigerate bread dough and pizza dough.

Cooking Session Two:
Magic Quiche with Asparagus

Time: 3 hours and 30 minutes

In this session you'll make two loaves of bread, pizza, cookies, quiche, two pasta sauces, and several recipes using two types of beans.

1. First thing in the morning, refrigerate yogurt and put away nest (see page 128). Continue cooking when ready.

2. Take bread dough out of refrigerator and set bowl on counter to warm.

3. Start beans (page 133). Add other ingredients at this time if the recipes call for it.

4. If you will be using fresh water for beans in a slow cooker, bring it to a boil. Drain beans, add hot water and salt, and turn slow cooker on high.

5. If you will be using a pot on the stove, drain beans if desired and then cover with fresh water. Add salt and bring to a boil. Turn heat down until water just barely boils.

6. Divide bread dough, shape, and let rise again. Put bread stone or heavy cookie sheet in oven.

7. Preheat the oven for dessert. Clean potatoes, wrap in foil, and bake in the oven corners or on another rack while you bake the dessert and bread.

8. Make cookies.

9. While cookies bake, make Magic Quiche with Asparagus (page 166). Use a big pot to cook asparagus so you can use the pot later.

10. Prepare rest of bean recipes. Cook onions and bell peppers in one big pot and divide up for recipes. Use that same pot later to make tomato and pizza sauce.

11. Bake bread and take a little break. Have a fresh cookie or cupcake if you'd like.

12. While bread bakes, make a tomato sauce for pasta. Then use the same saucepan to make pizza sauce.

13. Make another kind of pasta sauce.

14. Take bread out of the oven and cool on wire racks. Take quiche out of the oven when it is ready. Check to see if any baking vegetables are done. If so, take them out to cool. If not, let them cook more while you heat the oven for the pizza.

15. Turn up oven temperature for pizza. Make pizza, Green Salad (page 200), and Vinaigrette (page 201).

16. Have hot pizza and salad.

17. Refrigerate or put up the food when it is cool.

18. The next day, freeze food as needed, including any beans needed for Stoup at the end of the week.

13

Summer

Celebrate Independence Day and other summer holidays with Proud Black-Bean Burgers and Blueberry Pie. Let Speedy Grilled Pizza keep the heat outside.

Summer Menus

Summer Menu Week One

Breakfast every day unless mentioned otherwise ($0.50 / $0.30): two slices of toasted Whisk Sandwich Bread, peanut butter, and tea

Sunday ($4.36 / $2.44)
Lunch ($1.09 / $0.49): Speedy Grilled Pizza (one piece), carrot
Snack ($0.64 / $0.32): cantaloupe, Vanilla Yogurt
Dinner ($2.12 / $1.32): Proud Black-Bean Burgers on Good Burger Buns, Classic Cabbage Slaw, Blueberry Pie

Monday ($4.47 / $2.97)
Lunch ($1.05 / $0.76): Bean Salad with Fresh Corn, Peppers, and Tomatoes with black beans; carrot; cantaloupe

Snack ($0.37 / $0.18): Vanilla Yogurt
Dinner ($2.54 / $1.72): rotini with Tomato Sauce with Summer Squash, slice Cheddar, Marinated Green Beans, Blueberry Pie

Tuesday ($5.25 / $3.52)
Lunch ($2.06 / $1.38): rotini with Tomato Sauce with Summer Squash, Marinated Green Beans, cantaloupe
Snack ($0.69 / $0.39): walnuts

Summer Menu Week One (cont.)

Dinner ($2.00 / $1.45): Chickpea Stew on Couscous, tomato, Blueberry Pie with Sneaky-Wheat Butter Pie Crust

Wednesday ($4.08 / $2.85)

Breakfast ($0.69 / $0.46): Whisk Sandwich Bread toast with peanut butter, tea, pineapple-orange-banana juice

Lunch ($1.05 / $0.70): Bean Salad with Fresh Corn, Peppers, and Tomatoes with black beans; cucumber salad with Spicy Yogurt Sauce

Snack ($0.37 / $0.18): Vanilla Yogurt

Dinner ($1.97 / $1.51): Noodles in Spicy Peanut Sauce with Summer Vegetables, watermelon, Peach Ice Cream Supreme

Thursday ($4.53 / $2.86)

Breakfast ($0.57 / $0.42): Oatmeal with peanut butter, pineapple-orange-banana juice, tea

Lunch ($1.20 / $0.98): Chickpea Stew on Couscous

Snack ($0.30 / $0.16): Cocoa Cookies

Dinner ($2.46 / $1.30): Huevos Rancheros, Refried Beans, Zlaw, watermelon

Friday ($4.55 / $2.98)

Breakfast ($0.69 / $0.46): Whisk Sandwich Bread toast with peanut butter, tea, pineapple-orange-banana juice

Lunch ($1.50 / $1.14): Noodles in Spicy Peanut Sauce with Summer Vegetables, blueberries

Snack ($0.30 / $0.16): Cocoa Cookies

Dinner ($2.06 / $1.21): Tortilla Stacks, tomato and cucumber salad with Spicy Yogurt Sauce

Saturday ($5.05/ $2.82)

Lunch ($1.19 / $0.81): Stoup with black beans, cucumber, Cocoa Cookies

Snack ($0.14 / $0.14): watermelon

Dinner ($3.24 / $1.58): Speedy Grilled Pizza (two pieces), Grilled Summer Squash Two Ways, Peach Ice Cream Supreme

Summer Menu Week Two

Breakfast every day unless mentioned otherwise ($0.48 / $0.29):
two slices of toasted Good Whisk Bread, peanut butter, and tea

Sunday ($3.73 / $2.32)
Lunch ($1.06 / $0.67): Bean Salad with Fresh Corn, Peppers, and Tomatoes with lentils; cantaloupe

Snack ($0.69 / $0.39): walnuts

Dinner ($1.51 / $0.97): Pizza with Bell Peppers and Onions (two pieces), carrot, Feel-Good Peach Cobbler

Monday ($4.30 / $2.85)
Lunch ($2.18 / $1.42): rotini with Tomato Sauce with Summer Squash, slice or sprinkle mozzarella, Marinated Green Beans

Snack ($0.14 / $0.09): Peanut Butter Cookies, extra Cobbler biscuit

Dinner ($1.50 / $1.05): Cuban Black Beans, Rice, Classic Cabbage Slaw, cantaloupe, Feel-Good Peach Cobbler

Tuesday ($4.03 / $2.38)
Lunch ($0.84 / $0.49): Pizza with Bell Peppers and Onions (one piece), carrot, cantaloupe

Snack ($0.37 / $0.18): Vanilla Yogurt

Dinner ($2.34 / $1.42): Soft Tacos with Refried Beans, Grilled Summer Squash Two Ways with Spicy Yogurt Sauce, Feel-Good Peach Cobbler

Wednesday ($5.75 / $3.55)
Lunch ($1.46 / $0.93): Soft Tacos with Refried Beans and Spicy Yogurt Sauce, bell pepper strips

Snack ($0.14 / $0.14): watermelon

Dinner ($3.67 / $2.18): Southern Summer Pesto Pasta with Green Beans, blueberries, Chocolate Pudding

Thursday ($5.79 / $3.61)
Breakfast ($0.76 / $0.44): Oatmeal with peanut butter, tea, Vanilla Yogurt

Lunch ($3.24 / $1.94): Southern Summer Pesto Pasta with Green Beans, blueberries

Snack ($0.14 / $0.09): Peanut Butter Cookies

Dinner ($1.66 / $1.14): Hummus and Garlic Flatbread with tomato, cucumber, and Spicy Yogurt Sauce; watermelon

Friday ($4.28 / $2.64)
Lunch ($1.52 / $1.00): Hummus and Garlic Flatbread with tomato, cucumber, and Spicy Yogurt Sauce

Snack ($1.14 / $0.67): Vanilla Yogurt with blueberries

Dinner ($1.13 / $0.69): Vichyssoise Encore, bell pepper strips, Hard-Boiled Egg, watermelon, Peanut Butter Cookies

Saturday ($4.34 / $2.96)
Lunch ($1.01 / $0.71): Stoup with lentils, carrot, cantaloupe

Snack ($0.14 / $0.09): Peanut Butter Cookies

Dinner ($2.71 / $1.88): rotini with Tomato Sauce with Summer Squash, slice Cheddar, Marinated Green Beans, blueberries, Chocolate Pudding

Summer Menu Week Three

Breakfast every day unless mentioned otherwise ($0.48 / $0.29):
two slices of toasted Good Whisk Bread, peanut butter, and tea

Sunday ($4.86 / $2.71)
Breakfast ($1.18 / $0.74): Better Blueberry
Pancakes with real maple syrup, one
egg, tea
Lunch ($1.09 / $0.49): Speedy Grilled
Pizza (one piece), carrot
Snack ($0.64 / $0.32): Vanilla Yogurt with
cantaloupe
Dinner ($1.94 / $1.16): Proud Black-Bean
Burgers on Good Burger Buns, Zlaw,
Blueberry Pie with Sneaky-Wheat
Butter Pie Crust

Monday ($4.42 / $2.94)
Lunch ($0.78 / $0.57): Bean Salad with
Fresh Corn, Peppers, and Tomatoes
with kidney beans
Snack ($0.64 / $0.32): Vanilla Yogurt with
cantaloupe
Dinner ($2.52 / $1.76): rotini with
Tomato Sauce with Bell Peppers and
Onions, slice Cheddar, Green Beans
with Vinaigrette, Blueberry Pie

Tuesday ($6.22 / $3.43)
Lunch ($3.23 / $1.66): Greek Potato
Salad, cantaloupe
Snack ($0.14 / $0.09): Peanut Butter Cookies
Dinner ($2.38 / $1.39): Soft Tacos with
Refried Beans and Spicy Yogurt Sauce,
Grilled Summer Squash Two Ways,
Blueberry Pie

Wednesday ($7.00 / $4.37)
Breakfast ($0.80/ $0.57): Oatmeal with
tahini and tomato

Lunch ($1.79 / $1.10): Soft Tacos with
Refried Beans and Spicy Yogurt Sauce,
tomato, bell pepper strips
Snack ($0.69 / $0.39): walnuts
Dinner ($3.71 / $2.31): Southern Summer
Pesto Pasta with Green Beans,
watermelon, Peach Ice Cream Supreme

Thursday ($4.78 / $2.71)
Lunch ($2.55 / $1.63): Rotini with
Southern Summer Pesto, carrot,
blueberries
Snack ($0.14 / $0.09): Peanut Butter Cookies
Dinner ($1.61 / $0.71): Southwestern
Bean Stew, Rice, watermelon, Vanilla
Yogurt

Friday ($3.57 / $1.94)
Lunch ($0.86 / $0.46): Vichyssoise Encore,
Hard-Boiled Egg, green pepper strips
Snack ($0.58 / $0.39): Vanilla Yogurt with
blueberries
Dinner ($1.61 / $0.80): Southwestern
Bean Stew, Rice, Garlic Toast,
watermelon, Peanut Butter Cookies

Saturday ($5.17 / $2.79)
Lunch ($0.76 / $0.53): Southwestern
Bean Stew, Rice, cantaloupe
Snack ($0.69 / $0.39): walnuts
Dinner ($3.24 / $1.58): Speedy Grilled
Pizza (two pieces), Grilled Summer
Squash Two Ways, Rice, Peach Ice
Cream Supreme

Summer Menu Week Four

Breakfast every day unless mentioned otherwise ($0.50 / $0.30):
two slices of toasted Whisk Sandwich Bread, peanut butter, and tea

Sunday ($4.54 / $2.84)
Breakfast ($1.43 / $0.82): Better Blueberry
Pancakes with real maple syrup, eggs
(seven eggs for four people), tea
Lunch ($1.16 / $0.86): Bean and Tomato
Stew with black beans, Rice, bell pepper
strips
Snack ($0.27 / $0.14): cantaloupe
Dinner ($1.67 / $1.02): Pizza with Bell
Peppers and Onions (two pieces),
cucumber, Feel-Good Peach Cobbler

Monday ($4.08 / $3.04)
Lunch ($0.98 / $0.78): Bean Salad with
Fresh Corn, Peppers, and Tomatoes
with pinto beans; blueberries
Snack ($0.69 / $0.39): walnuts, extra
Cobbler biscuit
Dinner ($1.90 / $1.56): rotini with
Tomato Sauce with Bell Peppers and
Onions, slice Cheddar, Garlic Flatbread,
carrot, Feel-Good Peach Cobbler

Tuesday ($4.29 / $2.93)
Lunch ($0.71 / $0.49): Pizza with Bell
Peppers and Onions (one piece), carrot,
watermelon
Snack ($0.69 / $0.39): walnuts
Dinner ($2.39 / $1.75): rotini with
Tomato Sauce with Bell Peppers and
Onions, slice Cheddar, Green Beans
with Vinaigrette, blueberries, Peanut
Butter Cookies

Wednesday ($3.93 / $2.88)
Lunch ($0.98 / $0.78): Bean Salad with
Fresh Corn, Peppers, and Tomatoes
with kidney beans; blueberries
Snack ($ 0.58/ $0.39): Vanilla Yogurt
Dinner ($1.86 / $1.40): Noodles in Spicy
Peanut Sauce with Summer Vegetables,
watermelon, Feel-Good Peach Cobbler

Thursday ($3.80/ $2.92)
Lunch ($1.41 / $1.19): Chickpea Stew on
Couscous, blueberries
Snack ($0.14 / $0.09): Peanut Butter
Cookies
Dinner ($1.75 / $1.33): Huevos
Rancheros, Refried Beans, watermelon,
Vanilla Yogurt

Friday ($4.36 / $3.02)
Lunch ($1.50 / $1.14): Noodles in Spicy
Peanut Sauce with Summer Vegetables,
blueberries
Snack ($0.14 / $0.09): Chocolate Pudding
Dinner ($2.24 / $1.49): Tortilla Stacks,
Spicy Yogurt Sauce, peach

Saturday ($3.92 / $2.59)
Lunch ($0.95 / $0.80): Stoup with kidney
beans, Rice, watermelon
Snack ($0.37 / $0.18): Vanilla Yogurt
Dinner ($2.12 / $1.31): Proud Black-Bean
Burgers on Good Burger Buns, Zlaw,
blueberries, Chocolate Pudding

Summer Menu: Extra Days

Breakfast every day unless mentioned otherwise: two slices of toasted Whisk Sandwich Bread, peanut butter, and tea

Day one
Breakfast: Good Whisk Bread toast with peanut butter, tea, Yogurt with honey
Lunch: Cuban Black Beans, Rice, carrot, Vanilla Yogurt
Snack: walnuts, peach
Dinner: end-of-month Stoup, Parmesan, Garlic Flatbread, peach

Day two
Lunch: Tomato Sauce with Summer Squash on Couscous, remaining Cheddar and mozzarella, Zlaw, watermelon
Snack: Peanut Butter Cookies
Dinner: Proud Black-Bean Burgers, side of tomatoes with rice, carrot, peach

Day three
Lunch: peanut butter and honey sandwich on Good Whisk Bread, watermelon, salad from remaining vegetables: carrot, summer squash, and purple onion
Snack: Peanut Butter Cookies
Dinner: pinto beans in Tomato Sauce with Bell Peppers and Onions, Garlic Flatbread, Spicy Yogurt Sauce, remaining fruit

TABLE 13.1

Summer Shopping List

(All Food for One Month Using the Summer Menu)

GOT IT?	ITEM	CATEGORY	AMOUNT	GREEN PRICE	THRIFTY PRICE	% LEFT AT END OF MONTH
____	baking powder	baking	10 oz.		$1.49	88%
____	baking soda	baking	8 oz.		$0.46	93%
____	brown sugar	baking	1 lb.		$0.92	52%
____	cocoa	baking	8 oz.		$2.79	51%
____	cornstarch	baking	12 oz. or 1 lb.	$2.69	$1.30	62% or 71%
____	flour, all-purpose	baking	three 5-lb. bags	$4.69 ea.	$1.99 ea.	0%
____	flour, white whole wheat	baking	three 5-lb. bags	$8.99 ea.	$4.99 ea.	16%
____	pecans	baking	three 4-oz. bags or 1 lb.	$5.69 ea.	$8.71	14%
____	sugar	baking	5 lbs.		$3.44	–2%*
____	walnuts	baking	2 lbs.	$10.99/lb. bulk	$6.24 ea.	0%
____	yeast, rapid rise	baking	4 oz.		$5.49	13%
____	oats	cereal	2 lbs. or one 42-oz. box	$1.19/lb. bulk	$2.99	30% or 54%
____	wheat germ	cereal	1 lb.		$2.49	0%
____	tea	coffee and tea	three 80-bag boxes individual bags or two 24-bag boxes family-size bags	$3.99 ea.	$1.72 ea.	23% or 14%
____	butter	dairy	3 lbs.	$4.69 ea.	$2.19 ea.	30%
____	cheese, cheddar	dairy	six 8-oz. or four 12-oz. packages	$2.99 ea.	$2.89 ea.	0%
____	cheese, grated Italian mix	dairy	three 6-oz. or two 8-oz. packages	$5.99 ea.	$2.00 ea.	0%
____	cheese, mozzarella	dairy	two 12-oz. or one 1-lb. package	$4.69 ea.	$3.89	0%
____	cheese, parmesan	dairy	two 5-oz. or two 6-oz. packages	$3.99 ea.	$2.00 ea.	0%

* Use ¼ cup brown sugar for rest of white sugar.

(continues)

Summer Shopping List *(cont.)*

GOT IT?	ITEM	CATEGORY	AMOUNT	GREEN PRICE	THRIFTY PRICE	% LEFT AT END OF MONTH
____	eggs, large	dairy	four dozen	$3.99 ea.	$1.32 ea.	0%
____	juice, pineapple-orange-banana	dairy	64 oz.	$2.99	$2.50	0%
____	milk, fresh 2%	dairy	three gallons	$4.89 ea.	$3.10 ea.	−4%*
____	milk, fresh whole	dairy	half gallon	$3.29	$2.42	38%
____	yogurt for starter	dairy	three 6-oz. containers	$0.89 ea.	$0.56 ea.	25%
____	beans, black	grains	3 lbs.	$1.69/lb. bulk	$1.19/lb.	0%
____	beans, chickpea	grains	2 lbs.	$1.99/lb. bulk	$1.89/2 lbs.	0%
____	beans, kidney	grains	1 lb. (green list) or 2 lbs. (thrifty list)	$1.99/lb. bulk	$1.59/lb.	0%
____	beans, lentils	grains	1 lb.	$1.79/lb. bulk	$0.90/lb.	0%
____	beans, pinto	grains	4 lbs.	$1.99/lb. bulk	$2.29/2 lbs.	0%
____	beans, Yellow Indian Woman Beans (green list)	grains	1 lb.	$4.95	X	0%
____	couscous	grains	31.7-oz. box or three 10-oz. boxes	$7.99	$2.05 ea.	19% or 15%
____	rice, long-grain brown	grains	5 lbs. or two 2-lb. bags	$1.49/lb. bulk	$2.39 ea.	15%
____	honey	grocery	2½ lbs. or 2 lbs.	$3.99/lb. bulk	$6.91/2 lbs.	11% or −11%**
____	hot sauce (optional)	grocery	5 oz. or 12⅓ oz.	$3.99	$0.79	95% or 98%
____	ketchup	grocery	24 oz. or 20 oz.	$1.99	$1.35	80% or 76%
____	lemon juice (thrifty list)	grocery	two 15-oz. bottles	X	$1.99	36%
____	maple syrup, grade B or Canadian amber if available	grocery	32 oz. or 8½ oz.	$15.99	$4.99	87% or 50%
____	mayonnaise	grocery	11¼ oz. or 8 oz.	$5.69	$1.95	47% or 25%
____	mustard	grocery	8 oz. or 9 oz.	$1.99	$0.99	73% or 76%

---

* Use extra whole milk for rest of 2% milk.

** Use brown sugar in place of 3 tablespoons honey in vanilla yogurt.

Summer Shopping List *(cont.)*

GOT IT?	ITEM	CATEGORY	AMOUNT	GREEN PRICE	THRIFTY PRICE	% LEFT AT END OF MONTH
____	peanut butter	grocery	ten 18-oz. jars	$2.99 ea.	$2.00 ea.	1%
____	rotini, high-protein, or pasta	grocery	eleven 14.5-oz. boxes		$2.15 ea.	7%
____	tomatoes, crushed	grocery	eight 28-oz. cans	$1.79 ea.	$1.69 ea.	0%
____	tomatoes, diced	grocery	five 28-oz. cans	$1.89 ea.	$1.69 ea.	0%
____	vinegar, apple cider	grocery	16 oz.	$3.49	$1.23	71%
____	masa harina	int'l	one 52-oz. package		$2.97	3%
____	soy sauce	int'l	10 oz.	$2.49	$1.49	20%
____	tahini*	int'l	16 oz.	$7.69	$7.69*	57%
____	corn or canola oil	oil	16 oz. or 24 oz.	$4.69	$1.99	56% or 71%
____	olive oil	oil	four 16.9-oz. (½ liter) bottles or four 17-oz. bottles	$6.49 ea.	$5.39 ea.	19%
____	basil	produce	1 lb. plus one 2-oz. bunch or five 4-oz. bunches	$10/lb. plus $1.50/bunch	$0.99/bunch	0% or 10%
____	blueberries	produce	flat (18 pints)	$15.00/flat	$15.00/flat**	0%
____	cabbage, green	produce	4 lbs.	$1.49/lb.	$0.49/lb.	20%
____	cabbage, red	produce	1 lb.	$1.49	$0.49	20%
____	cantaloupes	produce	4 large	$3.25 ea.	$1.67 ea.	0%
____	carrots	produce	one 5-lb. bag	$3.99	$3.99	5%
____	cilantro	produce	one 4-oz. bunch	$1.49	$0.89	0%
____	corn	produce	one 20-ear bag		$8.00	15%
____	cucumber	produce	3 lbs.	$2.00/lb.	$0.99/lb.	8%
____	garlic	produce	8 heads	$0.59 ea.	$0.79 ea.	10%
____	ginger	produce	8 oz.	$5.99/lb.	$3.99/lb.	20%
____	green beans	produce	12 lbs.	$3.00/lb.	$1.50/lb.	4%
____	lemons (green list)	produce	two 10-lemon bags	$4.49 ea.	X	23%
____	onions, purple	produce	2 lbs.	$1.69/lb.	$1.29/lb.	25%

---

* Only organic tahini available this month, so using organic price.

** List shows same spray-free source for green and thrifty blueberries since it was the best price available.

(continues)

Summer Shopping List (cont.)

GOT IT?	ITEM	CATEGORY	AMOUNT	GREEN PRICE	THRIFTY PRICE	% LEFT AT END OF MONTH
____	onions, yellow or white	produce	three 3-lb. bags	$2.50 ea.	$2.39 ea.	2%
____	peaches	produce	½ bushel		$15.00	0%
____	peppers, green	produce	6 lbs. or 15 large peppers	$2.00/lb.	$0.50 ea.	13% or 3%
____	peppers, hot	produce	7 peppers or ½ lb.	$0.10 ea.	$2.99/lb.	0% or 36%
____	potatoes, all-purpose	produce	one 5-lb. bag or one 10-lb. bag	$4.49	$4.99	30% or 65%
____	squash, summer	produce	9 lbs.	$2.00/lb.	$0.79/lb.	3%
____	tomatoes	produce	12 lbs.	$2.00/lb.	$0.99/lb.	2%
____	watermelon	produce	5 small "personal" melons		$1.67 ea.	0%
____	bay leaves	spices	⅛ oz. or 0.12 oz.	$1.16/oz. bulk	$0.69	81%
____	cayenne	spices	1 oz.	$0.50/bulk	$2.86	76% or 54%*
____	chipotle (optional for thrifty list)	spices	1¾ oz. or 2 oz.	$5.69	$4.87	87% or 77%
____	cinnamon	spices	1 oz. or 2 oz.	$0.56/oz. bulk	$1.49	90% or 95%
____	cumin	spices	1 oz. or 7 oz.	$0.69/oz. bulk	$2.99	43% or 92%
____	oregano	spices	½ oz.	$0.75/oz. bulk	$0.75	21%
____	salt	spices	26 oz.		$0.47	39%
____	sesame seeds	spices	1½ oz.		$0.59	60%
____	vanilla	spices	4 oz. or 8.4 oz.	$9.69	$1.99	41% or 72%
____	almond extract	spices, optional	2 oz.	$4.69	$3.63	96%

* For thrifty list, percent left assumes using cayenne in place of chipotle.

Summer Cooking Plan

The summer cooking plan is my favorite. With one big cooking weekend a month, you can make delicious meals to enjoy all month long. Cooking throughout the week and for the other weekends of the month will be much easier because you've made such a great start.

The cooking doesn't even take that long—just five hours of cooking, spread over two days! You'll cook three kinds of beans (fifty-two servings!), two loaves of bread, homemade burger buns, blueberry pie, an extra pie crust for later in the month, tomato and summer-squash pasta sauce, pesto, hummus, bean burgers, bean salad, and homemade yogurt.

Do the first cooking session in the afternoon or evening of one day and the second session the next day. That gives time a chance to work for you on the yogurt, beans, and bread.

Cook big once a month and then take a cooking vacation. Sure, you'll still be cooking some, but you will have a big head start on many meals.

Cooking Session One

 Time: 1 hour

In this session, you'll mix dough for two loaves of bread, clean and soak three kinds of beans, and make yogurt. Optionally, mix dough for burger buns.

Pick Your Buns

If you don't have a bread machine or stand mixer, make Whisk Burger Buns instead of Good Burger Buns. The first cooking session will take 10 more minutes and the second session 15 to 20 minutes less. This option saves a little time, money, and calories. Good Burger Buns are tens on the Bun Perfection Scale, well worth making if you can.

---

1. Make one or two recipes of dough for Good Whisk Bread (page 153). Cover bowl and set on counter to rise. Make the second recipe if you are making Whisk Burger Buns instead of Good Burger Buns.

2. Make yogurt. While milk comes to a boil, set out a slow cooker and two big pots for beans.

3. While milk cools, clean and soak two pounds each pinto and black beans (page 132), putting black beans in the biggest pot.

4. Clean one pound chickpeas and soak in slow cooker with six cups of water and 1½ teaspoons of salt, stirring to mix. Turn slow cooker on low so beans cook overnight.

5. About fifteen minutes later, when milk cools to around 110°F, finish making yogurt. Put bread dough in refrigerator after it has risen for one to five hours.

Cooking Session Two

Time: 4 hours

In this session you'll make three kinds of beans plus bean burgers and bean salad, two loaves of bread, burger buns, pesto, tomato and squash sauce for pasta, hummus, blueberry pie, and an extra pie crust for later in the month.

1. First thing in the morning, take bread dough out of refrigerator and put yogurt in. Turn off heating pad and put yogurt nest away.

2. Start Good Burger Buns (page 157) by measuring ingredients and letting dough knead in stand mixer or bread machine, if making.

3. Start cooking pinto and black beans. Cool and bite a few chickpeas. If they are tender, pour into a bowl and pour a cup or two of pinto beans into the slow cooker. (Putting beans into the slow cooker in two steps reduces the temperature shock to the hot crock.) Add salt to pintos and to black beans. Turn black beans on high and let come to a boil. Add rest of pintos to slow cooker, cover, and turn on high. When black beans come to a boil, turn heat down until water barely boils. (You are cooking black beans on the stove because you use them sooner. If the pintos aren't done when you need them, just finish refried beans later.)

4. Oil a big bowl for the bun dough. When dough has finished kneading, put it in a bowl, cover, and let rise for at least an hour until doubled.

5. Make one recipe of Sneaky-Wheat Butter Pie Crust (page 227), measuring dry ingredients for second recipe into a medium bowl to be used in a few minutes. Freeze crust for 10 minutes while you prepare filling for Blueberry Pie (page 226). Finish making pie and refrigerate for 30 minutes. Meanwhile, preheat oven to 425°F. Make second recipe of pie crust for later in the month, wrap well, and freeze.

6. Cut up melon and put in covered container while pie continues to cool. Take pie out of refrigerator and put melon in.

7. Put foil strips on pie and bake. Set timer to remind you to remove foil strips after the first thirty minutes.

8. Scrape any scraps of pie dough out of your food processor. Use food processor to make slaw and chop bell peppers, onions, and garlic for remaining recipes. Rinse food processor with water when done.

9. Make Tomato Sauce with Summer Squash (page 174).

10. Finish making Classic Cabbage Slaw (page 202) and refrigerate.

11. Make Bean Salad with Fresh Corn, Peppers, and Tomatoes (page 136) and refrigerate. Add black beans later, after they cook and cool. Pasta sauce should be done simmering, so turn off heat and put pan on cool burner or trivet.

12. Take pie out when ready, turn oven temperature to 350°F, and take a ten-minute break. This may be best spent admiring your pie.

13. Bake bread for 35 to 40 minutes. Check black beans and turn off burner if they are tender.

14. Shape burger buns and let rise for 30 to 40 minutes.

15. Make Southern Summer Pesto (page 177). Save ¼ cup for burgers and freeze rest.

16. Make Proud Black-Bean Burgers (page 137) and prepare cookie sheets for burgers. Let burger mixture rest for at least 15 minutes.

17. Refrigerate Tomato Sauce with Summer Squash you will be using this week and freeze the rest. Cook onions for Refried Beans (page 146) in the pan you used for tomato sauce.

18. When bread is done, remove from oven and cool on wire racks. Turn oven temperature to 375°F.

19. Glaze burger buns with egg yolk and sprinkle with sesame seeds, if using. Bake buns at 375°F for 15 minutes.

20. Make Hummus (page 142) and freeze. It's not on the menu until week two, but you needed to cook chickpeas for this week anyway and the food processor is in play.

21. Shape bean burgers. Remove buns from oven when done and put on wire racks to cool. Set the oven temperature to 425°F. Bake bean burgers at 425°F for 30 minutes, setting timer to flip them in 15 minutes.

22. Finish Refried Beans (page 146) if pintos are tender. Flip bean burgers. When refried beans are done, turn off stove and remove from heat. (If the pinto beans aren't tender, check them again after lunch and make the refrieds when the pintos are tender.)

23. Get ready to eat lunch. Set out slaw and toppings for burgers (ketchup and mustard are on the *Wildly Affordable Organic* shopping list, but you know your favorites). Slice buns that you will be using. Wrap remaining buns well and freeze.

24. Take bean burgers out of oven. Eat!

25. After lunch, cover, refrigerate, or freeze food as needed.

14

Fall

Indulge in a feast every month with Harvest Lasagna and Baked Pears with Cinnamon Yogurt Sauce. Thrift enables luxury!

Fall Menus

Fall Menu Week One

Breakfast every day unless mentioned otherwise ($0.46/ $0.30): two slices of toasted Good Whisk Bread, peanut butter, and tea

Sunday ($5.22 / $3.42)
Breakfast ($0.98 / $0.57): Two-for-One Apple-Streusel Coffee Cake, egg, tea
Lunch ($1.90 / $1.23): Cuban Black Beans, Nutty Rice Salad, banana
Snack ($0.30 / $0.20): Oatmeal-Raisin Cookies
Dinner ($2.04 / $1.41): Pizza with Bell Peppers and Onions (two slices), Green Salad with Vinaigrette, orange

Monday ($6.11 / $4.16)
Lunch ($2.20 / $1.50): rotini with Parsley Pesto, carrot, banana

Snack ($0.30 / $0.20): Oatmeal-Raisin Cookies
Dinner ($3.15 / $2.15): Black Beans in Baked Winter Squash with Persian Tomato Sauce topped with Yogurt, Nutty Rice Salad, apple

Tuesday ($3.89 / $2.75)
Lunch ($1.16 / $0.88): Pizza with Bell Peppers and Onions (one slice), carrot, orange
Snack ($0.60 / $0.40): Oatmeal-Raisin Cookies and milk
Dinner ($1.67 / $1.17): Bean Burritos, Green Salad with Vinaigrette, banana

Wednesday ($5.80 / $3.33)

Breakfast ($0.88 / $0.59): Two-for-One Apple-Streusel Coffee Cake, peanut butter, tea

Lunch ($1.30 / $1.02): Bean Burritos, carrot, apple

Snack ($0.30 / $0.20): Oatmeal-Raisin Cookies

Dinner ($3.32 / $1.52): Green Eggs Scramble, microwaved or baked sweet potato, banana

Thursday ($4.95 / $3.44)

Lunch ($1.73 / $1.43): rotini with Persian Tomato Sauce, carrot, orange

Snack ($0.41 / $0.26): Chocolate Pudding

Dinner ($2.35 / $1.45): Potato Peanut Curry, steamed broccoli with Vinaigrette, banana, Vanilla Yogurt

Friday ($5.22 / $3.74)

Lunch ($2.20 / $1.50): rotini with Parsley Pesto, carrot, banana

Snack ($0.30 / $0.20): Oatmeal-Raisin Cookies

Dinner ($2.27 / $1.73): Bean and Tomato Stew with black beans, Rice, Green Salad with Vinaigrette, orange, Bright Popcorn

Saturday ($4.19 / $3.05)

Breakfast ($0.37 / $0.37): Oatmeal with peanut butter, tea

Lunch ($1.44 / $0.99): Stoup with black beans, Garlic Toast, apple

Snack ($0.46 / $0.30): banana

Dinner ($1.92 / $1.39): rotini with Persian Tomato Sauce, Green Salad with Vinaigrette, Chocolate Pudding

Fall Menu Week Two

Breakfast every day unless mentioned otherwise ($0.48/ $0.32): two slices of toasted Whisk Sandwich Bread, peanut butter, and tea

Sunday ($5.21 / $3.37)

Breakfast ($1.27 / $0.70): Two-for-One Apple-Streusel Coffee Cake, two eggs, tea

Lunch ($1.09 / $0.79): Red Bean Chili, Spanish Rice, carrot

Snack ($0.60 / $0.50): orange

Dinner ($2.25 / $1.48): Pizza with Kale, Garlic, and Onions (two slices); Green Salad with Vinaigrette; apple; Chocolate Pumpkin Snack Cake

Monday ($4.79 / $3.32)

Lunch ($1.09 / $0.79): Red Bean Chili, Spanish Rice, carrot

Snack ($0.40 / $0.25): banana

Dinner ($2.83 / $1.96): rotini with Tomato Sauce with Bell Peppers and Onions, steamed broccoli with Vinaigrette, orange, Chocolate Pudding

Tuesday ($5.11 / $3.30)

Lunch ($1.64 / $0.94): Pizza with Kale, Garlic, and Onions (one slice); broccoli; apple

Fall Menu Week Two (cont.)

Snack ($0.91 / $0.56): walnuts, Vanilla Yogurt

Dinner ($2.09 / $1.48): Spicy Black-Eyed Peas, Couscous, Tasty Tahini Greens, orange

Wednesday ($4.62 / $3.18)

Lunch ($1.88 / $1.23): Spicy Black-Eyed Peas, Couscous, Tasty Tahini Greens, banana

Snack ($0.29 / $0.17): Vanilla Yogurt

Dinner ($1.97 / $1.46): Noodles in Spicy Peanut Sauce with Fall Vegetables, orange

Thursday ($4.79 / $3.27)

Breakfast ($0.37 / $0.37): Oatmeal with peanut butter, tea

Lunch ($2.08 / $1.51): rotini with Tomato Sauce with Bell Peppers and Onions, broccoli, orange

Snack ($0.40 / $0.25): banana

Dinner ($1.95 / $1.14): Potato Pudding (main-dish serving), Glazed Carrots, Chocolate Pumpkin Snack Cake

Friday ($4.29 / $3.07)

Breakfast ($0.97 / $0.62): Two-for-One Apple-Streusel Coffee Cake, Vanilla Yogurt, tea

Lunch ($1.97 / $1.46): Noodles in Spicy Peanut Sauce with Fall Vegetables, orange

Snack ($0.30 / $0.20): Oatmeal-Raisin Cookies

Dinner ($1.05 / $0.79): Cuban Black Beans, Rice, Glazed Carrots, apple

Saturday ($4.48 / $2.96)

Lunch ($1.48 / $0.91): Stoup with black-eyed peas, Potato Pudding (side-dish serving), carrot

Snack ($0.74 / $0.47): Vanilla Yogurt, banana

Dinner ($1.80 / $1.28): rotini with Tomato Sauce with Bell Peppers and Onions, Green Salad with Vinaigrette, Chocolate Pudding

Fall Menu Week Three

Breakfast every day unless mentioned otherwise ($0.46 / $0.30):
two slices of toasted Good Whisk Bread, peanut butter, and tea

Sunday ($4.70 / $3.14)
Breakfast ($1.38 / $0.84): Pumpkin Bread
(two pieces), peanut butter, tea
Lunch ($0.91 / $0.65): Babe's Split Pea
Soup, Corn Bread (one piece), banana
Snack ($0.35 / $0.23): Chocolate
Pumpkin Snack Cake
Dinner ($2.04 / $1.41): Pizza with Bell
Peppers and Onions (two slices), Green
Salad with Vinaigrette, orange

Monday ($5.32 / $3.42)
Lunch ($1.63 / $1.29): Bean Burritos,
Corn Bread (one piece), carrot, orange
Snack ($0.62 / $0.39): walnuts
Dinner ($2.62 / $1.43): Potato Peanut
Curry, steamed broccoli with lemon
juice, banana, Vanilla Pudding

Tuesday ($4.32 / $2.87)
Lunch ($1.80 / $1.13): Pizza with Bell
Peppers and Onions (one slice),
broccoli, orange
Snack ($0.40 / $0.25): banana
Dinner ($1.67 / $1.19): Babe's Split Pea
Soup, Corn Bread (two pieces), orange,
Vanilla Pudding

Wednesday ($4.02 / $2.93)
Lunch ($1.49 / $1.22): Bean Burritos,
carrot, orange
Snack ($0.30 / $0.20): Oatmeal-Raisin
Cookies
Dinner ($1.77 / $1.21): Noodles in Spicy
Peanut Sauce with Fall Vegetables,
banana

Thursday ($6.12 / $3.84)
Lunch ($2.37 / $1.68): rotini with Persian
Tomato Sauce, broccoli, orange
Snack ($0.30 / $0.20): Oatmeal-Raisin
Cookies
Dinner ($3.00 / $1.66): Green Eggs
Scramble, microwaved or baked potato
with butter, carrot, apple

Friday ($5.47 / $3.78)
Breakfast ($1.38 / $0.84): Pumpkin Bread
(two pieces) with peanut butter, tea
Lunch ($1.97 / $1.46): Noodles in Spicy
Peanut Sauce with Fall Vegetables,
orange
Snack ($0.41 / $0.30): apple
Dinner ($1.70 / $1.18): Chickpea Stew on
Couscous, Oatmeal-Raisin Cookies

Saturday ($4.42 / $3.22)
Breakfast ($0.37/ $0.37): Oatmeal with
peanut butter, tea
Lunch ($1.06 / $0.69): Stoup with pinto
beans, Garlic Toast, banana
Snack ($0.72 / $0.50): apple, milk
Dinner ($2.27 / $1.66): rotini with Persian
Tomato Sauce, Green Salad with
Vinaigrette, apple, Chocolate Pumpkin
Snack Cake

Fall Menu Week Four

Breakfast every day unless mentioned otherwise ($0.48/ $0.32):
two slices of toasted Whisk Sandwich Bread, peanut butter, and tea

Sunday ($4.79 / $3.38)
Lunch ($2.06 / $1.52): Chickpea Stew on Couscous, carrot, orange
Snack ($0.35 / $0.29): Bright Popcorn
Dinner ($1.90 / $1.25): Pizza with Kale, Garlic, and Onions (two slices); Green Salad with Vinaigrette; apple

Monday ($4.53 / $3.08)
Lunch ($1.64 / $1.07): rotini with Tomato Sauce with Bell Peppers and Onions, broccoli
Snack ($0.40 / $0.25): banana
Dinner ($2.01 / $1.44): Red Bean Chili, Corn Bread (two pieces), carrot, orange, Cocoa Cookies

Tuesday ($4.13 / $2.70)
Lunch ($1.82 / $1.15): Pizza with Kale, Garlic, and Onions (one slice); broccoli; orange
Snack ($0.26 / $0.17): Cocoa Cookies
Dinner ($1.56 / $1.07): Red Bean Chili, Corn Bread (two pieces), carrot, apple

Wednesday ($5.29 / $3.37)
Lunch ($2.04 / $1.32): rotini with Tomato Sauce with Bell Peppers and Onions, broccoli, banana
Snack ($0.29 / $0.17): Vanilla Yogurt
Dinner ($2.48 / $1.56): Roasted Vegetables with Hummus, apple

Thursday ($10.46 / $6.79)
Breakfast ($0.82 / $0.51): Pumpkin Bread with peanut butter, tea

Lunch ($1.57 / $1.19): Red Bean Chili, Rice, orange
Snack ($0.26 / $0.17): Cocoa Cookies
Dinner ($7.80 / $4.92): Harvest Lasagna (large serving), Garlic Flatbread, Green Beans with Vinaigrette, baked acorn squash, Roasted Apples, Baked Pears with Cinnamon Yogurt Sauce

Friday ($6.97 / $4.49)
Breakfast ($0.82 / $0.51): Pumpkin Bread (one piece) with peanut butter, tea
Lunch ($1.43 / $1.00): Red Bean Chili, Corn Bread (one piece), carrot, apple
Snack ($0.40 / $0.25): banana
Dinner ($4.32 / $2.73): Harvest Lasagna (small serving), Garlic Flatbread, Marinated Green Beans, Baked Pears with Cinnamon Yogurt Sauce

Saturday ($4.40 / $3.30)
Breakfast ($0.37 / $0.37): Oatmeal with peanut butter, tea
Lunch ($1.71 / $1.12): Jack O' Lantern Soup with chickpeas, Garlic Flatbread, banana
Snack ($0.60 / $0.50): orange
Dinner ($1.73 / $1.32): rotini with Tomato Sauce with Bell Peppers and Onions, Green Salad with Vinaigrette, Bright Popcorn

Fall Menu: Extra Days

Day one
Breakfast: Oatmeal with tahini, tea
Lunch: rotini with Persian Tomato Sauce, carrot
Snack: apple, Bright Popcorn
Dinner: Green Eggs Scramble with remaining ricotta, Garlic Flatbread, carrot, orange

Day two
Breakfast: Couscous with honey, half apple, half orange, six ounces milk, tea
Lunch: Stoup, Corn Bread (two pieces), carrot, orange
Snack: walnuts
Dinner: Roasted Vegetables with Hummus, Garlic Flatbread, banana, Bright Popcorn

Day three
Breakfast: Oatmeal, peanut butter, tea
Lunch: burritos with black-eyed peas and onions in Enchilada Sauce, remaining cheese, Corn Bread (one piece), apple
Snack: walnuts
Dinner: Stoup, Garlic Flatbread, carrot, raisins

TABLE 14.1

Fall Shopping List

(All Food for One Month Using the Fall Menu)

GOT IT?	ITEM	CATEGORY	AMOUNT	GREEN PRICE	THRIFTY PRICE	% LEFT AT END OF MONTH
____	baking powder	baking	10 oz.		$1.49	76%
____	baking soda	baking	8 oz.		$0.46	82%
____	brown sugar	baking	2 lbs.		$1.09/lb.	36%
____	cocoa	baking	8 oz.		$2.79	28%
____	cornmeal	baking	2 lbs.	$0.99/lb. bulk	$1.25/2 lbs.	47%
____	cornstarch	baking	1 lb.		$1.30	79%
____	flour, all-purpose	baking	two 5-lb. bags	$4.69 ea.	$1.89 ea.	29%
____	flour, white whole wheat	baking	two 5-lb. bags	$8.99 ea.	$4.99 ea.	35%
____	sugar	baking	5 lbs.		$3.15	16%
____	walnuts	baking	3 lbs.	$9.99/lb. bulk	$6.24/lb.	11%
____	yeast, rapid rise	baking	4 oz.		$5.49	63%
____	oats	cereal	3 lbs. or three 18-oz. boxes	$1.19/lb. bulk	$2.45 ea.	7% or 18%
____	wheat germ	cereal	1 lb.		$2.49	11%
____	tea	coffee and tea	three 80-bag boxes of individual bags or two 24-bag boxes of family-size bags	$3.99 ea.	$1.79 ea.	23% or 14%
____	butter	dairy	3 lbs.	$3.99 ea.	$2.99 ea.	13%
____	cheese, cheddar	dairy	8 oz.	$4.99	$2.49	0%
____	cheese, mozzarella	dairy	five 8-oz. packages or 2 lbs. plus 8 oz.	$2.69 ea.	$3.50 ea. plus $2.49	13%
____	cheese, parmesan	dairy	five 5-oz. packages or four 6-oz. packages	$3.99 ea.	$2.49 ea.	15% or 11%
____	eggs, large	dairy	5 dozen	$3.50 ea.	$1.49 ea.	1%
____	milk, fresh 2%	dairy	3 gallons	$4.89 ea.	$3.23 ea.	8%
____	ricotta cheese	dairy	15 oz.	$5.69	$2.49	0%
____	yogurt for starter	dairy	two 6-oz. containers	$0.89	$0.50	38%

Fall Shopping List *(cont.)*

GOT IT?	ITEM	CATEGORY	AMOUNT	GREEN PRICE	THRIFTY PRICE	% LEFT AT END OF MONTH
____	raisins	fruit	4 lbs. or two 24-oz. boxes	$3.19/lb. bulk	$3.45 ea.	7% or 17%
____	beans, black	grains	2 lbs.	$1.69/lb. bulk	$1.19 ea.	0%
____	beans, black-eyed peas	grains	1 lb.	$1.99/lb. bulk	$1.19	20%
____	beans, chickpea	grains	2 lbs.	$1.89/lb. bulk	$1.55 ea.	0%
____	beans, kidney	grains	2 lbs.	$1.99/lb. bulk	$1.59 ea.	0%
____	beans, pinto	grains	2 lbs.	$1.99/lb. bulk	$2.29/2 lbs.	0%
____	beans, split peas	grains	1 lb.	$1.79/lb. bulk	$1.55	0%
____	couscous	grains	31.7-oz. box or three 10-oz. boxes	$7.99	$1.97 ea.	19% or 15%
____	rice, long-grain brown	grains	2 lbs. or one 2-lb. bag	$1.49/lb. bulk	$2.39	0%
____	burritos, 10-inch flour	grocery	two 10-count packages		$1.99	0%
____	honey	grocery	1 lb. or one 24-oz. jar	$3.99/lb. bulk	$5.49	35% or 57%
____	lasagna noodles, no boil if available	grocery	one 8-oz. box or one 9-oz. box	$2.99	$1.35	0%
____	lemon juice (thrifty list)	grocery	15 oz.	X	$1.99	58%
____	peanut butter	grocery	eight 18-oz. jars or four 40-oz. jars	$2.99 ea.	$4.99 ea.	3% or 13%
____	popcorn	grocery	1 lb. or one 2-lb. package	$1.99/lb. bulk	$2.99	0% or 50%
____	pumpkin	grocery	four 1-lb. or four 15-oz. cans*	$2.69 ea.	$1.50 ea.	17% or 11%
____	rotini pasta	grocery	twelve 14.5-oz. boxes		$2.15 ea.	0%
____	tomatoes, crushed	grocery	fifteen 28-oz. cans	$1.79 ea.	$1.59 ea.	2%
____	tomatoes, diced	grocery	nine 28-oz. cans	$1.89 ea.	$1.39 ea.	6%
____	vinegar, apple cider	grocery	16 oz.	$3.49	$1.19	6%

(continues)

Fall Shopping List (*cont.*)

GOT IT?	ITEM	CATEGORY	AMOUNT	GREEN PRICE	THRIFTY PRICE	% LEFT AT END OF MONTH
____	soy sauce	int'l	10 oz.	$2.49	$1.49	20%
____	tahini	int'l	16 oz. or 15 oz.	$7.99	$6.29	35% or 31%
____	corn oil	oil	16 oz. or 24 oz.	$4.69	$1.99	54% or 85%
____	olive oil	oil	four 16.9-oz. (½ liter) bottles or four 17-oz. bottles	$6.49 ea.	$4.79 ea.	11%
____	apples	produce	eight 3-lb. bags or 24 lbs.	$3.69 ea.	$0.89/lb.	3%
____	bananas	produce	42 lbs.	$0.79/lb.	$0.50/lb.	0%
____	bell peppers, green	produce	14	$1.00 ea.	$0.33 ea.	0%
____	broccoli	produce	9 lbs. or seven bunches	$3.49/lb.	$1.99 ea.	2% or 6%
____	cabbage, green	produce	3 lbs.	$1.49/lb.	$0.49/lb.	7%
____	carrots	produce	three 5-lb. bags	$3.99 ea.	$2.99 ea.	5%
____	chard or mustard	produce	four bunches or 3 lbs.	$2.00 ea.	$0.99/lb.	7%
____	collards or kale	produce	one 11-oz. bundle	$2.00	$0.99	40%
____	garlic	produce	8 heads	$0.59 ea.	$0.79 ea.	8%
____	ginger	produce	8 oz.	$5.99/lb.	$3.00/lb.	20%
____	green beans	produce	2 lbs.	$2.50/lb.	$1.79/lb.	0%
____	lemons (green list)	produce	1	$0.79	X	16%
____	lettuce	produce	4 lbs. or two 2-lb. heads	$2.49/lb.	$1.79 ea.	20%
____	mushrooms, button	produce	two 8-oz. packages	$2.49 ea.	$2.29 ea.	0%
____	onions, green	produce	one 4-oz. bunch	$1.29	$1.00	0%
____	onions, yellow or white	produce	four 3-lb. bags	$2.49 ea.	$2.79 ea.	0%
____	oranges	produce	ten 4-lb. bags	$5.99 ea.	$4.99 ea.	4%
____	parsley	produce	two 4-oz. bunches	$1.00 ea.	$0.89 ea.	38%
____	pears	produce	8	$0.83 ea.	$0.56 ea.	0%
____	potatoes, all-purpose	produce	two 5-lb. bags or one 10-lb. bag	$3.99 ea.	$4.99 ea.	0%

Fall Shopping List *(cont.)*

GOT IT?	ITEM	CATEGORY	AMOUNT	GREEN PRICE	THRIFTY PRICE	% LEFT AT END OF MONTH
_____	potatoes, sweet	produce	4 lbs.	$1.75/lb.	$0.50/lb.	0%
_____	squash, acorn	produce	4 squash	$1.49 ea.	$0.99 ea.	0%
_____	bay leaves	spices	⅛ oz. or 0.12 oz.	$1.16/oz. bulk	$0.69	81%
_____	cayenne	spices	1 oz.	$0.50/oz. bulk	$2.86	66%
_____	chipotle	spices	1 3/4 oz. or 2 oz.	$5.69	$4.87	60% or 65%
_____	cinnamon	spices	1 oz.	$0.56/oz. bulk	$1.49	15%
_____	cumin	spices	3 oz. or two 2 oz. jars	$1.12/oz. bulk	$1.59 ea.	18% or 39%
_____	nutmeg	spices	1 oz.	$2.25/oz. bulk	$2.14	82%
_____	oregano	spices	1 oz.	$0.75/oz. bulk	$0.59	81%
_____	salt	spices	26 oz.		$0.47	52%
_____	turmeric	spices	1 oz. or 0.95 oz.	$0.91/oz. bulk	$3.72	71% or 69%
_____	vanilla	spices	2 oz. or 4 oz.	$6.69	$1.99	0% or 50%
_____	cardamom	spices, optional	1 oz. or 2 oz.	$2.69/oz. bulk	$9.38	93%
_____	thyme	spices, optional	1 oz. or 0.7 oz.	$1.16/oz. bulk	$2.77	98% or 96%

---

* To save even more, use fresh pumpkin baked from decorative pumpkins in place of canned pumpkin.

Fall Cooking Plan

The fall cooking plan shows how to make a feast for Thanksgiving or any of the big fall holidays. Decide when your feast will be each month. Up to four days in advance, do Cooking Session One below. The day of your feast, do Session Two to make a celebration meal that includes Harvest Lasagna, Baked Pears with Cinnamon Yogurt Sauce, and more.

The other three weeks, follow the core Winter Cooking Plan (page 78).

What About Our Traditional Family Dishes, Old or New?

Most Americans have roast turkey for Thanksgiving. If that's important to you, look for a smaller, well-raised bird and load up on the vegetable side dishes. Consider making Black Beans in Baked Winter Squash with Persian Tomato Sauce (page 138) to enjoy along with or instead of the turkey.

If your family counts on familiar favorites to celebrate, try cooking them the *Wildly Affordable Organic* way: from scratch and with healthy ingredients. Even if you can't do that, a few servings of canned cranberry sauce, green bean casserole, and hot-pink peppermint ice cream won't undo all the positive steps you've taken all year long. The holidays are when I most often put on my flexitarian hat. Don't start a family feud over lox, kielbasa, or tofurkey.

Cooking Session One: Can Be Done Up to Four Days in Advance

 Time: 1 hour

In this session you'll mix the dough for Garlic Flatbread and make Yogurt.

   1. Mix Whisk Pizza Dough (page 185) for Garlic Flatbread and let rise for at least an hour.
   2. Make Yogurt (page 127).
   3. Wash the dishes.
   4. When milk for yogurt cools to about 110°F, finish making yogurt.
   5. Refrigerate dough.

Cooking Session Two:
Feast Cooking Plan with Lasagna

 Time: 3 hours and 15 minutes

In this session, you'll make Harvest Lasagna, Garlic Flatbread, Roasted Apples, Green Beans with Vinaigrette, baked acorn squash, and Baked Pears with Cinnamon Yogurt Sauce.

1. First thing in the morning, refrigerate yogurt and put away nest. Continue cooking 3 hours and 15 minutes before you plan to start your feast.

2. Make lasagna, taking a ten-minute break after finishing the sauce and before assembling. Put bread stone or heavy cookie sheet in oven and then set to 375°F. Assemble lasagna.

3. Cut acorn squash in half, remove seeds and fiber. Put butter, brown sugar, and cinnamon in cavities. Bake lasagna and butternut squash.

4. Take 15 minutes for a break or to set out serving dishes and set the table.

5. Make Baked Pears with Cinnamon Yogurt Sauce, setting pears aside to bake later. Refrigerate sauce.

6. Clean green beans and put in pot ready to boil. Make Vinaigrette.

7. Prepare apples for roasting (page 209).

8. Take dough for Garlic Flatbread out of refrigerator, divide, and let rest on floured surface. Shape, and let rise.

9. Cook green beans. When tender, drain and toss with Vinaigrette. Keep warm until ready to serve.

10. Uncover lasagna and return to oven to bake 5 more minutes. Put apples in oven with lasagna.

11. Roll out Garlic Flatbread and top with olive oil and garlic.

12. Remove lasagna and acorn squash from oven and turn temperature to 450°F, leaving apples in oven.

13. When oven reaches temperature, bake Garlic Flatbread.

12. Put acorn squash and green beans on the table. When ready, remove Garlic Flatbread and Roasted Apples from oven, turn temperature down to 350°F, and put pears in oven to bake while you eat. Serve lasagna and enjoy your feast.

13. When pears are ready, serve topped with Cinnamon Yogurt Sauce.

14. Refrigerate or freeze extra.

Part IV
Recipes

15

The Basics

Use these recipes one at a time or as part of a *Wildly Affordable Organic* seasonal menu or cooking plan. They are full of fresh vegetables and fruit, whole grains, and fiber.

You *can* afford to cook with local, sustainably grown, and organic ingredients. Just squeeze every last drop of flavor and nutrition out of the food you buy. Get the best ingredients that your budget allows. When you cook from scratch, you can mix and match.

All the recipes are thrifty, especially the ones in the section called Something from Nothing (page 191). Use these recipes to make delicious dishes out of food that many people throw away and to develop new habits that will provide you with "free" meals every month.

See Cook Clean (page 42) for information on rinsing and peeling produce and keeping germs at bay.

Core Recipes
If you are new to cooking from scratch, start with these recipes:

- Good Whisk Bread (page 153)
- Basic Dried Beans and Peas (page 132)
- Noodles Cooked in Very Little Water (page 170)
- Good Tomato Sauce (page 171)
- Southern Summer Pesto (page 177)
- Rice (page 203)
- Roasted Vegetables (page 208)
- Vinaigrette (page 201)
- Strawberry Ice Cream (page 216)
- Chocolate Pudding (page 212)

Ingredients

- Use large eggs.
- Use salted butter. If you have unsalted butter, add a pinch salt for each stick used.
- When two ingredients are listed, the first one is recommended and is the one included in the shopping list and cost calculations. For example: white whole wheat or all-purpose flour.

Also see the Scrimp or Splurge Twenty (page 20).

Temperatures

A rapid-read thermometer helps you make sure live yeast and yogurt culture thrive. But if you don't have one, think baby bottles. A baby would howl if given a bottle at 120°F, a temperature that will kill yeast and make your bread flat. Yogurt, too, likes the happy-baby range of temperatures for milk—from 105° to 110°F.

Weights and Measures

Here are some of the most common measurements used in this book. I taped a copy of this chart inside one of my kitchen cupboards for easy reference. Find an easy-to-print version at CookforGood.com/wao.

TABLE 15.1

Weights and Measures of Ingredients

TYPE	INGREDIENT	MEASURE	GRAMS	OUNCES
Dairy	milk	1 cup	244	8.6*
	yogurt	1 cup	227	8.0*
Flours	cornmeal	1 cup	122	4.3
	all-purpose,	1 cup	120	4.2
	white whole wheat,	½ cup	60	2.1
	and whole wheat flour	⅓ cup	40	1.4
	masa harina	¼ cup	30	1.1
Beans & Legumes	black beans	1 cup	185	6.5
	black-eyed peas	1 cup	171	6.0
	chickpeas	1 cup	164	5.8
	kidney beans	1 cup	177	6.2
	lentils	1 cup	198	7.0
	peanut butter	1 cup	258	9.1
	pinto beans	1 cup	171	6.0
Sweeteners	brown sugar, packed	1 cup	220	7.8
		½ cup	110	3.9
		⅓ cup	73	2.6
		¼ cup	55	1.9
	honey	1 cup	336	11.9
		½ cup	168	5.9
		⅓ cup	111	3.9
		¼ cup	84	3.0
	sugar	1 cup	200	7.1
		½ cup	100	3.5
		⅓ cup	66	2.3
		¼ cup	50	1.8
Vegetables	cabbage, grated	1 cup	50	1.8
	carrot, grated	1 cup	110	3.9
	carrot, whole	large	72	2.5
	onion, chopped	1 cup	160	5.6
	onion, whole	medium	110	3.9
	potato, diced	1 cup	150	5.3
	potato, whole	medium	213	7.5
	tomato, diced	1 cup	150	5.3
	tomato, whole	medium	123	4.3
	zucchini, grated	1 cup	60	2.1

* Ounces shown are for *dry* ounces (weight), not *fluid* ounces (volume), and given for convenience in weighing milk and yogurt. A cup is always 8 fluid ounces in size, no matter what the contents weigh.

16

Breakfast

Two-for-One Apple-Streusel Coffee Cake

This cake reminds me of fall color tours when I was growing up. We'd look at the changing leaf colors and stop by an apple orchard for cider and apple cake.

Mix up two cakes' worth of batter base (a.k.a. cake mix) and streusel ahead of time, maybe at the beginning of a holiday month. Make one cake right away and the other later.

 Active time: 35 minutes for first cake, 15 minutes for the second
Total time: 1 hour, 25 minutes for first cake, 1 hour 10 minutes for the second
Makes 16 servings (2 cakes)

Streusel (makes 2 cakes)
1 cup chopped walnuts (110 grams)
⅓ cup packed brown sugar (73 grams)
¼ cup white whole wheat flour (30 grams)
½ teaspoon cinnamon
3 tablespoons butter, room temperature

Batter base (makes 2 cakes)
2 cups white whole wheat flour (240 grams)
2 cups all-purpose flour (240 grams)
1½ cup sugar (300 grams)
2 tablespoons baking powder
1 teaspoon cinnamon
1 teaspoon nutmeg
1 teaspoon salt
1 teaspoon cardamom, optional
10 tablespoons butter (1¼ sticks), room temperature

For each cake
1 apple
butter or shortening for pan
1 cup milk
1 egg
¼ teaspoon almond or vanilla extract

1. Pulse all streusel ingredients together in food processor fitted with cutting blade until crumbly, about 10 pulses. Set half aside (¾ cup, or 100 grams) and refrigerate the rest to make a second cake later.

2. Core and quarter apple and put in food processor. Pulse until chopped, about 6 times, then set aside.

3. Put batter-base ingredients except butter in food processor. Pulse about 3 or 4 times to mix. Cut butter into 10 pieces and add to flour mixture. Pulse about 10 times until mixture has the texture of coarse sand. Take out half (just under 4 cups, or 425 grams) and refrigerate in a covered container to make a second cake later.

4. Preheat the oven to 350°F. Grease or butter an 8-inch-square or a 9-inch-round baking pan.

5. Add milk, egg, and almond extract to flour mixture for one cake. Process briefly until batter is smooth, about 6 seconds. Longer processing develops the gluten, the protein structure in wheat flour that helps bread rise but also makes for a tough cake.

6. Pour half the batter into the pan. Sprinkle evenly with half the apple and half the streusel. Repeat. Bake for 50 to 55 minutes. The cake is done when a tester inserted into the center comes out clean.

7. Serve warm or at room temperature. Keeps covered at room temperature for up to 4 days.

Better Blueberry Pancakes

More protein, less salt, bigger pancakes . . . what's not to like? Better Blueberry Pancakes have about 40 percent less salt than the recipe I grew up with, but they taste just as good. The trick? Use just one-sixth as much baking powder to cut the sodium, then add lemon zest or juice to keep the flavor bright. I also added more milk and flour, so the pancakes are slightly larger and flatter but cook more quickly and thoroughly. These changes also boost the protein in a serving, from 7.7 grams to 9.3 grams.

They still taste like classic blueberry pancakes, one of the best breakfasts ever. They're healthy too, made with all white whole wheat flour and full of juicy blueberries, one of the "super-food" fruits. Top your stack with real maple syrup, not fake "table syrup," which is loaded with high-fructose corn syrup and artificial flavors.

 Active time: 20 minutes
Total time: 20 minutes
Makes 4 servings, 3 pancakes each

2 tablespoons butter
1 cup 2% or whole milk
1 egg
1 cup white whole wheat flour (120 grams)
½ teaspoon baking powder
1 tablespoon sugar
½ teaspoon salt
½ teaspoon lemon zest or 1 tablespoon lemon juice
½ cup blueberries (75 grams)
2 teaspoons corn or vegetable oil for the griddle

Topping
2 tablespoons butter, optional
½ cup real maple syrup

1. Heat a flat skillet or griddle to medium-high, or 370°F. Melt butter in a microwave-safe container also suitable for serving maple syrup at the table, about 30 seconds on high. Whisk together milk and egg in a measuring cup or small bowl.

2. Whisk flour, baking powder, sugar, and salt together in a medium bowl. Stir lemon zest into flour or lemon juice into milk mixture. Stir in milk mixture, melted butter, and blueberries just until combined. There shouldn't be any dry spots left, but remember that shorter mixing means lighter pancakes.

3. Brush the skillet with oil. Use a ladle or measuring cup to spoon batter onto the skillet. Cook until bubbles forming in top of batter stop rising and the bottom is golden brown, about one minute. Use a spatula to flip pancakes and cook for another minute, until other side is golden brown.

4. While pancakes cook, put maple syrup in container used to melt butter and microwave on high until warm, about 30 seconds.

5. Serve pancakes at once or keep warm for a few minutes in a 200°F toaster oven or oven. Top each serving with butter, if using, and maple syrup. Freeze extra pancakes in plastic bags. To reheat, thaw overnight in refrigerator or at room temperature for about 20 minutes. Toast in a single layer in toaster oven until hot, the same as you would toast a slice of bread.

Notes

Frozen blueberry pancakes are a wonderful backup for mornings when you're out of bread to make toast or want something more luxurious than oatmeal. Make a double batch, cool on wire racks, and freeze in freezer bags.

Lemon zest gives a more lemony flavor than juice and is essentially free if you buy lemons for juice.

Saltiness was the only difference between pancakes made with one teaspoon of baking powder and those made with six times as much. The half teaspoon used here produces short but light pancakes. Thanks to Dick Tucker and his wife Carol Moore for inspiring me to rework this recipe.

Oatmeal for Breakfast Six Ways

Start the day with healthy, thrifty hot oatmeal. Many people love it just boiled in water with a bit of salt or sugar. But if you, like me, were traumatized as a child by being forced to eat oatmeal, try the wonderfully flavored mix-ins and toppings below. They may help you rediscover this useful breakfast option.

Use oatmeal as a sponge to soak up flavors and nutrients that would otherwise go down your drain. Try bean broth, pasta water, and broth from your broth jar (page 191). According to the USDA, bean broth has about 4 grams of protein a cup and loads of vitamins and minerals.[1]

Why bother cooking oatmeal for breakfast? Oatmeal is a whole-grain food that may lower your bad cholesterol, raise your good cholesterol, and help control your weight. Nutritionist Jane Brody called oatmeal "the nutritional Cadillac among grains" back when that was a good thing—high in protein, vitamins, and minerals.[2] Unlike a Cadillac, however, oatmeal is inexpensive and lasts a long time on the shelf.

Active time: 7 minutes
Total time: 12 minutes
Makes 4 servings

**2 cups old-fashioned rolled oats
    (not instant) (160 grams)
4½ cups water or broth
½ teaspoon salt if using water, less
    with salty broth**

Suggested mix-ins and toppings

- Cook oats in bean broth instead of water. Top with 1 cup diced ripe tomatoes.
- Cook oats in saved pasta water instead of plain water. Mix in ¼ cup tahini and top with 1 cup diced ripe tomatoes and 2 tablespoons snipped fresh chives.
- Mix in ½ cup peanut butter, ½ cup raisins (80 grams), and a dash of hot sauce.
- Mix in ¼ cup tahini and top with ¼ cup chopped spring onions. Season with chipotle hot sauce, salt, and pepper to taste.
- Cook ½ cup raisins with oats. Top with ¼ cup chopped walnuts.
- Mix in 4 ounces shredded or cubed Cheddar and 2 tablespoons butter.

1. In medium saucepan, bring oatmeal, liquid, and salt to a boil over medium heat. Stir in raisins, if using. Turn heat down to low so oatmeal barely boils and then cook for 5 minutes, stirring frequently. Remove from heat, cover, and let finish cooking for 5 minutes.

2. Meanwhile, prepare one set of mix-ins and toppings. When oatmeal is done cooking, mix in and top as appropriate. Serve immediately.

Notes

The version made with bean broth and topped with tomatoes is my favorite. I've had it as a quick and filling main course for dinner too, with or without grated Cheddar on top.

The version made with saved pasta water is a close second, especially when the pasta water contains traces of pesto.

Sweet Raisin Flatbread or Breakfast Focaccia

I love the speed and garlicky, salty taste of traditional focaccia. And I love the sweet homeness of cinnamon-raisin bread. One night I decided to make a breakfast focaccia by replacing olive oil with butter, most of the salt with sugar, and adding cinnamon and raisins. Voilà! A scrumptious pan of breakfast bread that makes a weekend breakfast special and freezes well for mid-week enjoyment. Enjoy Sweet Raisin Flatbread plain or spread with butter or peanut butter.

Sweet Raisin Flatbread is ready almost as fast as a quick bread because it uses a full pack of yeast for one pan of bread and a warm oven to speed the rising. Because it's short and sturdy, you can cut it while it's still warm.

This recipe uses all white whole wheat flour, which requires more kneading than most bread recipes in this cookbook. I use a bread machine to do the kneading, but you can use a heavy-duty mixer or just knead by hand. See Notes below.

 Active time: 15 minutes
Total time: 1 hour and 15 minutes
Makes 8 servings

1 cup water (about 110°F)
1 tablespoon butter, plus shortening or
    butter to grease pan
2 ¼ teaspoons rapid-rise or instant
    yeast (one package)
2 ½ cups white whole wheat or
    all-purpose flour (300 grams)
1 teaspoon cinnamon
¼ teaspoon salt
2 tablespoons honey (42 grams)
1 cup raisins (160 grams)

Topping
1 tablespoon butter
1 tablespoon sugar

1. **Get ready.** Warm the water to about 110°F. Melt one tablespoon of butter. Put a bread stone or heavy cookie sheet on bottom shelf of oven. Preheat oven to 200°F. Use shortening or butter to grease an 11 x 7-inch baking pan.

2. **Mix and knead.** If using a bread machine, put yeast, flour, cinnamon, salt, melted butter, honey, and warm water into the bowl of the bread machine in the order listed. Start machine running on one kneading or dough cycle. Add raisins after five minutes or just before the end of the machine's cycle. You want them to be stirred in but not mashed.

3. **Put dough in the pan to rise.** Oil hands and remove dough from bread machine. Put it in the greased baking pan and then pat and stretch dough until it covers the bottom of the pan. If any raisins are sticking out, poke them down into dough so they won't burn. Put bread in the oven and immediately turn off heat. Let bread rise for 20 minutes.

4. **Top and bake.** Remove bread from oven. Turn oven up to 400°F. Melt remaining tablespoon of butter. Gently poke dough to make a regular pattern of dimples to catch butter. I usually make twelve dimples, with four rows of three. Pour remaining melted butter on dough and spread with your fingers or a brush. Sprinkle top with sugar. Let dough rise on the counter until your oven reaches 400°F. Bake for 23 minutes until deep golden brown. Cool in the pan on a rack.

5. **Serve warm** from the oven or toasted to reheat. To toast, split pieces in two and

put in a toaster oven sugar-side up. Store bread at room temperature in pan or cut it into sections and remove to store on plate or in bag. Because you will be toasting this bread, it doesn't matter if the bottom gets a little soggy from cooling in the pan. Or wrap in foil and freeze.

Notes

Other kneading methods: Stir flour and yeast together before adding salt to keep the yeast alive. Knead dough using a stand mixer with the dough-hook attachment for about 8 minutes. Or just knead by hand until stretchy for 8 to 10 minutes. Add the raisins a minute or two before you are done kneading.

If you're not in a hurry, let the bread rise for about two hours at room temperature instead of in the oven.

Yogurt

Yogurt is amazingly easy to make at home once you know how, and it tastes at least as good as the store-bought kind. The trick is to use the ways perfected over centuries in Turkey and India. Many modern recipes call for all sorts of unneeded extra steps and ingredients. But in fact, cleanliness, time, and gentleness are the keys to thick yogurt. Live yogurt starter and milk are the only ingredients. You don't need to add powdered milk or gelatin. Just bring milk to a boil and cool it slowly to change the protein so it thickens.

Before using this recipe the first time, read about yogurt starter and making a yogurt nest.

Yogurt Basics

Yogurt Starter

Yogurt starter is just fresh yogurt in which the yogurt culture is still alive. Most yogurt sold in stores contains live yogurt. Look for a statement like this on the package: "Contains active yogurt cultures including *L. acidophilus.*"

Buy plain, unflavored yogurt, made with milk, yogurt culture, and sometimes pectin, which is made from fruit. Avoid gelatin, which is made from animal skin and bones. I usually use Stonyfield Farm's plain organic fat-free yogurt or Dannon's All Natural plain yogurt.

If you can't find plain yogurt, look for "fruit on the bottom" or unmixed flavored yogurt. You are after the yogurt culture, not the jam.

When you buy a container of yogurt for starter, freeze any you don't need immediately in a clean ice cube tray. The next day, pop yogurt cubes into a freezer bag or container and keep them in the freezer. The culture will stay alive for months. Just take out a yogurt cube when you are ready to make a fresh batch of yogurt.

If you make yogurt every day or two, you can just use a spoon full of yogurt from one batch to start another. That's how people in Turkey and Indian have done it for centuries. But if you make it just once a week or so, bad cultures will start to take over the good cultures. Most people start each batch with commercial yogurt.

Making a Yogurt Nest

Yogurt culture grows best between 86° and 113°F.[3] Using lower heat takes longer, but doing so produces silkier yogurt. Yogurt made at higher temperatures also releases more of its whey, making it more watery. Bumping, stirring, or moving the yogurt can disrupt the formation of the protein network that makes yogurt yogurt.

So the job of your yogurt nest is to keep the milk and yogurt starter warm enough and cozy enough to make good yogurt. I use a cake keeper, a heating pad, and an old, clean bath towel. A box works fine too.

Put the towel on the counter and the heating pad on the towel. Put the containers with hot milk and yogurt culture on the heating pad, wrap the towel over the containers, and put the cake keeper or box over the whole shebang. Turn on the heating pad and let the yogurt culture grow.

Before you make your first batch of yogurt, test the nest by filling your containers with water heated to about 110°F and putting them in the yogurt nest. Turn the heating pad to a low setting. After a couple of hours, check the water temperature. Adjust the setting until you find one that keeps the water temperature in the safe range between 90° and 110°F. Write in this book or on the heating pad's label which setting works best.

Confused? Watch the yogurt-making video at CookforGood.com/wao.

Making Yogurt

Active time: 30 minutes, mostly of occasional stirring
Total time: 8 to 11 hours.
Servings: 8 half-cup servings
Divides or doubles easily

2 tablespoons fresh live yogurt or 1 ice-cube-sized chunk frozen live yogurt
4 cups milk (2%, whole, or skim)

1. Set out live yogurt in a small, very clean bowl or cup so it will come to room temperature while milk is heated and then cooled. Set out one or more very clean containers or jars.

2. Heat milk over medium heat in a medium pot just until it starts to boil. At first, cover the pot and stir milk occasionally so it doesn't burn. As it gets hotter, uncover the pot and stir frequently. At the end, stir constantly except when you are checking to see if the milk is boiling. Scrubbing burnt milk off the bottom of a pot wastes any time you might have saved by ignoring milk that was about to boil.

3. Set up the yogurt nest between stirs. As soon as milk starts to boil, take it off the heat and pour into containers. Let milk cool to between 105° and 110°F, about 30 minutes. Use a clean thermometer to check the temperature or dip out some milk with a spoon and put it on the inside of your wrist. Milk should be just right for a baby bottle.

4. Stir yogurt starter until it is creamy and then stir into the warm milk. Cover the container and nestle it in the yogurt nest. Turn on the heating pad. Leave yourself a

note so you will remember to refrigerate the yogurt after seven to ten hours.

5. When the time comes, gently place the container in the refrigerator. Let it cool thoroughly before stirring or it will release its whey and become watery. Keeps refrigerated for at least a week. Some say yogurt keeps for three weeks in an unopened jar and then a week after that, but I've never kept it that long myself. Do not eat yogurt that smells bad or has mold.

Notes

To get dishes and containers "very clean," wash them thoroughly using detergent and hot water or run them through the dishwasher. If your yogurt turns out sour, try using glass jars and lids and boiling them in water. Don't stir cooling yogurt with your finger or with a spoon you've used for something else.

If you will be making Whisk Sandwich Bread soon (page 155), boil extra milk for that recipe while you boil milk for yogurt.

Boil milk to make yogurt and then use the same pot to make pudding.

If your yogurt is thin and watery, try letting the culture develop at a lower temperature for a longer time.

Flavoring Yogurt

Cinnamon Yogurt Sauce

Start with ½ cup of plain yogurt. Mix in 4 teaspoons brown sugar and ½ teaspoon each of cinnamon and vanilla. Let flavors combine for 5 minutes and then serve over baked pears or sweet potatoes.

Spicy Yogurt Sauce

Start with ½ cup of plain yogurt. Mince 1 garlic clove, about ½ teaspoon. Stir together yogurt, garlic, ¼ teaspoon cumin, and ¼ teaspoon chipotle hot sauce. Taste and adjust seasonings, adding salt if desired. Let the flavors blend for five minutes before serving. Keeps for a week if made with fresh yogurt. Excellent as a garnish for burritos, bean dishes, salads, or steamed vegetables such as broccoli.

Vanilla Yogurt

Start with 4 cups of plain yogurt. Stir in 2 tablespoons of honey and 1 teaspoon of vanilla extract. Eat as is or mix in fruit.

17

Beans, Beautiful Beans

Kidney beans, pinto beans, black beans, white beans, chickpeas, split peas: I love them all. I eat beans at least once a day. Usually twice, if you count the chickpea flour in high-protein pasta.

A Few Benefits of Beans

Beans Are Delicious Countless Ways

The recipes in this book just hint at the many ways to cook beans. Eat them hot or cold, whole or mashed, and in stews, soups, salads, or burritos. You can even roast cooked beans to make a crunchy snack almost like peanuts or make sweet bean cakes for dessert. Make pancakes or gravy with bean flour.

Beans Are a Bargain

Dried beans are the second cheapest form of protein I found, next to flour. As of this writing in July 2010, you can make a ½-cup serving of organic cooked beans with 10 grams of protein for 17 cents. A serving of conventionally grown beans costs a dime.

Start with dried beans to use every scrap of the food you paid for. There's no fat, bone, gristle, or innards to throw away. Cooking beans produces a delicious, healthy vegetable broth. A cup of broth from stewed kidney beans contains 4 grams of protein, plus iron, calcium, zinc, folate, and other nutrients.[1]

Beans Are Good for the Planet

Shipping dried beans is about as environmentally friendly as it gets. No water, no can or label, and no refrigeration or refrigerators are needed. They don't break or spoil, so few beans are wasted between field and table.

Beans Store Well Dried, Cooked, or Canned

Dried beans keep practically forever, although they cook faster when they are less than a year old. If you watch your leftovers, you never have to throw away beans. Cooked beans freeze and reheat beautifully. It's a snap to make a big pot of beans and freeze several servings.

Canned beans keep for years. Buy organic ones on sale and keep them for emergencies. Drain and rinse before using; canned bean broth tastes metallic.

Beans Are Easy to Cook, Even Without a Kitchen

Even if you don't have a kitchen, you can cook beans and vegetables in a slow cooker and eat them with tortillas or bread. Add a rice cooker for variety if you can. When I'm on the road, I travel with a rice cooker so I can cook canned-bean stews and rice in hotels.

Beans Are Good for You

They are high in protein and fiber, have loads of vitamins and minerals, and have almost no fat. According to the National Institutes of Health, beans are a good source of folate, an essential vitamin needed in higher levels by pregnant and nursing women. Folate also helps people with kidney or liver disease and drinking problems.[2]

What about Beans' Other F Word?

Unfortunately, folate isn't the first thing some people mention to me when they hear I'm a bean evangelist. They talk about farts.

The questions and jokes come from people who don't eat beans often. We bean eaters know that gas is not a problem if you are used to eating beans or have a high-fiber diet. As Steve Sando says, the best way to control "nature's little joke" is to "eat more beans."[3]

Ironically, you'll probably smell "more attractive, more pleasant, and less intense" if you switch from red meat to beans, according to a study from Charles University in Prague.[4]

Just make sure to:

- Start slowly. If you are eating mostly white bread and meat right now, start with one serving of beans every other day for the first week or two.
- Cook beans thoroughly. At first, you may want to soak beans and then cook them in fresh water. Skim off any foam that appears when beans first start boiling.
- Avoid other gas-producing foods in the same meal, such as broccoli or cabbage.

If you are still having problems, try including some of the traditional herbs used to help digestion: turmeric from India, epazote from Mexico, kombu from Japan, bay leaves from Europe. Or use Beano from the United States. Very soon you'll be able to eat beans every day without embarrassment or discomfort.

The Unseen Bean: Soy

There's one bean that you won't find here: soybeans. Soybeans have a high level of phyto-estrogen, the plant form of the female hormone estrogen. Because of this, the National Institutes of Health cautions women who have or are at increased risk of breast cancer or other hormone-sensitive conditions to be cautious about soy and to talk with their doctors about eating it.[5] One study linked a high-soy diet to lower sperm counts. Men and women may increase their risk of thyroid problems, cancer, and even memory problems.[6]

This is a shame because soybeans are cheap and have more protein than other beans. Many versions of soybean "meat" are hard to tell from the real thing. Years ago I discovered this meat and started cooking with it three or four times a week. We were eating some form of soy most days because I was already cooking with soy milk and tofu. My husband began to feel bad and then to feel worse. After reading up on soy problems, we went cold turkey on the soy. He started feeling more energetic in days and is now back up to full strength.

Clearly we need more in-depth research on the effects of soybeans on our health. In the meantime, the recipes in this book stick with the other beans.

Basic Beans and Peas:
Cooking Dried Legumes

Pick the bean and cooking method that suits your schedule. Times will vary based on the age of the beans; older beans take longer to cook.

Soaking beans before you cook them will shave 30 minutes to an hour off the cooking time. Not only will the beans cook more evenly, but you'll also save a little energy. Even a short soak can help: beans absorb half the water possible in just two hours and all of it in six to ten hours.[7]

Cooking beans longer makes them softer but doesn't do any harm. If you want to cook beans overnight or while you are gone all day, pick a recipe that calls for soft beans, such as refried beans or black-bean soup, and fire up your slow cooker.

Special Caution for Kidney Beans

The FDA recommends always soaking kidney beans for at least 5 hours and throwing away the soaking liquid to avoid problems with a rare toxin sometimes found in kidney beans. Then cook them at a full boil for at least 10 minutes. If the kidney beans are toxic, they are at their deadliest when partly cooked, so never swallow raw or crunchy kidney beans.[8] Although the FDA says this toxin is most reported in the United Kingdom and no outbreaks are known as of this writing in the United States, being careful with kidney beans still makes sense.

 Active time: 10 minutes
Total time: varies, see chart below
Makes 20 servings, a generous ½ cup each

2 pounds dried beans (4 ½ cups)
1 tablespoon of salt
12 cups of water (10 cups for split peas or lentils)

TABLE 17.1
Approximate Cooking Times for
Beans Cooked Various Ways

BEAN TYPE, NOT PRE-SOAKED	TIME ON STOVE	TIME IN SLOW COOKER ON HIGH WITH HOT WATER	TIME IN SLOW COOKER ON LOW WITH COLD WATER
split peas, lentils, black-eyed peas	40 minutes	1 hour, 15 minutes	6 hours
black beans, chickpeas, kidney beans, pinto beans	2½ hours	3½ hours	7½ hours

1. Clean beans by putting about a cup of them on the far side of a light-colored plate and pulling them towards you a few at a time. Pick out anything that is not a bean, such as small stones or stems. Also pick out any beans that look much smaller and more wrinkled than the rest. These "mummy beans" tend to stay hard no matter how long you cook them. After you've worked beans over to the near side of the plate, dump them into a colander and pick over another batch until you've checked them all. Rinse beans well under running water.

2. If soaking the beans, put beans and water in the slow cooker or pot that you will be cooking them in or in a large bowl and let soak at room temperature.

3. Cook beans in their soaking liquid unless you have just started eating lots of beans or unless they are kidney beans. In those cases, replace soaking water with fresh water, covering beans by an inch or two. Add salt and then cook beans covered in a slow cooker or on the stove until they are creamy and tender, adding extra water if needed to keep them covered. Test three or four beans when you check for doneness; they don't always cook evenly.

- **In a slow cooker, the slow way.** Put beans into a slow cooker that will hold at least 14 cups. Add water and salt. Turn the slow cooker on low.
- **In a slow cooker with the quick-soak method.** Bring fresh water to a boil before adding it to drained beans in the slow cooker. Add salt and turn the slow cooker on high.
- **On the stove.** Bring beans to a boil over high heat, then turn heat to low and simmer until beans are tender.

Notes

If you've never sorted dried beans before, start with kidney beans or chickpeas. They are bigger than most and are a different color than most of the stones or stems you're likely to find.

Most beans these days are very clean, but sometimes a batch seems like it came from the bottom of the bag, having more stems and stones than usual. Pick a batch like that over twice: you don't want to miss a stone.

Bean and Tomato Stew

You can make this tomato stew with any cooked beans. When I make a big pot of dried beans, I save some to make this stew. Serve over hot rice or with bread.

 Active time: 8 minutes
Total time: 12 minutes
Makes 4 servings, ¾ cups each. Recipe is easily halved or doubled.

2 garlic cloves
2 teaspoons olive oil
1 onion
2 cups cooked beans
One 28-ounce can diced tomatoes

1. Mince garlic and set aside. Heat oil in a medium pan over medium heat. Chop onion and add to pan. Cook until soft, stirring occasionally, about 5 minutes.

2. Add garlic to pan, stirring once. Add beans and tomatoes, including tomato juice. Stir and bring to a boil over high heat. Turn heat down to low, cover, and simmer for 5 minutes until heated through.

3. Serve hot. Refrigerate or freeze any extra.

Bean Burritos

Bean burritos are as fast to make as sandwiches but more festive.

*Active time: 5 minutes, starting
     with cooked beans
Total time: 8 minutes
Makes 4 servings, 1 burrito each*

**2 cups cooked pinto or black beans
4 large flour tortillas
½ onion, chopped
1 cup Enchilada Sauce (page 181)**

1. Heat beans in medium pot on medium heat. When warm, use potato masher or large spoon to mash beans until they hold together but still have some whole beans for texture.

2. To warm tortillas so they roll easily, stack them on a microwave-safe plate, cover with a damp tea towel or paper towel, and microwave on high for about 40 seconds, until warmed through and flexible. You can also heat them one at a time in a large skillet over medium heat for about 30 seconds each.

3. Divide beans and onion evenly among tortillas. Picture the tortilla as a clock, then spread filling from 11 o'clock straight down until level with 8 o'clock. To roll, fold the left side of the tortilla over the filling, fold the bottom of the tortilla up to hold the bottom of the filling, then finish rolling to the right.

- **For here.** Roll tortilla up and then pour enchilada sauce on top. Microwave on high until hot, about one minute on high. Serve immediately.
- **To go.** Spread enchilada sauce on top of beans and onions before rolling up tortilla. At this point, you can wrap each one in foil. Refrigerate if they will be eaten in a day or two or freeze for later. Serve at room temperature or warm by putting on a microwave-safe plate or waxed paper, covering with a damp paper towel, and microwaving on medium-high until hot, about 90 seconds.

Notes

Tuck leftover vegetables or rice into the burritos before you roll them up.

Top sauce with grated cheese, chopped parsley, or chopped cilantro.

Bean Salad with Fresh Corn, Peppers, and Tomatoes

Make bean salad when it's too hot to cook. It's practically a party in a bowl. Beans provide a dramatic backdrop to a bright confetti of corn, tomatoes, purple onions, and herbs.

 Active time: 12 minutes, starting with cooked beans
Total time: 12 minutes
Makes 4 main-dish servings, about 1 ½ cups each

2 cups cooked beans (black, kidney, chickpeas, lentils, or black-eyed peas)
2 ears corn
1 cup chopped fresh tomatoes
½ cup diced purple onion
¼ cup Greek Dressing (page 201)
2 tablespoons basil, sliced crossways into thin ribbons

1. Rinse beans well so the bean broth doesn't make salad look muddy, then put in a big bowl.

2. Cut corn kernels off cobs and add corn and tomatoes to beans.

3. Rinse diced onions in cold water so they don't overwhelm other flavors. Add onion and dressing to bean mixture and toss to combine. Top with basil ribbons just before serving.

4. Serve immediately or let sit at room temperature for up to 2 hours. To keep longer, refrigerate but allow to come to room temperature before serving. Just before serving, stir salad to make sure dressing coats every bite.

Notes

Using fresh corn and home-cooked beans makes this salad one of the delights of summer. However, you can make a pretty good bean salad using rinsed canned beans, canned diced tomatoes, and 1½ cups drained canned corn. This pantry version works well when you are traveling or in a rush.

Proud Black-Bean Burgers

My Taster inspired me to create this recipe when he said, "Quit trying to make your bean burgers taste like hamburgers. Make the best bean burger you can." The resulting burgers have a spicy, green, and beany taste. They're their own delicious burgers, not a substitute for anything.

Walnuts deepen the flavor and give a sassy crunch. Because these burgers are baked instead of grilled, it's easy to double the recipe and cook 12 burgers at once. Serve a crowd or freeze the extra for superfast meals later.

Never fear, though. Once baked, Proud Black-Bean Burgers can be reheated on the grill so you can take them to cookouts. Serve on Good Burger Buns (page 157) or Whisk Burger Buns (page 155).

 Active time: 20 minutes, starting with cooked beans and prepared pesto
Total time: 50 minutes to 1 hour and 20 minutes
Makes 8 burgers

4 garlic cloves
3 cups cooked black beans
2 onions
1 egg
1 cup walnuts (110 grams)
1 cup old-fashioned rolled oats (80 grams)
¼ cup Southern Summer Pesto (page 177) or Parsley Pesto (page 178)
2 teaspoons cumin
1 teaspoon chipotle

1. Preheat oven to 425°F now if you won't have time to let burgers rest in step 3. Set up your food processor with the cutting blade or use a blender. Turn the machine on and drop garlic in while the blade is turning. Turn off when garlic is minced, after about 10 seconds.

2. Put beans in strainer or colander to drain. Too much moisture will keep burgers from holding their shape.

3. Cut onions into quarters. Put in food processor and pulse until chopped. Add remaining ingredients to food processor and pulse until well combined but still rough: you want a burgerish texture here, not baby food. If you have time, let mixture sit for 15 to 30 minutes so the oatmeal has time to absorb some of the liquid. About 10 minutes before starting step 4, preheat oven to 425°F.

4. Line a cookie sheet with parchment paper or grease it. Divide the bean mixture into 8 even balls and put on cookie sheet. Shape into burgers.

5. Bake for 15 minutes and then use a spatula to turn burgers over. Bake for another 15 minutes until burgers are crispy and browned on the outside and still creamy on the inside.

6. Serve at once. Cool extra on wire racks so they don't get soggy, and then refrigerate or freeze. Reheat in toaster oven or on grill to maintain crispiness.

Notes

Make a batch of these burgers right after you've made pesto. You don't waste a drop of pesto and will clean the food processor only once.

Use an ice cream scoop with a release trigger to scoop the bean mixture out of the food processor. The one I have makes right-size burgers very quickly. As a bonus, I barely have to touch the sticky burger mixture.

To keep burgers from sticking together when freezing, separate them with pieces of parchment paper saved from lining the pan.

Black Beans in Baked Winter Squash with Persian Tomato Sauce

Stuffed acorn squash is easy enough to make for a casual lunch and fancy enough to take the place of turkey at Thanksgiving. Enjoy the blend of flavors, textures, and temperatures as you scoop up squash, spicy beans, and yogurt with each bite. It's great with Nutty Rice Salad (page 203).

Active time: 6 minutes
Total time: about 20 minutes
Makes 4 servings

2 small acorn squash, about 14 ounces each
2 cups black beans, drained (see Basic Beans recipe, page 132)
½ cup Persian Tomato Sauce (page 172)
¼ cup plain yogurt, optional (page 127)

1. Wash the outside of the squash with mild detergent and rinse well. Cut squash in half from stem to pointed end. Scrape out seeds and fibers. Put cut-side down on a shallow microwave-safe dish, cover loosely with waxed paper, and cook on high for 12 minutes. Turn squash over, replace wax paper, and cook on high until fork tender, about 2 more minutes.

2. Meanwhile, mix beans and sauce in another microwave-safe dish. When squash is done, let squash rest in dish still covered by waxed paper while beans cook. Cover beans and microwave on high until hot, about 4 minutes.

3. To serve, arrange squash on a platter or on individual plates. Use a fork to roughen up the inside of each squash a bit so that beans don't slide right out. Put ½ cup of bean mixture into each squash and top with a tablespoon yogurt, if using.

Notes
In a time crunch, use shortcuts: canned beans, bottled tomato sauce or salsa, and ready-made yogurt. This version can be made wherever you have access to a microwave, such as a dorm or hotel. Try Frontera Chipotle Salsa if you like spicy food.

Chickpea Stew on Couscous

This exotic stew mixes flavors and textures: spicy, creamy, sweet, robust, and fluffy. It's fast enough for a weeknight and complex and attractive enough for company, especially if you add some optional toppings (see Notes).

If you haven't tried couscous before, get ready to meet a new friend. Couscous is a North African way of serving steamed semolina, made from Durham wheat. It's easier and faster to make than rice.

 Active time: 20 minutes, using cooked
    chickpeas
    Total time: 25 minutes
    Makes 4 servings

2 garlic cloves
2 teaspoons olive oil
1 onion
1 bell pepper
2 carrots
One-half 28-ounce can diced tomatoes
    or one 14.5-ounce can
2 cups cooked chickpeas (see Basic
    Beans, page 132)
½ teaspoon cayenne
½ teaspoon salt
1 teaspoon oregano, optional
½ cup raisins, optional (80 grams)

Couscous
1 cup dry couscous (175 grams)
1 ¼ cups water or chickpea broth
¼ teaspoon salt if using water

1. Mince garlic and set aside. Heat oil in a medium pan over medium heat. Chop onions and bell peppers and add to the pan as you chop them, stirring occasionally.

2. Peel carrots, slice lengthwise, then cut into half-moons about ½-inch wide. When onions are soft, add garlic and stir once. Add carrots, tomatoes, chickpeas, spices, and raisins, if using. Bring to a boil and then reduce heat to low. Cover and simmer until carrots are tender.

3. Meanwhile, make couscous. Bring water to a boil in a small pan. Add couscous and salt, if using. Stir briefly, cover saucepan, and remove from heat. Couscous will be done in 5 minutes, but leave it covered until you are ready to serve it so it stays warm.

4. To serve, fluff couscous with a fork and put on plates or in bowls. Serve stew on top of couscous. Refrigerate or freeze any extra.

Notes
Use other dried fruits instead of raisins if you have them, such as apricots or dried plums, cutting large pieces into halves or quarters.

Top the stew with banana slices, a sprinkling of salted cashews, a spoonful of plain yogurt, or chopped parsley.

Because raisins are not on the summer shopping list, leave them out during that time unless you have some on hand.

Cuban Black Beans and Black Bean Soup

Reader Amy B. wrote that her family "absolutely adores" Cuban Black Beans, including her children, aged four and two. She serves beans with steamed vegetables, avocado, and fresh tomatoes, saying, "We call them yum bowls."

Enjoy Cuban Black Beans as a change from tomato-based bean dishes, serving them over rice or wrapping them in a burrito. To make black bean soup, just whirl beans and broth in a blender or food processor until smooth.

 Active time: 20 minutes
Total time: 2 hours 20 minutes to
7 hours 20 minutes, depending on
cooking method used for beans
Makes 8 servings, ¾ cups each

12 ounces dried black beans
    (1¾ cups dried or 4 cups cooked)
3 bay leaves
2 teaspoons salt
3 garlic cloves
1 onion
1 bell pepper
1½ teaspoons dried ground cumin
½ teaspoon dried crushed oregano
½ teaspoon dried chipotle or cayenne

1. Cook beans using the Basic Beans recipe (page 132), adding bay leaves when you add salt.

2. About an hour before beans should be done, bite a few to check for tenderness. When beans give but are still crispy, mince garlic, chop onion and bell pepper, and then stir into beans. Cover and simmer for another hour, until beans and vegetables are tender.

3. Remove bay leaves. Serve over rice, wrapped in a burrito, or whirled into soup. Optionally, top with a spoonful of plain yogurt, diced tomatoes, or salsa.

Note

Always count bay leaves when you put them in so you know how many to take out, especially if you will be making soup or serving children or the visually impaired.

Hoppin' John

Hoppin' John is a tradition on New Year's Day in the South. Have seconds: the more black-eyed peas and greens you eat, the more luck and money you'll have in the coming year. Make it the main dish for your holiday open house or enjoy it all winter long. Serve with Tasty Tahini Greens (page 173) and Corn Bread (page 158).

 Active time: 30 minutes
Total time: 1 hour, 30 minutes using a slow cooker
Makes 10 servings, 1 cup each

5 cups cooked black-eyed peas
  (see Basic Beans, page 132)
5 cups cooked rice
Two 28-ounce cans diced tomatoes
6 ounces spring onion
8 ounces Cheddar, optional
hot sauce to taste, optional

1. Cook black-eyed peas and rice while preparing other ingredients. Grate cheese, if using, and drain tomatoes, saving liquid for other uses. Chop spring onions crossways into circles.

2. Drain peas when tender, saving broth for another use. Fluff rice with a fork, then add to peas. Stir gently to mix, then stir in tomatoes. Heat until warm, about 10 minutes. At this point, dish will keep for an hour or so in a slow cooker on low. Mix in spring onions just before serving.

3. To serve, top with grated cheese, if using, and pass the hot sauce. Refrigerate or freeze any extra.

Notes

Bring the whole slow cooker of Hoppin' John to a potluck dinner. It will stay hot during a short trip and you can plug it in when you get there.

Hummus

Making hummus takes only about 10 minutes if you start with cooked beans. Use it as a dip for vegetables, on toast, as sandwich filling, and as a delicious "gravy" for roast vegetables such as carrots, white and sweet potatoes, onions, and bell peppers.

Active time: 10 minutes
Total time: 10 minutes, plus 2 to
7½ hours for cooking beans
(see Basic Bean recipe, page 132)
Makes 8 servings, generous ½ cup each

4 garlic cloves
4 cups cooked chickpeas
   (see Basic Beans, page 132)
⅓ cup chickpea broth, reserved from
   cooking chickpeas, or water
½ cup tahini
⅓ cup olive oil
2 to 4 tablespoons lemon juice (the
   juice from one or two lemons)
2 teaspoons ground cumin
1½ teaspoons salt
½ teaspoon cayenne or chipotle
black pepper to taste, optional

1. Set up your food processor with the cutting blade or use a blender. Turn the machine on and drop garlic in while the blade is turning. Turn off machine when garlic is minced, after about 10 seconds.

2. Add chickpeas, broth, tahini, olive oil, and juice of one lemon. Process or blend until smooth.

3. Add cumin, salt, cayenne, and black pepper, if using. Process to blend. Taste and adjust seasonings. If it tastes right but is too thick, add more chickpea broth or water. If it lacks zing, add more lemon juice.

4. Use hummus right away or put in a container, cover, and refrigerate until ready to serve. It freezes beautifully.

Notes

If you use canned chickpeas, rinse them thoroughly and use warm water in the recipe instead of chickpea broth.

Turn humdrum hummus and celery into a festive Yule tree with a few quick chops of the knife. The first time I brought this appetizer to a holiday party, people snapped it up in only 5 minutes. Before filling the celery, slice a thin ribbon from the bottom edge of each stalk, creating a flat resting place. (This will keep the celery from flopping over.) Spread hummus into the curve of each stalk and then arrange "tree branches" on a long, narrow plate or foil-covered cardboard.

Red Bean Chili

Colorful and spicy, red bean chili is nearly a whole meal by itself. It's full of beans, of course, but it also has tomatoes, onions, peppers, and garlic. Use chipotle pepper if you can for a smoky, rich taste. Serve with garlic toast, corn bread, or over rice.

Active time: 25 minutes, starting with nearly cooked beans
Total time: 55 minutes
Makes 12 servings, 1 cup each

6 cups cooked kidney beans
   (see Basic Beans, page 132)
2 teaspoons corn or canola oil
2 onions
2 bell peppers
8 garlic cloves
1 to 1½ teaspoons chipotle or cayenne
2 tablespoons plus 2 teaspoons cumin
Two 28-ounce cans diced tomatoes
   with juice

1. Cook the beans. About 30 minutes before beans should be done, dice garlic and chop onions and bell peppers. Heat oil in a medium pan over medium heat. Add onions and bell peppers as you chop, stirring occasionally. When onions are soft, in about 5 minutes, add garlic and stir once. Add spices and stir to coat vegetables. (If beans are not tender when onions are done, add tomatoes to onion mixture and simmer on low so spices don't burn while beans continue to cook.)

2. Drain beans when tender. Stir beans and tomatoes into onion mixture. Cover and simmer on low for 30 minutes. Taste and adjust spices as needed.

3. Serve hot. Refrigerate or freeze any extra.

Notes

The tomatoes will stop beans from becoming more tender, so make sure beans are soft before adding them to the tomatoes.

Adding hot pepper is easier than taking it out, so start slowly, taste, and then add more. If you do go over your comfort limit, refrigerate chili and taste again the next day. Beans will absorb some of the heat from the sauce, reducing the heat level.

To make **Black Bean Chili**, use black beans instead of kidney beans.

Red Bean Chili Casserole with Corn Bread Topping

Dress up nearly any bean stew by baking it in a casserole topped with corn bread batter. It makes a hearty family dinner or a welcomed contribution to a potluck dinner.

 Active time: 15 minutes, starting with prepared chili
Total time: 40 minutes
Makes 8 servings

butter or shortening for pan
8 cups Red Bean Chili (page 143)
1 recipe Corn Bread (page 158)

1. Preheat oven to 400°F. Butter or grease a 9 x 13-inch casserole dish that is at least 2 inches deep.

2. Heat chili on stove or in microwave. Mix up corn bread batter, stirring melted butter and corn oil into batter instead of putting them in a skillet.

3. Pour chili into casserole and level with a spoon. Top with corn bread batter, leveling quickly. Bake for about 25 minutes until corn bread is golden brown and tester inserted into the center of the corn bread comes out clean.

4. Serve hot or warm. To serve in two neat layers, cut casserole into rectangles and serve using a spatula. For a more casual approach, dip out servings with a ladle or big spoon. Refrigerate or freeze any extra.

Notes

When you check the corn bread for doneness, put the tester through just the corn bread layer. The chili will always make the skewer wet.

Preheating the chili makes sure that the corn bread cooks evenly. If you start with cold chili, the top of the corn bread will burn before the bottom cooks.

To freeze, cut casserole into individual servings and wrap in freezer-weight aluminum foil.

Lentil Stew with Spring Onions

Lentils cook so quickly that you will want to keep them on hand for nights when you need a high-protein dish in a hurry. They come in various colors. Brown lentils are bargains. Green or French lentils hold their shape while cooking. Beautiful red lentils are one of the fastest cooking of all legumes. A glass jar full of lentils elevates storage to decoration.

 Active time: 20 minutes
Total time: 40 to 50 minutes
Makes 8 servings, a generous ¾ cup each

2 garlic cloves
1 ⅓ cups spring onions
2 teaspoons olive oil
1 teaspoon turmeric
⅘ pound brown, green, or red lentils
   (scant 2 cups or 360 grams)
4 cups water
2 teaspoons salt, or to taste
4 carrots

1. Mince garlic and set aside. Cut spring onions into ¼-inch rounds, discarding root and tip ends.

2. Heat olive oil in a medium pot over medium heat. Add garlic and turmeric. Stir until fragrant, about 30 seconds. Add spring onions and cook until softened, about 2 minutes. Stir frequently to keep from burning.

3. Meanwhile, pick through lentils to remove nonlentil objects and rinse well (see Basic Beans page 132).

4. Add lentils, water, and salt to onion mixture and bring to a boil. Cut carrots lengthwise and then crossways into half-moons about ¼ inch wide, discarding leaf ends. Add carrots to pot as you cut them. Reduce heat to low and cover pot, simmering until lentils and carrots are tender, about 20 minutes.

5. Serve hot. Refrigerate or freeze any extra.

Notes

What's with the odd measurement for lentils? It's an awkwardness coming from the Imperial measurement system (pounds, ounces, cups, and so forth). It's a result of using 2 pounds of lentils in two recipes that make 8 servings each and one recipe that makes 4 servings. If you aren't following the menu plan to the letter, feel free to use a whole pound with a bit more water.

For a super-speedy dish, microwave sliced carrots in a covered dish for 4 minutes on high before adding to stew. You'll save 5 or 10 minutes of total cooking time.

Refried Beans

Time is your friend once again with this recipe. Cook onions slowly until golden brown to give your refried beans the rich flavor at the core of so many Mexican dishes.

 Active time: 25 minutes, starting with cooked beans
Total time: 25 minutes
Makes 8 servings, ½ cup each

2 tablespoons corn oil
1 onion
4 garlic cloves
4 cups of cooked pinto beans,
  with some bean broth
salt to taste

1. Warm oil in a medium pan over medium heat. Chop onion and put in pan. Turn heat down to medium-low and cook until golden brown, about 10 minutes. Stir from time to time to keep onion from burning.

2. Meanwhile, mince garlic and set aside. If pinto beans are not already warm, heat them on the stove or in the microwave until they are at about room temperature. Warm beans are easier to mash.

3. When onions are deep golden brown but not black, stir in garlic. Then add beans to onions in steps, putting in about ⅓ of beans at a time. Mash beans with a potato masher or big spoon, then add more. Add enough bean broth to make beans a bit softer than you like to eat them, since they firm up as they cool. Taste and add salt if needed.

4. Serve immediately or keep warm over very low heat until ready to serve, stirring occasionally to keep from burning. Use in a recipe or serve as a side dish, topped with a little chopped tomato or grated cheese if you like. Refrigerate or freeze any extra.

Notes
The broth from home-cooked beans is essential to making tasty refried beans. If you have to use canned beans, just buy canned refried beans.

Soft Tacos with Refried Beans

For each serving, warm 3 tortillas and ½ cup refried beans separately in the microwave or on the stove. Bend each tortilla across the middle to make a taco shape and then spread with few spoonfuls of refried beans. Top with ½ cup Fresh and Easy Salsa and one ounce grated Cheddar. Recipes: Tortillas (page 160), Refried Beans), Fresh and Easy Salsa (page 182).

Southwestern Bean Stew: Heirloom Beans with Tomatoes and Roasted Corn

Beans gone gourmet! Here's a bean dish you can serve to your most upscale foodie friends with your head held high. I love this stew with Yellow Indian Woman Beans, but you can use other heirloom beans. The thrifty menu recommends making this dish with kidney beans, but it would also be delicious with pinto beans or black beans.

Serve a bowl of Southwestern Bean Stew topped with chopped ripe tomatoes, garlicky fresh corn, and cilantro as a colorful dish with—or instead of—the usual grilled offerings of summer.

According to the website Local Harvest (www.localharvest.org), a Swedish family first brought Yellow Indian Woman beans to Montana. I got my first ones as part of a big birthday-check splurge at Rancho Gordo, the epicenter of heirloom-beandom, and I have been a loyal customer ever since.

 Active time: 25 minutes
Total time: 3 hours, plus at least 5 hours soaking if using kidney beans
Makes 12 servings

1 onion
1 pound Yellow Indian Woman Beans
   or kidney beans
6 cups water
2 teaspoons salt

Toppings
   kernels from 5 ears corn
   1 tablespoon olive oil
   2 garlic cloves
   1 pound ripe tomatoes
   1 cup fresh chopped cilantro leaves
   1 lemon or 2 tablespoons lemon juice

1. Chop onion and cook with beans until beans are creamy but still hold their shape (see Basic Beans, page 132).

2. Mince garlic. Shuck corn, rinse, and cut kernels off cobs. Heat olive oil in a large skillet over medium heat. Add garlic and stir once. Add corn kernels and cook mixture until it starts to brown, stirring occasionally so corn doesn't stick to the skillet or burn.

3. Meanwhile, chop tomatoes and cilantro. If using fresh lemon, slice into 12 moon-shaped pieces. Otherwise, stir lemon juice into beans.

4. To serve, put hot beans in a bowl with a lemon moon on the side, if using. Top with tomatoes, corn mixture, and cilantro. Refrigerate or freeze any extra. Refrigerate any extra toppings.

Notes

Prepare only as much of the tomatoes and cilantro as will be used right away.

To serve buffet style, leave beans in slow cooker to retain heat. Let guests ladle up beans and add toppings themselves.

My cost calculations for this recipe using green prices include 80 cents in shipping charges, assuming you ordered several pounds of beans at once, either for yourself or with friends. The thrifty prices use kidney beans. But even if you ordered only one pound of beans from Rancho Gordo (www.ranchogordo.com), so the flat $8 shipping charge fell only on these beans, the cost per serving would be only $1.55 regular and $1.62 green using prices from July 2010. That's hardly extravagant when eating like Napa Valley connoisseurs.

Spicy Black-Eyed Peas

As easy as it gets, these spicy, soupy black-eyed peas bring a taste of the Mediterranean to your table. Black-eyed peas cook so quickly that you don't need to presoak them. This is a great dish to start and then let cook while you go to the market or run errands. I love this dish so much that I sometimes make it for my birthday dinner, topped with Madhur Jaffrey's lemon-walnut sauce (see Notes).

 Active time: 20 minutes
Total time: about 1½ hours
Makes 12 servings, ½ cup of black-eyed peas each plus plenty of sauce. Serve with brown rice, white rice, bread, or just as a bowl of soupy goodness.

6 cups water
1 pound dried black-eyed peas
1½ teaspoons salt
4 bay leaves
2 teaspoons oregano
1 teaspoon chipotle or cayenne
1 teaspoon thyme
2 teaspoons paprika
2 tablespoons olive oil
6 garlic cloves

1. Turn slow cooker on high. Bring water to a boil in a tea kettle or on the stove.

Meanwhile, pick over and rinse black-eyed peas (see Basic Beans, page 132). Put hot water, peas, salt, and spices into the slow cooker, stir to mix, and then cover.

2. Start tasting the black-eyed peas to see if they are tender in forty minutes if you presoaked beans or in an hour if you didn't. When beans are tender, turn slow cooker down to low. Do not drain peas.

3. Dice garlic and put it in a small microwave-safe bowl with olive oil. Microwave on high until the oil bubbles and garlic is fragrant, about 1 minute. Add garlic oil to peas and stir to mix. Simmer for about 10 more minutes to blend flavors.

4. Serve over rice or with bread, especially brown rice or flatbread. Refrigerate or freeze any extra.

Notes

You must start with dried black-eyed peas rather than canned ones to create the rich broth essential to this dish.

Inspired by a recipe in Madhur Jaffrey's *World Vegetarian*, this version uses ingredients in the *Wildly Affordable Organic* kitchen, simplifies the cooking process, and reduces the number of pots to wash. I can't improve on her Walnut Sauce, but you'll get some of that sauce's zing with Greek Dressing (page 201).

Babe's Split Pea Soup

Here's a vegan twist on the classic split pea and ham soup, with tahini and chipotle adding the smoky taste and silky texture. Split peas cook so quickly that you can serve this comforting, hearty soup less than an hour after starting it—more quickly if you soak the split peas.

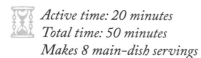

Active time: 20 minutes
Total time: 50 minutes
Makes 8 main-dish servings

1 pound split peas
5 cups water
2 teaspoons salt
2 teaspoons corn oil
1 onion
½ teaspoon chipotle or cayenne
4 carrots
1 tablespoon tahini

1. Clean split peas and bring to a boil with water and salt in a big pot (see Basic Beans, page 132). Heat oil in a medium skillet over medium heat. Chop onion and add to skillet with chipotle. Cook until onion is soft, about 5 minutes, stirring occasionally. Stir onion mixture into split peas.

2. Meanwhile, scrub carrots, cut off ends, then slice lengthwise and across to get half-moons. Add to peas with tahini. When soup begins to boil, reduce heat to low until it barely boils.

3. Simmer covered for about 30 minutes until peas are very soft. Add salt as needed.

4. Serve hot in bowls. Refrigerate or freeze any extra.

Notes

Use sweet potatoes instead of carrots for a Caribbean touch.

I like some texture in this soup, but if you want it smoother, simmer for 5 more minutes.

Disclaimer: this soup is named in honor of my favorite movie pig, but to my knowledge, Babe has neither tried nor commented on this soup.

Tortilla Stacks

Tortilla stacks are as easy to make as a sandwich once you've made the ingredient recipes for soft tacos or burritos. They are also attractive and interesting enough for a casual get-together.

 Active time: 10 minutes, starting with prepared refried beans, tortillas, and salsa
Total time: 10 minutes
Makes 4 main-dish servings

2 cups Refried Beans (page 146)
12 Tortillas (page 160)
1 cup shredded cabbage
1 cup shredded zucchini
4 ounces grated Cheddar
1 cup Fresh and Easy Salsa (page 182)

1. Heat refried beans in pot on stove or in microwave in microwave-safe dish if needed. If needed, heat tortillas in microwave on high for about 30 seconds, covered with a slightly damp towel. Shred cabbage, zucchini, and cheese.

2. On a plate for each person, make a stack that repeats three times with a tortilla, refried beans, cheese, and salsa. Top with shredded cabbage and zucchini.

3. Serve immediately.

Notes

If you are feeding a crowd or want to prepare several servings to pack for lunch, make tortilla stacks into a Mexican lasagna by assembling all layers except shredded vegetables in a casserole dish. Bake at 350°F for 20 minutes. To serve, cut into squares and top with shredded vegetables.

Try other fresh shredded or finely chopped salad vegetables as toppings, including lettuce, spring onions, tomatoes, bell peppers, and carrots. To make this vegan, use more beans and skip the cheese.

18

Breads

For many people, the fragrance of bread baking says "home" and "comfort" like nothing else. Making bread is like nothing else too. You are developing the gluten, the stretchy, high-protein "muscle" of the wheat that provides the bread's structure. You're also awakening the living yeast that inflates the structure so the bread rises. Depending on your mood, making bread may thrill your inner scientist or artist. Either way, you'll be part of a tradition that goes back thousands of years.

Best of all, homemade bread is easy, good for you, and so delicious you'll wonder why you ever bought manufactured bread.

The New, No-Knead Whisk Breads

The no-knead recipes in *Wildly Affordable Organic* are my pride and joy, the results of eighteen months of research and bread making. I wanted very nutritious bread that was fast and easy to make and didn't require any special equipment.

My no-knead whisk breads, buns, and pizza dough are incredibly easy to make. No kneading. No bread machine, mixer, or food processor is necessary. Just whisk part of the ingredients together to develop the gluten that gives the dough the structure needed to rise. Let the dough rise first on the counter and then overnight in the refrigerator. You'll get good results by using half as much yeast, the most expensive component in the recipe, because it will party on overnight, budding and breeding to make more yeast.

No-knead breads are great bargains too. In July 2010, a loaf of Good Whisk Bread (page 153) cost $1.73 per loaf using top-quality organic ingredients and only $1.02 using thrifty, good ingredients.

The taste is complex and interesting for adults while still being kid friendly. The crispy crust protects the tender inside. The texture is light but without the big holes that might let your peanut butter escape.

I studied and tried dozens of recipes, with three sources inspiring the key steps. Thanks to Mark Bittman and Jim Lahey's Sullivan Street Bread for the idea of letting the dough develop overnight instead of kneading it. Thanks to Jeff Hertzberg and Zoe Francois for the idea of creating a gluten cloak. And thanks to Rose Levy Beranbaum for the idea of mixing all-purpose flour with wheat germ and her encouragement to measure by weight instead of volume.

Traditional Breads

Classic bread recipes also have a place in the *Wildly Affordable Organic* kitchen. For speed, try Corn Bread and Pumpkin Bread, which use baking soda or baking powder to rise immediately. Tortillas don't use any leavening, so they are thrifty, flat, and fast.

Traditional yeast breads require kneading and more yeast but are ready in just a few hours. Try Good Burger Buns and the Sweet Raisin Flatbread (page 126) in the Breakfast section. I bet you'll find they are worth it.

Tips for Successful Bread Making

- Use nonstick loaf pans for sticky, no-knead bread dough.
- Yeast bread rises best at temperatures between 72° and 90°F. In the winter my kitchen is at 68°F or colder, so I put my bread pans on a heating pad turned to low, cover them with a cake carrier, and then cover that with a clean bath towel.
- Yeast bread rises best in a humid oven. Use the regular bake setting instead of convection. Some recipes raise the oven's humidity by putting ice cubes in along with the loaves. Use an old or disposable pan for the cubes because the big change in temperature will warp it and minerals in the ice will stain.
- Keep all bread at room temperature or frozen. Refrigerating bread makes it go stale faster.

Good Whisk Bread

Start here if you've never made yeast bread before. This recipe takes little time and uses few ingredients. Whisk up a bowl of dough and bake it anytime over the next two weeks. The taste gets a sourdough tang during the second week. Visit Cookfor-Good.com/wao for videos on whisking and shaping bread dough.

 Active time: 20 minutes
Total time: 4 hours, plus rising at least overnight
Makes 2 loaves, with 16 servings of 2 slices each

2 ½ cups white whole wheat flour or whole wheat flour (300 grams)
2 ¼ teaspoons rapid-rise or instant yeast (1 package)
1 tablespoon salt
½ cup wheat germ (64 grams)
1 tablespoon honey (21 grams)
3 cups warm water, about 110°F
4 cups all-purpose, unbleached flour (480 grams)

1. **Mix the dough.** In a one-gallon or larger bowl, whisk white whole wheat flour and yeast to mix. Add salt, wheat germ, honey, and the first 2 cups of water. Whisk slowly to dampen flour, then rapidly for a minute. Swish your whisk in remaining cup of water (or water, milk, and melted butter, if you're making Whisk Sandwich Bread) so you don't waste anything. Add all-purpose flour and then the last cup of liquid to dough, then stir with a big slotted spoon until all flour is damp.

2. **Let it rise.** Cover the bowl with something tight enough to keep it from drying out but loose enough that the yeast gas can escape. I use a plate, but any loose lid or even a piece of waxed paper would do fine. Let dough rise at room temperature for one to five hours (see Tips if the room is cold, page 152). Refrigerate dough overnight or for up to two weeks. This will let yeast develop, making bread taste better and rise more.

3. **Divide the dough.** When you are ready to bake, take dough out of the refrigerator. (If you have time, do this up to 30 minutes before you start to handle dough so it won't feel so cold.) Grease a spatula and 1 or 2 nonstick 9.25 x 5.25 x 2.75-inch loaf pans with shortening or butter. Oil or flour your hands so dough doesn't stick. Sprinkle a little flour on dough and then use a serrated knife to cut it in half. Coax half out of the bowl with the greased spatula. To preserve the gluten structure and trapped bubbles, try to keep dough together without tearing it. Sprinkle other side of dough with a little flour too. If you are making only one loaf, return rest to the refrigerator in its covered bowl.

4. **Stretch the dough.** Hold your hands underneath dough and slowly spread them so dough almost falls through. As it falls, dough will stick to your hands a little and stretch, creating the gluten web that will support crust as it rises. Gather stretched dough at the top like an outie belly button. Turn dough about 30° and repeat, keeping the belly button on top, until you have dropped, stretched, and gathered dough five or six times, going all the way around. Stretching dough should take about a minute.

5. **Shape the dough.** Turn dough sideways so its belly faces a wall and then shake

it until it is nearly loaf shaped. Then put it belly-side down in the pan. Press dough down gently until it covers the bottom of the pan and fills the corners. Repeat with other loaf if you are baking two.

6. **Let the dough rise again.** Put dough in a small, warm place so it can rise without drying out, such as a cake carrier or a microwave, or cover with a clean, smooth towel (not terry cloth). Let rise for about two hours until it has doubled in size. It should be at or near the top of the bread pan.

7. **Bake.** Preheat your oven to 350°F. Do not use convection baking because it will take away steam that gives bread its final height. Put an empty pan on the very bottom of your oven. Put a bread stone or heavy cookie sheet on the bottom rack of your oven. Put several ice cubes in a bowl or scoop so you can put them into the empty pan in the oven without burning yourself. Open the oven, put bread pans directly on the bread stone, and slide ice cubes into the empty pan. Quickly close the oven door to trap steam. Bake for 35 to 40 minutes until golden brown and interior temperature is 205°F.

8. **Remove bread from oven.** Remove loaf from the pan. (If bread doesn't pop out of the pan when you turn it over, slide a plastic knife or thin spatula between bread and the pan to loosen it.) If you like a crisper crust, slide loaf out of the pan and put it back into the oven on the bread stone for about 3 minutes. Cool bread on a wire rack. Let it cool all the way to room temperature before slicing so that its structure sets. If you cut it while it's hot, the bread will become a gummy mess. Slice with a serrated knife. Store at room temperature, wrapped in a clean tea towel or piece of cotton, plastic wrap, or in a paper bag. To keep longer, wrap the bread well in plastic or foil and then freeze.

Whisk Sandwich Bread

Whisk Sandwich Bread is the richer cousin to Good Whisk Bread (page 153). Because it has milk and butter in it, Whisk Sandwich Bread keeps longer once baked and has a softer texture. Ironically, the milk also limits its time safely rising at room temperature to two hours and time resting in the refrigerator to a week.

Extra ingredients
⅔ cup scalded milk to replace ⅔ cup water
2 tablespoons butter

Make this bread just like Good Whisk Bread, except after adding the last flour, use ⅔ cup warm milk and ⅓ cup water instead of all water and add 2 tablespoons melted butter. Scald milk by bringing it just to a boil and then remove from heat. Put butter in hot milk to melt and then add ⅓ cup water to speed the cooling process. Let cool to about 110°F before adding to mixed dough.

I like to make this bread and yogurt at the same time because both call for scalding milk. Otherwise, microwave milk in a 2-cup Pyrex measuring cup for about 2 minutes on high or heat on the stove.

Whisk Burger Buns

Try these thrifty, no-knead burger buns for casual family dinners or vegan gatherings.

Make dough for Good Whisk Bread (page 153) or Whisk Sandwich Bread, following the recipe through shaping dough. A full bread recipe will make 16 buns, but you can use as much as you need at the time and refrigerate the rest for up to a week, using it for more buns or for bread.

Cut dough into as many burger buns as you need. Stretch dough for each bun as you would for a whole loaf. Then follow the directions in Good Burger Buns (page 157) for letting dough rise and baking it. The glaze and sesame-seed topping are optional.

Garlic Toast

My Taster loves garlic toast so much that I use it to make an otherwise not-so-exciting meal bring a sparkle to his eyes. Good Whisk Bread makes the best garlic toast, but any bread that is not too sweet will do. You can use first-quality bread, but garlic toast is just as good with crust ends or bread that's going stale.

 Active time: 3 minutes
Total time: 8 minutes
Makes 4 servings, 2 slices each

2 garlic cloves
2 tablespoons olive oil or melted butter
8 slices of Good Whisk Bread (page 153) or Whisk Sandwich Bread (page 155)
salt to taste

1. Mince garlic or put it through a garlic press. Put garlic and olive oil in a small, microwave-safe dish, such as a Pyrex custard cup. Microwave on high until the oil starts to bubble and mixture is fragrant, about 40 seconds.

2. Brush oil on bread and salt to taste. Toast in a toaster oven oil-side-up until golden brown.

3. Serve immediately.

Notes

If you have salt with large crystals, such as kosher salt, use it here.

In the first two steps, you are making garlic-infused oil. If you have it on hand, this recipe is even faster. The oil keeps for up to a week in the refrigerator but no longer. Garlic can spoil without any sign, so throw out any that may be too old.

If you are feeling extravagant, sprinkle on a little grated Parmesan before toasting.

Good Burger Buns

I laughed out loud the first time I made these. It seemed unbelievable that I could make burger buns that looked so perfectly normal, just like what you might get at the grocery store. But I wasn't laughing after I took the first bite; I was mmmm-ing. These buns are light, tender, and faintly sweet, but they are strong enough to hold up to a big burger and lots of toppings. No one will guess that they are more nutritious than most buns.

Good Burger Buns take 5 or 10 minutes more time than Whisk Burger Buns (page 155), but the results will stand up to finicky relatives and important national holidays. And because you make 12 buns at once and freeze the ones you don't use right away, you may agree that it's time well spent.

 Active time: 30 minutes
Total time: 3 hours
Makes 12 buns

1½ cups warm water, about 110°F
3 tablespoons butter, melted
1 egg plus 1 egg white (save extra yolk for glaze)
3⅓ cups plus 2 teaspoons all-purpose flour (400 grams), plus extra for kneading
1½ cups white whole wheat flour (180 grams)
¼ cup sugar (50 grams)
1 tablespoon salt
1 tablespoon plus 1 ½ teaspoons rapid-rise yeast (2 packets)
2 teaspoons oil for plastic wrap

Glaze
1 egg yolk
1 tablespoon water
2 tablespoons sesame seeds, optional

1. Combine all dough ingredients in a big bowl and stir to mix. Put extra egg yolk in a small bowl and refrigerate until needed for the glaze.

2. Knead dough using a bread machine or a stand mixer fitted with a dough hook for about 8 minutes or knead by hand for about 10 minutes. Dough will be very soft, sticky, and smooth.

3. Oil a big clean bowl and put dough in to rise. Cover with a plate or lid so it doesn't dry out. Let dough rise for an hour or so until it has doubled in size.

4. Line two cookie sheets with parchment paper or grease the sheets. Oil or flour your hands just enough to keep dough from sticking. (Too much flour will make the buns tough.) Put dough on a floured surface and cut into 12 even pieces. Shape each piece into a ball and then flatten. Space dough disks evenly on cookie sheets, 6 buns to a sheet.

5. Oil plastic wrap and cover each cookie sheet, stretching it barely tight to keep the buns from rising too high. Let rise for 30 to 40 minutes, until they have doubled in size.

6. Position two oven racks in the middle of the oven with enough room to put one set of buns on the lower rack without touching the rack above. Preheat oven to 375°F.

7. Carefully remove plastic wrap. Add water to egg yolk and whisk until smooth. Use your fingers or a brush to coat buns gently with glaze. Sprinkle glazed buns with sesame seeds if desired. Bake for 12 to 15 minutes until golden brown.

8. Remove buns from the oven. Transfer to a wire rack to cool completely. Slice crossways with a serrated bread knife before serving. Keep extra in container at room temperature or wrap well and freeze.

(continues)

Note

I hate having half an egg left over at the end of a recipe. Making 12 buns at a time lets you use 2 complete eggs—one yolk in the glaze and the rest in the dough.

Corn Bread

Cooking bread in a skillet makes me feel like a pioneer right out of *Little House on the Prairie*. But even if you've worked all day at the most high-tech job imaginable, you'll be glad to have a bread that comes together fast, with a rich taste and bright color.

If you love sweet corn bread, add a tablespoon or two of sugar with the other dry ingredients. But try it without sugar. It's less expensive, of course, and more like what the pioneers actually ate because sugar was so hard to get. It's better for you too.

 Active time: 10 minutes
Total time: 40 minutes
   Makes 12 servings, with one wedge or muffin each. Doubles well when cooked as muffins.

1 tablespoon butter
1 tablespoon corn oil
2 cups finely ground cornmeal
   (265 grams)
2 teaspoons baking powder
1 teaspoon baking soda
1 teaspoon salt
1 egg
1¾ cups Yogurt (400 grams) (page 127)

1. Preheat oven to 400°F. Put butter and oil into a cast-iron skillet or 9-inch round metal cake pan into the oven. See Notes if making corn muffins.

2. Stir together cornmeal, baking powder, baking soda, and salt in a medium bowl. Break egg into a small bowl and stir briefly with a fork to blend. Add egg and yogurt to dry ingredients and stir quickly until just blended and smooth.

3. Take the hot skillet out of the oven, if using, and tilt if needed so butter mixture covers entire bottom. Pour batter into the skillet or muffin pan and bake at 400°F until golden brown, about 30 minutes.

4. Serve hot, warm, or at room temperature. Best eaten fresh, but keeps covered at room temperature for a day or two. Freezes well.

Notes

To make corn muffins, butter or grease muffin pan or use paper liners. Stir melted butter and corn oil into batter. Do not preheat pan. Bake for 25 minutes.

If you don't have enough yogurt, make up the difference with milk. As little as ½ cup yogurt provides the acidity needed to let muffins rise.

Do not preheat a glass or pottery casserole and then pour cold batter into it. The change in temperature could break the container.

Look for stone-ground cornmeal, which has more taste and nutrition than steel-ground cornmeal. If you don't have a good local source, try Hodgson Mill's plain yellow cornmeal, which is also available by mail order.

Pumpkin Bread

Pumpkin bread tastes like a treat even though it's packed with nutrition. Pumpkin is a vegetable, after all, and here it's joined by nuts, raisins, and whole wheat flour. It's delicious toasted with peanut butter or served by the slice as a snack or dessert.

 Active time: 15 minutes
Total time: 1 hour, 35 minutes
Makes 24 servings, 1 slice each

10 tablespoons butter (1¼ sticks),
    at room temperature
2½ cups sugar (500 grams)
4 eggs
2½ cups pumpkin puree
3⅓ cups white whole wheat flour
    (400 grams)
2 teaspoons salt
2 teaspoons baking soda
½ teaspoon baking powder
1 teaspoon cinnamon
½ teaspoon nutmeg
⅔ cup walnuts, chopped coarsely
    (300 grams)
⅔ cup raisins (100 grams)

1. Preheat oven to 350°F. Grease bottom of two 9.25 x 5.25 x 2.75-inch loaf pans.

2. Beat butter and sugar in a mixing bowl on medium-low until fluffy, about 1 minute. Add eggs and pumpkin puree; stir to mix. Add flour, salt, baking soda, baking powder, cinnamon, and nutmeg. Stir in walnuts and raisins. Pour into loaf pans and bake for 1 hour and 10 minutes.

3. Cool on wire racks for about 10 minutes and then remove from pans. Cool completely before slicing.

4. Serve at room temperature or toasted. Wrap extra and refrigerate for up to 10 days or freeze for up to a year.

Note

If you don't have homemade pumpkin puree, use a 16-ounce can plain pumpkin plus ⅓ cup water. Do not use pumpkin pie mix.

Tortillas

Homemade tortillas were another revelation when I developed the summer menu. I couldn't believe that they were easier to make than pancakes! This recipe looks long, but that's because it describes the process of making the tortillas step-by-step in case it's as new to you as it was to me.

I think of these as "After You Tortillas" because the sweeping motion you make with your hand to put a tortilla flat on a hot grill is like the polite gesture you make to let someone go in front of you through a door: "After you, my dear tortilla!"

We're lucky to have a big Hispanic population in my community, so masa harina, the corn flour for tortillas, is easy to get at many grocery stores.

 Active time: 15 minutes
Total time: 45 minutes
Makes 8 servings, 3 tortillas each

1 cup plus 2 tablespoons water
2 cups masa harina (240 grams)
½ teaspoon salt (optional but good)

1. Bring water to a boil. Put masa harina and salt into a medium bowl and stir to mix. Pour boiling water over masa harina and stir to form a soft dough. Cover and let rest for 30 minutes.

2. Meanwhile, make your own tortilla press by cutting a freezer-weight plastic bag along the sides so it is joined only at the bottom. A quart-size bag will be just the right size. I label mine, wash it afterward, and reuse it. Line a basket or dish with a clean towel or cloth napkin to hold cooked tortillas.

3. Preheat a big flat skillet or griddle to medium-high. Form dough into 12 balls and put on a plate. Cover with a damp cloth.

4. Put the cut bag on a flat surface. Center dough balls one at a time inside the bag and press gently with the flat of your hand until you have a flat disk about 5 inches across. Pick up the bag and hold it in one hand while you peel back the top of the plastic, starting with a section of tortilla that has a fairly thick edge. Flip tortilla over so it rests on your hand and peel the plastic off the other side.

5. When the skillet is hot, hold one hand palm-side up and parallel to the floor. Drape tortilla over your fingers so a little more than half the tortilla is on your hand and the rest drapes over. Lay the tortilla flat on the skillet by brushing the back of your hand just above the skillet so the raw edge of the tortilla touches and catches, pulling the rest of the tortilla off your hand, but not close enough to burn your hand. This brushing motion will give you flat tortillas and will become second nature after a few tries.

6. Now start the dance of cooking some tortillas while pressing the next ones. You will flip each tortilla twice, cooking three times for about 30 seconds each time. They will be slightly puffed and have brown patches on each side when done.

To keep track of how many times you've flipped a tortilla, start it at one position on the grill and flip it "around the clock." I start at 9 o'clock because that's a good position for a right-hander to brush the tortilla onto the grill, then flip it to 1 o'clock and 5 o'clock. Finally, it gets tucked under the cloth in a basket to steam. In between flips, press out the next tortillas.

7. If you have time, let tortillas steam themselves in the basket for about 10 minutes and then serve hot or use in a recipe. Put any extras in a bag or small container and keep at room temperature for up to two days.

Notes

Tortilla dough should be just wet enough to hold its shape when you squeeze it. If you have trouble peeling the plastic off, make the tortilla thicker with edges as thick as its middle. If that doesn't work, add more masa harina to the dough.

If you have a real tortilla press, use the cut bag to line it. A press would be a great time saver if you were making lots of tortillas every day. But for *Wildly Affordable Organic* purposes, pressing the dough by hand works just fine.

Thanks to Rick Bayless and his excellent *Mexican Kitchen* cookbook for the idea of letting dough rest for 30 minutes. This simple step greatly improves the taste of the tortillas.

19

Eggs and Potatoes

Eggs and potatoes add variety and nutrition to *Wildly Affordable Organic* meals. Make dinner in ten minutes by scrambling eggs, microwaving potatoes, and cutting up carrots or broccoli. Or take time to go exotic with Swiss Chard Frittata or Potato Peanut Curry. Either way, you'll be getting high nutrition and taste at a very low price.

Eggs and potatoes are both kitchen chameleons, changing wildly depending on how you prepare them. It's hard to believe that a hard-boiled egg is related to a quiche or that a plain baked potato is just a sauce away from Potato Peanut Curry.

Egg and Spring-Onion Burritos

Your family will say "olé!" any time of the day that you serve these quick and fresh burritos. The tortilla wrapping makes them portable enough for breakfast on the run and somehow important enough for dinner. Enjoy one when dining by yourself rather than reaching for a packaged frozen dinner.

 Active time: 5 minutes
Total time: 5 minutes
Makes 4 servings

2 teaspoons corn oil
1 cup spring onions
6 eggs
2 ounces grated Cheddar
¼ teaspoon salt
4 large flour tortillas
2 teaspoons hot sauce

1. Heat corn oil in medium skillet over medium heat. Cut spring onions into ¼-inch rounds, discarding root and tip ends, and put in skillet. Cook until soft, about 2 minutes.

2. Break eggs in medium bowl and stir with a fork to combine. Add eggs, Cheddar,

and salt to pan. Stir to scramble until eggs are set, for about 2 minutes.

3. Meanwhile, put tortillas on a microwave-proof plate and cover with a damp tea towel or paper towel. Microwave on high for 40 seconds until tortillas are flexible.

4. Divide egg mixture among tortillas, sprinkle with hot sauce, and roll up tortillas (for how to roll a burrito, see Bean Burritos, step 3, page 135). Serve immediately.

Green Eggs Scramble

When I'm scrambling myself, I rely on Green Eggs Scramble to put a filling dinner on the table in about 20 minutes, including time to scrub and microwave sweet potatoes to complete the meal.

See Notes for preboiling robust greens such as kale or mustard. For a similar dish suitable for guests, see Swiss Chard Frittata (page 164).

 Active time: 20 minutes
Total time: 20 minutes
Makes 4 servings

4 cups chopped greens, preferably tender Swiss chard but robust kale or mustard are also good
2 teaspoons olive oil
1 onion
2 garlic cloves
¼ cup raisins (40 grams)
8 eggs
½ teaspoon salt, or to taste
2 ounces Parmesan

1. If using robust greens, preboil as described in Note in next column.

2. Heat oil over medium heat in a large skillet. Chop onion and put in the skillet, stirring frequently to prevent burning. Mince garlic and set aside.

3. Meanwhile, rinse and chop greens (page 42). Add stems to skillet as you chop and stir. Repeat for remaining greens. Cook for about 5 minutes, turning heat down to medium-low if the mixture starts to burn. Slice leaves into narrow ribbons.

4. Add garlic to skillet and stir once. Add leaves and raisins, stir, and cover skillet. Reduce heat to low and cook for about 5 minutes, until greens are tender.

5. Meanwhile, break eggs into medium bowl. Add salt and whisk until light yellow, about 30 seconds. Grate Parmesan if needed.

6. When greens are tender, add eggs to skillet and stir to combine. Raise heat to medium, stirring frequently until eggs are set, about 2 minutes.

7. Top with Parmesan and serve immediately.

Note

Preboil robust greens to minimize bitterness. Bring 6 to 8 cups of water to a boil in a medium pot. Meanwhile, clean and chop greens. Add stems to boiling water first, reducing heat to keep water at a low boil. Add leaves to pot about 2 minutes later. Boil covered for 5 minutes. Drain greens and press dry with a spoon. Add to skillet after garlic.

Swiss Chard Frittata

This fancier version of Green Eggs Scramble (page 163) calls for heating up the oven, but that one extra step plus a little waiting time turns a casual dish into something fancy. A frittata is a flat omelet, Italian style.

I cooked this frittata for a friend who exclaimed, "I feel like I'm eating at Moosewood!" Try this recipe yourself to see how easy it is to give your guests the experience of eating in a famous restaurant for a fraction of the cost.

Any chard will work, but use ruby or rainbow chard if you can get it. The red, yellow, and orange stems add a festive touch.

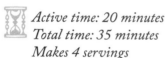 *Active time: 20 minutes*
Total time: 35 minutes
Makes 4 servings

4 cups Swiss chard
2 teaspoons olive oil
1 onion
2 garlic cloves
¼ cup raisins (40 grams)
8 eggs
½ teaspoon salt, or to taste
2 ounces Parmesan

1. Preheat the oven to 400°F and use a large oven-proof skillet, but otherwise follow Green Eggs Scramble recipe until adding eggs.

2. Add eggs to skillet and stir very briefly to combine, using a spatula to push down any chard that sticks up above the eggs. Continue cooking on stove without stirring until bottom is golden brown, about 10 minutes. (Use the spatula to lift up the edges and check). Put in oven and bake until cooked through, about 10 minutes.

3. Top with grated Parmesan, cut into wedges, and serve hot or warm. Refrigerate any extra.

Notes

An "oven-proof" skillet in this recipe is one that can handle a 400°F oven. A cast-iron skillet will be fine, as will many other skillets, but you don't want the handle to scorch, melt, or put out toxic gasses.

If Parmesan doesn't melt right away, return the skillet to the oven for about 30 seconds.

Hard-Boiled Eggs

Put eggs in a medium pot and cover with about an inch of water. Put lid on pot, turn heat to high, and bring water to a boil. Turn off heat and remove pot from burner. Let eggs sit in covered pot for 9 to 11 minutes. (Large eggs from the grocery store tend to cook in 9 minutes; larger and more yolky pastured eggs take longer.) Prepare a bowl of ice water. When eggs are done boiling, put in ice water until cold, about 10 minutes. The icy plunge helps prevent a green ring from forming between the yolk and the white. For easier peeling, use older eggs and refrigerate for several hours or up to a week.

Huevos Rancheros

"Ranch-Style Eggs" is a classic Mexican breakfast dish originally served to hungry ranchers after their early-morning chores. The vivid flavors and colors make it a popular choice for dinner too. Serve with refried beans (page 146).

This recipe is a good example of the value of mix-and-match cooking. Tortillas, salsa, and refried beans appear in other *Wildly Affordable Organic* meals, such as Tortilla Stacks and Soft Tacos (pages 150 and 146). The presentation is different enough for variety, yet using the same core recipes cuts back on the time spent cooking and washing dishes.

Active time: 10 minutes, with premade tortillas and salsa
Total time: 10 minutes
Makes 4 main-dish servings

8 Tortillas (page 160)
1 cup of Fresh and Easy Salsa (page 182)
2 teaspoons corn or vegetable oil
8 eggs
4 ounces Cheddar, grated

1. Make tortillas and salsa. If the tortillas aren't warm, put them on a microwave-safe plate, cover them with a barely damp towel, and microwave on high for about 40 seconds.

2. Heat oil over medium heat in a large skillet. Break eggs one at a time into a small bowl and carefully slide each egg onto the hot oiled skillet. Cook until white is firm but yolk is still somewhat liquid.

3. Meanwhile, set out a plate for each person. Arrange two tortillas on each plate and top with 2 tablespoons of salsa. When eggs are cooked, use a spatula to gently transfer two eggs to each plate on top of the tortillas and salsa. Sprinkle with Cheddar. Serve at once.

Notes

Instead of using a microwave, heat tortillas on a dry skillet on medium-high heat for about 20 seconds on each side.

Sunny-side up eggs are the most dramatic, but cook the eggs the way you like them: cooked until yolks are hard, over easy, or even scrambled.

Magic Quiche with Asparagus

Here's a quiche for folks who tremble at the thought of making a pie crust . . . or who just don't have time to put one together. With Magic Quiche, you mix up the crust ingredients with eggs and milk and, ka-zaam, it makes itself! For your second magic trick, save woody asparagus ends to make Double Asparagus Pasta (page 193).

 Active time: 30 minutes
Total time: 1 hour and 20 minutes
Makes 8 servings

butter or shortening for greasing
    casserole
4 eggs
2 cups milk
½ cup white whole wheat or
    all-purpose flour (60 grams)
1 teaspoon salt
¼ teaspoon nutmeg
1 cup asparagus pieces
½ cup spring onions
2 teaspoons olive oil
4 ounces Cheddar, grated

1. Preheat oven to 350°F. Butter or grease a 9 x 13 x 2-inch baking pan.

2. In a medium bowl, beat eggs until thoroughly mixed and light yellow, about 45 seconds. Beat in milk, flour, salt, and nutmeg.

3. Trim about ¼ inch from the bottoms of asparagus stalks, enough to get rid of any dirty or damaged parts. Gently flex each stem so that it breaks just above woody part, usually ¼ to ⅓ up stalk. Save woody ends for another recipe. Cut top part of asparagus into bite-size pieces about 1½ inches long.

4. Cut spring onions into ¼-inch rounds, throwing away the tips and root ends. Heat oil in a medium skillet over medium heat. Add asparagus pieces. Cook about a minute and then add spring onions. Cook for another minute or two until asparagus is bright green and crunchy-tender and onions begin to soften. Grate cheese if needed.

5. Spread asparagus and onions evenly in baking pan and then sprinkle with cheese. Pour egg mixture gently over vegetables and cheese.

6. Bake for 40 minutes at 350°F. Quiche is done when eggs are set and a skewer or knife inserted into the middle comes out clean. Cool for 5 to 10 minutes before serving. Refrigerate any extra.

Note

Fill up the oven when you bake this quiche with white potatoes or sweet potatoes. If you bake it with Whisk Sandwich Bread, the quiche will provide extra moisture in the oven that will help the bread rise. Put quiche in at least 10 minutes before bread so it can start to heat up.

Greek Potato Salad

Get a different taste with every bite in this summery main-dish salad. It's a great way to show off tomatoes and green beans at their peaks. This is best with wide Italian green beans and a mix of heirloom tomatoes, large and small. Make this salad vegan by using two cups of cooked, drained chickpeas instead of eggs and cheese.

 Active time: 25 minutes, starting with hard-boiled eggs and Greek Dressing
Total time: 30 minutes
Makes 4 main-dish servings, 2½ cups each

4 hard-boiled eggs
4 cups water
½ teaspoon salt
3 cups diced potatoes
3 cups green beans in bite-size pieces
2 cups chopped tomatoes, cut into bite-size pieces
1 bell pepper
½ cup Greek Dressing (page 201)
8 leaves fresh basil, optional
½ cup crumbled feta cheese, optional

1. Boil eggs at least a day before if possible for easy peeling.

2. Bring water and salt to a boil in a covered medium pot over high heat.

3. Meanwhile, scrub potatoes. Cut into ¾ inch cubes. Add to water as you cut so they don't turn brown.

4. Rinse green beans and cut off tips. Cut into bite-size pieces at a diagonal. Add to pot as you cut.

5. When water begins to boil, reduce heat to medium low and simmer, partly covered, until potatoes and green beans are tender but still firm, about 8 minutes.

6. Meanwhile, cut tomatoes into bite-sized pieces. If using cherry tomatoes, cut each in half. Put in a medium bowl. Cut bell pepper into bite-size pieces and add to bowl. Peel eggs, cut into bite-size pieces, and set aside.

7. Drain potatoes and green beans as soon as they are done, saving water in your broth jar. Add potatoes, green beans, and dressing to tomatoes and bell peppers. Toss to mix and coat evenly with dressing. Add eggs and toss gently. If using, cut basil ribbons just before serving (page 43).

8. Serve slightly warm or at room temperature, topped with feta cheese and basil ribbons, if using. Refrigerate any extra. Keeps for 2 or 3 days in the refrigerator.

Potato Peanut Curry

Looking for a spicy, rich dish suitable for company? This is it. Yet it's fast enough to make from scratch on a weeknight. Serve over hot rice or with Garlic Flatbread (page 188). Double the recipe to enjoy the next day just reheated or made into a dynamite burrito with scrambled eggs or sautéed bell peppers.

 Active time: 35 minutes
Total time: 45 minutes
Makes 4 main-dish servings or
8 side-dish servings

4 garlic cloves
One-half 28-ounce can diced tomatoes
  (14 ounces total)
1 cup water
¼ teaspoon salt
1 pound potatoes
2 tablespoons corn or canola oil
2 tablespoons tahini
2 tablespoons peanut butter
1 teaspoon chipotle or cayenne
½ teaspoon turmeric, optional but
  very good
2 tablespoons chopped parsley leaves
  or basil ribbons

1. Mince garlic and put in a small microwave-safe bowl. Put tomatoes with their juice, the water, and salt in a medium pot, but don't heat yet. This tomato bath will keep the potatoes from turning brown.

2. Cut potatoes into ½-inch cubes, stirring into pot as you go.

3. Cover pot and bring to a boil over medium-high heat, then simmer on medium-low so mixture barely boils.

4. Put oil, tahini, peanut butter, and chipotle in bowl with garlic. Stir to combine, cover bowl, and microwave on medium-high for about 2 minutes until the mixture is fragrant. Stir in turmeric if using, and then stir into potato mixture.

5. Simmer for about 10 minutes, until potatoes are tender. Chop parsley.

6. Serve hot in bowls, with rice if desired, or wrapped in flour tortillas. Refrigerate any extra. Freezing makes potatoes mushy.

Note

A recipe in Raghavan Iyer's *660 Curries: The Gateway to the World of Indian Food* inspired this recipe. This version is easier and faster, made with ingredients already in the *Wildly Affordable Organic* kitchen.

Potato Pudding

Think scalloped potatoes; think creamy savory custard; think comfort food supreme. You're thinking about Potato Pudding. Have it one day as the main dish with a salad or green vegetable and the next as a side dish. Use garlic when serving for lunch or dinner, but skip it if serving for brunch.

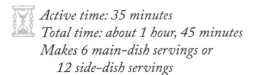

Active time: 35 minutes
Total time: about 1 hour, 45 minutes
Makes 6 main-dish servings or
*   12 side-dish servings*

1 tablespoon butter
2 garlic cloves, optional
4 potatoes
1 teaspoon salt
8 ounces Cheddar
1 onion
4 eggs
2 cups milk, 2% or whole
¼ cup white whole wheat or whole
   wheat flour (30 grams)
1 teaspoon salt
½ teaspoon nutmeg, optional
¼ teaspoon thyme, optional
2 tablespoons wheat germ (16 grams)

1. Put butter in a 3-quart baking pan to soften. Mince garlic, if using, and set aside.
2. Fill a medium pot about halfway full of water, cover, and bring to a boil over high heat. Cut potatoes in half length-wise, then cut crossways into ¼-inch slices. Boil potato slices for 10 minutes and then drain, saving liquid to boil a vegetable side dish or in your broth jar (page 191).

3. Preheat the oven to 350°F. Slice or grate cheese and chop onion. Whisk eggs in a medium bowl until blended. Add milk, flour, garlic, salt, and spices, if using, and whisk again to blend.
4. Butter baking pan. Make two or three sets of three even layers: potatoes, onions, and then cheese. The number of layers depends on the shape of your baking dish.
5. Whisk egg mixture once or twice and then pour over layers. Sprinkle with wheat germ.
6. Bake for 60 minutes, until golden brown and solid, with bubbles just around edges. Potatoes should seem tender when you insert a knife or skewer. Let cool for about 10 minutes and then cut to serve in wedges, lifting carefully with a spatula to preserve layers. Refrigerate any extra. Potatoes turn mushy when frozen.

Notes

Instead of grating cheese for casseroles, try slicing it into very thin pieces using a cheese slicer with a wire cutter. This is faster and easier on the wrists.

If you have any bread crumbs, sprinkle a handful over the pudding just before baking. Make bread crumbs from toasted, leftover bread, especially the crusts, or just the crumbs you've collected when cutting bread. Keep bread crumbs frozen so they don't get moldy.

The recipe is based on one from my very first cookbook, *The Vegetarian Epicure* by Anna Thomas. My version uses Cheddar instead of three more expensive cheeses, adds wheat germ and garlic, and has minor changes throughout.

20

Pasta and Sauces

The *Wildly Affordable Organic* menus call for pasta nearly every day. It's quick to cook and easy to dress up with a variety of sauces. It's light to ship and easy to store. I love the way rotini holds sauces and is so easy to get from plate to mouth, but you might want to mix it up by using other shapes. By cooking pasta in very little water, you can take rotini from box to plate in only twelve minutes. Angel-hair pasta cooks even faster.

Make double batches of sauce and pasta to cut your cooking and cleaning time more. If you cook two meals' worth of pasta at a time, sauce the extra pasta right away.

For most tomato-based sauces, I recommend topping with Cheddar instead of Parmesan. Why? To save money while still getting a big cheesy taste.

See Scrimp or, Splurge for more on high-protein pasta and organic options (page 20).

Noodles Cooked in Very Little Water

Save energy, water, and time by cooking your pasta in just enough water to cover it. You can use half as much salt too. The savings add up. If you cook pasta 3 times a week, in one year you'll save 5 hours of burner time, 5 hours of your time, 1½ cups of salt, and 100 gallons of water.

 Active time: 12 minutes, mostly of occasional stirring
Total time: 12 minutes
Makes 4 servings, ¾ cup each

3 cups high-protein pasta
½ teaspoon of salt
6 cups water

1. Put pasta and water in a small pan, cover, and bring to a boil over high heat, stirring occasionally.

2. Turn the heat down so that water barely boils. Stir occasionally and then test for doneness about 7 minutes after the water starts to boil. Drain, sauce, and serve.

Save even more by starting a broth jar. Don't pour flavor and nutrients down the drain (page 191).

I've always cooked pasta in less water than my Italian aunties recommend, but Harold McGee's *New York Times* article,[1] "How Much Water Does Pasta Really Need?" inspired me to experiment with how little I could use and to taste the broth.

Use this technique with 100 percent whole wheat and other pasta too.

Good Tomato Sauce

Make your own tomato sauce using canned, crushed tomatoes while your pasta cooks. Start by mincing garlic and setting it aside. Exposing it to air enhances its healthy properties (see page 43). Load the sauce up with seasonal vegetables.

Plain crushed tomatoes work well for all these recipes. But to emphasize the variety and seasonal change, try crushed tomatoes with basil for summer sauces and fire-roasted tomatoes for fall and winter sauces.

These recipes serve six because they call for a 28-ounce can of crushed tomatoes, the biggest size commonly available in grocery stores. For a family of four, double the recipes to get three meals from a pot of sauce.

Serve Good Tomato Sauce or any of the following variations on high-protein pasta with carrot sticks, salad, or a green vegetable for a complete meal.

Active time: 5 minutes
Total time: 10 minutes
Makes 6 servings, ¾ cups each.
Doubles well.

2 garlic cloves, minced
2 teaspoons olive oil
seasonal additions (see variations below)
One 28-ounce can crushed tomatoes
½ teaspoon dried oregano
¼ teaspoon cayenne or chipotle, optional
1 tablespoon fresh basil, optional

1. Heat olive oil in a large skillet over medium heat.

2. Chop vegetables and put them in the skillet, stirring frequently to keep from burning. Turn heat down to medium-low. Cook until soft, about 2 minutes for spring onions and 5 minutes for other vegetables.

3. Add garlic to vegetable mixture. Stir once and then add crushed tomatoes and oregano. Bring to a boil over medium heat and then reduce heat to low. Cover skillet and let sauce simmer for about 5 minutes. Cool a spoon of sauce and taste it, then adjust seasonings as desired.

4. Add sauce to the pot with drained hot pasta in it. Let the sauce get to know the pasta for about a minute. Cut basil ribbons if using (page 43). Serve hot pasta garnished with basil. Refrigerate or freeze any extra.

(See Good Tomato Sauce variations on pages 172–174)

Persian Tomato Sauce

I came up with this fast and exotic sauce to help a friend whose husband and sons loved ground beef in their pasta sauce. This sauce uses chopped walnuts instead of the ground beef and adds raisins to take the edge off the walnuts, which can be a little bitter. The result reminds me of the fabulous savory-sweet dishes we used to get at Persian restaurants when we lived in the Washington, DC, area. This recipe is best with crushed tomatoes with basil or fresh basil.

 Active time: 10 minutes
Total time: 20 minutes

Seasonal additions
1 onion, chopped
½ cup walnuts, chopped
½ cup raisins

To prepare sauce
1. Cook onion and walnuts in olive oil before adding garlic.
2. Add raisins with crushed tomatoes.

Tomato Sauce with Bell Peppers and Onions

This is my favorite pasta sauce. I cook it all year round but especially in the summer and fall when bell peppers are so cheap and delicious. Use red bell peppers if you have them. They are the ripe form of green bell peppers and are sweeter and even more nutritious. This recipe is best with crushed tomatoes with basil or fresh basil. Add chipotle during cold months.

 Active time: 10 minutes
Total time: 20 minutes

Seasonal additions
1 onion, chopped
1 bell pepper, chopped

Tomato Sauce with Robust Greens and Onions

This is one of my go-to recipes all winter. Collards are among the least expensive of the winter greens. They add body to the sauce and the sauce hides the collards from picky eaters who won't eat their greens. Sometimes I use kale instead when it is a better buy.

To cut the strong taste of the greens, boil them first in the pot you will use to make the pasta. Use fire-roasted crushed tomatoes and chipotle to warm up a cold-weather meal.

 Active time: 20 minutes
Total time: 30 minutes

Seasonal additions
1 cup chopped collards or kale
1 onion, chopped

To prepare greens
In a medium pan bring 6 to 8 cups of water to boil. Rinse collard leaves, remove leaves from stems, and chop (page 42). Add the chopped stems to the pot of boiling water as you get them ready. Cut leaves into thin ribbons, about ¼ inch wide. Add leaves to boiling water about 2 minutes after you added stems. Boil for 5 minutes and drain. Stir into sauce with tomatoes, simmering sauce until greens are tender, about 10 minutes.

Tomato Sauce with Spring Onions

Spring onions are sweeter and more colorful than the mature, stemless onions available year round. Look for the big spring onions at your farmers' market, ones with white ends an inch or two across and thick, long, green ends. They radiate a sense of joyous growth, the very essence of spring. The smaller spring onions available in most groceries will be fine too, if not quite so rambunctious. Tender spring onions cook quickly, so this sauce comes together in a flash. This recipe is best with plain crushed tomatoes and without chipotle.

 Active time: 7 minutes
Total time: 12 minutes

Seasonal addition
2 cups chopped spring onions, cut into ¼-inch rounds

Tomato Sauce with Summer Squash

Summer squash is one of the great buys of the summer markets. It grows so well that it's a good choice if you have even a small vegetable garden. You may find yourself getting free squash from your friends who are overwhelmed by them in their own gardens.

All these good qualities may mean that you get tired of eating squash by midsummer. This recipe hides shredded zucchini or yellow squash in a rich tomato sauce, so your family won't even guess that they are having squash for dinner *again*. It freezes well too, giving you a way to store summer's bounty for the colder months. This recipe is best with crushed tomatoes with basil or fresh basil.

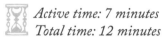 *Active time: 7 minutes*
Total time: 12 minutes

Seasonal additions
**1 cup grated summer squash
(zucchini, yellow squash, or a mix)**

Noodles in Spicy Peanut Sauce with Seasonal Vegetables

This brightly colored, spicy dish tastes like it comes from a fancy Thai restaurant, but it takes only few minutes more time than it takes to just boil noodles. It's super healthy, too: high in protein and full of veggies. Make a double batch of sauce, refrigerating or freezing it for a quick meal later.

 Active time: 18 minutes
Total time: 18 minutes
Makes 4 servings, about 1 cup each

Seasonal Vegetables

Spring
2 carrots, cut into matchsticks but not peeled
2 cups shredded green cabbage
24 pods sugar snap peas, strings removed and cut into bite-size pieces
½ cup chopped spring onions, cut into ¼-inch rounds

Summer
1 cup chopped green beans, ends trimmed and cut into bite-size pieces
2 cups shredded green cabbage
1 bell pepper, cut into matchsticks
½ cup thinly sliced purple onion
basil ribbons, optional

Fall and winter
2 carrots, cut into matchsticks
1 cup broccoli florets and peeled stems, cut into matchsticks
2 cups shredded green cabbage
2 spring onions, cut into ¼-inch rounds

Noodles
3 cups high-protein rotini or other pasta shape
7 cups water

Sauce
2 teaspoons minced or pressed garlic
2 teaspoons finely grated or minced ginger
½ cup plus 1 tablespoon peanut butter (144 grams)
¼ cup soy sauce
1½ teaspoons sugar
½ teaspoon chipotle or cayenne, or to taste
¼ cup hot water

1. Prepare vegetables that will be cooked—carrots, green beans, and broccoli.

2. In a medium pot, cook rotini in one more cup of water than usual to make room for vegetables (page 170). Once water boils, set timer for two minutes less than usual and add green beans to pasta.

3. To make sauce, mix all sauce ingredients in a large bowl, taking hot water from pasta pot. Stir sauce until smooth. Taste and adjust seasonings.

4. Prepare vegetables that will be used raw—again, depending on the season: cabbage, sugar snap peas, spring onions, bell peppers, purple onions, or basil.

5. Two minutes before rotini should be done, put carrots and broccoli into the pot. Continue boiling for another two minutes, until noodles are tender. Drain and add noodle mixture to sauce. Stir in cabbage, sugar snaps, and half the onions, saving a few snow peas, remaining onions, and basil for garnish. Stir to combine.

6. Just before serving, slice basil ribbons if using (page 43). Top noodles with basil and remaining garnish and serve immediately. Refrigerate any extra. The sauce freezes well by itself.

Notes

This recipe shows the exact amount of vegetables used in the menus and shopping lists, but be flexible. Get the best quality produce for the best price and be open to trying other vegetables.

This dish reheats well if it will then be eaten right away. But although it seems like a great dish for a party or picnic, it does not keep well at room temperature or over low heat. The pasta will absorb the sauce and the whole thing will turn into a rubbery brick.

Southern Summer Pesto

Here's a new twist on the classic pesto made with pine nuts or walnuts: basil with pecans. The slightly sweet, lighter taste of the pecans complements the full taste and aroma of the basil. This recipe uses more leaves and more nuts and less cheese than my standard pesto recipe, making it better for both your body and your pocketbook. If you live where pecans grow but walnuts and pine nuts don't, this will also appeal to your inner locavore.

Try my favorite **Southern Summer Pesto with Green Beans** to save energy and dishwashing. Boil pasta in an extra cup of water. Cut green beans into bite-sized pieces and add to boiling pasta when it has about 6 minutes cooking time left. Toss pasta and green beans with pesto.

 Active time: 18 minutes
Total time: 18 minutes
Makes 18 servings, ¼ cup each

6 ounces Parmesan, optional
    (128 grams)
8 garlic cloves (40 grams)
4 cups tightly packed basil leaves
    (100 grams)
3 cups pecan pieces (300 grams)
1 teaspoon salt
2 cups olive oil
freshly ground black pepper to taste,
    optional

1. Rinse basil well in a bowl of water. Let it soak until needed.

2. Grate Parmesan and set aside. Set up your food processor with the cutting blade or use a blender. Turn the machine on and drop garlic in while the blade is turning. Turn off when garlic is minced, after about 10 seconds.

3. Give basil a good swish in water, then dry by spinning in a salad spinner or rolling gently in a towel. Remove stems and put leaves in food processor or blender. Put pecans and salt on top of leaves. Process until finely chopped but still a bit rough.

4. With the machine going, slowly pour in olive oil.

5. Stop the machine and add Parmesan. Process briefly to mix. Taste and adjust seasonings.

6. To serve, stir pesto into hot cooked pasta, spread on bread or crackers, or stir into hot green beans. Eat warm or at room temperature. Refrigerate or freeze any extra, pressing plastic wrap onto surface to prevent browning.

Notes

Save the basil stems and cheese rind, if you are using block Parmesan, for Vichyssoise Encore (page 199). The high level of tannin in basil stems turns pesto dark faster.

Spread out the expenses when making a big batch to freeze by leaving out the cheese. When ready to use, thaw pesto and stir in grated cheese.

Parsley Pesto

Most people think "basil" and "summer" when they think pesto, but parsley pesto packs a rich, garlicky taste even in the winter. It's easier to make because you use parsley stems and all.

To make, follow directions for Southern Summer Pesto (page 177), using walnuts instead of pecans and parsley instead of basil. Before putting parsley in the food processor, cut ends off stems and then cut rest of parsley two or three times so it will fit in your food processor.

Active time: 12 minutes
Total time: 12 minutes
Makes 8 servings, ¼ cup each

6 ounces Parmesan, grated (128 grams)
4 garlic cloves (20 grams)
2 cups tightly packed parsley, including stems (110 grams)
1 cup walnut pieces (110 grams)
½ teaspoon salt
1 cup olive oil
freshly ground black pepper to taste, optional

Harvest Lasagna

Two layers of filling make this a holiday-worthy main course. You can stretch the servings to 12 for normal days, but I like to dish out 4 big servings for a feast and then 4 smaller ones the next day.

 Active time: 90 minutes
Total time: just under 3 hours
Makes 8 to 12 servings

Sauce
2 teaspoons olive oil
2 garlic cloves, minced
1 onion, quartered
One 28-ounce can crushed tomatoes
   with basil
1 teaspoon dried oregano
⅛ teaspoon cayenne or chipotle

Fillings
2 teaspoons olive oil
1 onion
1 pound Swiss chard
1 pound ricotta
1 egg
⅛ teaspoon salt
pinch nutmeg, optional
1 pound fresh button mushrooms
1 teaspoon olive oil

Noodles and cheese
butter or shortening for baking pan
2 ounces Parmesan, grated
1 pound shredded mozzarella
One 9-ounce box no-cook lasagna
   noodles

1. Set out a medium pot for sauce and a large pot for filling. Add 2 teaspoons olive oil to each. Warm oil for sauce over medium heat.

2. In a food processor fitted with the cutting blade, start processor on high. Drop in garlic. Turn off machine, quarter onion, and add to processor. Pulse 4 or 5 times to chop and then scrape into sauce pot. Cook until onion is soft, stirring occasionally, about 5 minutes.

3. Warm oil in filling pot over medium-low heat. Quarter another onion and chop in processor, pulsing 4 or 5 times, then scrape into filling pot. Cook until onion is soft, stirring occasionally, about 5 minutes.

4. Rinse chard, separate leaves from stems, and chop (see page 42), saving time by chopping stems in food processor. Add chopped stems to filling pot and stir. Slice chard leaves into ribbons about ¼ inch across and add to filling pot. Stir, cover pot, and reduce heat to low. Cook for about 10 minutes until leaves are wilted and tender.

5. Add tomatoes, oregano, and cayenne to sauce pot. Stir and then turn up heat to medium. Let sauce come to a boil and then turn down heat to low and simmer uncovered for at least 10 minutes.

6. Put ricotta in a medium bowl and stir with a fork until fluffy, about 30 seconds. Add egg, salt, and nutmeg, then stir again.

7. Taste sauce and chard, adjusting seasonings as needed. Preheat oven to 375°F.

8. Rinse mushrooms quickly in a colander, rubbing with your hands as needed to dislodge any dirt. Cut off thin slice of stem.

(continues)

Put trimmed mushrooms into food processor and pulse 4 or 5 times to chop into pieces about ¼ inch across.

9. Empty filling pot, putting chard mixture on a plate or in a bowl. Add 1 teaspoon olive oil to filling pot and warm over medium heat. Add mushrooms and cook until nearly dry, stirring occasionally.

10. Grease a 9 x 13 x 2-inch baking pan. Add layers to pan in this order, from bottom to top:

- ½ cup sauce
- 4 lasagna noodles
- ½ ricotta mixture
- mushrooms
- 1 cup mozzarella
- 1 cup sauce
- 4 lasagna noodles
- rest of ricotta mixture
- chard mixture
- 1 cup mozzarella
- ½ cup sauce
- 4 lasagna noodles
- rest of sauce, about 1 cup

11. Cover lasagna with a tent of aluminum foil. Bake for 50 to 60 minutes, until sauce begins to bubble around the edges. Remove foil, quickly top with remaining cheese, and bake uncovered for another 5 to 10 minutes, until top is melted and browned. Remove from oven and let stand for 15 minutes before serving.

12. Serve hot. Refrigerate any extra for up to 4 days or freeze.

Note

If you can't find no-boil lasagna noodles, use a box of regular noodles, boiling as directed on the package.

Enchilada Sauce

Use this sauce for burritos or other dishes you want to spice up Mexican style.

Active time: 7 minutes
Total time: 12 minutes
Makes 18 servings, ¼ cups each

2 garlic cloves
2 teaspoons corn oil
1 onion
1 teaspoon chipotle or cayenne, or to
   taste
One 28-ounce can crushed tomatoes
2 teaspoons lemon or lime juice,
   optional

1. Mince garlic and set aside. Heat oil in a skillet over medium heat. Chop onion and add to skillet. Cook until soft, stirring occasionally, about 5 minutes.

2. Add garlic and chipotle, stirring once.

3. Add tomatoes and citrus juice, if using. Turn heat up to high, bring sauce to a boil, and then turn down heat to low and simmer for 5 minutes.

4. Use immediately, refrigerate for up to 4 days, or freeze.

Fresh and Easy Salsa

Here's salsa stripped down to the basics. You can make it in about the time it takes to open a bottle of salsa. The results are so fresh and bright you'll never use bottled salsa during tomato season again.

 Active time: 5 minutes
Total time: 5 minutes
Makes 8 servings, ¼ cup each

1 garlic clove, minced
2 cups chopped ripe tomatoes
1 jalapeño pepper, diced
1 teaspoon lemon or lime juice
¼ onion, diced

1. Combine garlic, tomatoes, pepper, and citrus juice in a small bowl.

2. Rinse diced onion in cold water and then stir into tomato mixture.

3. Serve within 2 hours at room temperature or refrigerate for a day or 2.

Notes

Rinsing the onion takes away some of the bite that will otherwise dominate the salsa, but if you eat raw onion sandwiches, skip the rinsing step.

Jazz up this salsa by using lime juice instead of lemon juice, adding chopped cilantro, or even adding chopped peaches.

21

Pizza

Homemade pizza is a joy: really hot, topped just the way you like, and with ingredients as healthy as you choose. Plus, you don't have to tip the delivery person.

Having three recipes plus a list of toppings may make pizza seem complicated, but if you'll take fifteen minutes the night before to make the dough, you can probably make a hot pizza in less time than it would take to have one delivered. You can make the sauce and prepare the toppings the day before too.

In a rush and have a grill? Try Speedy Grilled Pizza (page 189).

Pizza: Putting It All Together

Make Whisk Pizza Dough (page 185), Pizza Sauce (page 186), and a Seasonal Pizza Topping (page 189), then follow these steps to finish the pizza.

Active time: 20 minutes for 1 pizza, plus 8 minutes for each additional pizza, which can be done while another pizza is baking
Total time: 45 minutes for one pizza; 1 hour and 15 minutes for three made at the same time
Makes 24 slices as either 2 large pizzas, 3 medium pizzas, or 6 flatbreads. The menus recommend two pizza slices for dinner and one for lunch.

1. **Prepare the oven.** Put pizza stone or heavy cookie sheet on the bottom rack of your oven. If the cookie sheet has a rim, put it in rim-side down. Move other oven racks to the top of the oven to give you room to work. Preheat oven to 450°F for at least 30 minutes.

2. **Divide the dough.** Take dough out of the refrigerator. (If you have time, do this up to 30 minutes before you handle dough so it won't feel so cold.) Oil a spatula and your hands so dough doesn't stick. Sprinkle a little flour on dough and then use a serrated knife to cut off a pizza-sized piece, about half or a third of the recipe. Coax dough out of the bowl with the greased spatula. Try to keep dough together without

183

tearing it to preserve the gluten structure and trapped bubbles. Sprinkle other side of dough with a little flour too. If you are not making all pizzas at once, return remaining dough to the refrigerator in its covered bowl. Stretch dough (see page 153), creating a belly button on top. Put dough ball belly-side down on the floured surface to rest for 10 to 30 minutes. Heat pizza sauce if it's cold.

3. **Roll out the dough.** Lightly flour a sheet of parchment paper that is at least as large as the finished pizza will be (a large pizza will be about the size of a cookie sheet) and get another sheet the same size ready. Put one dough ball in the center of the floured sheet, flour dough lightly, and top with other sheet. Use a rolling pin to roll dough into a circle or oval as thin as you like. Peel off the first sheet of parchment paper and set it aside to use with the next pizza. Pinch around edges of dough circle to make a rim.

4. **Top it.** Spread olive oil over dough, including rim, with your fingers or a brush. Spread warm pizza sauce over dough. Sprinkle with greens, if using, then cheese and other toppings. Put greens under cheese to keep them from burning.

5. **Bake it.** Slide a rimless cookie sheet or pizza peel under bottom sheet of parchment paper. Open oven door and slide out the rack with the pizza stone on it. Grab the back edge of the parchment paper and slide it with pizza onto the hot stone. Quickly slide the rack back in and close the door. Bake for about 14 minutes, until crust browns, cheese starts to brown, and sauce bubbles. Overcooking the pizza a little is better than undercooking it.

6. **Make the rest.** Meanwhile, roll out and top remaining dough balls, using the sheet of parchment saved from pizza in the oven, plus a new sheet.

7. **Serve.** Remove pizza from the oven by carefully grabbing the front of the parchment paper and sliding it onto the rimless cookie sheet. Let cool for about 5 minutes before cutting. Serve hot. Refrigerate any extra for up to 4 days or freeze.

Notes

Start preheating the oven by baking something else with the pizza stone or heavy cookie sheet already in place. Roast vegetables at 450°F because they aren't so fussy about oven temperature. Or bake cookies or bread and then raise the temperature for the pizza.

If you like a very crisp crust and are using an oven stone, slide the parchment paper out from underneath the cooking pizza after it has baked 10 minutes and the crust is firm. You may need to use a spatula to hold the pizza back while you slide out the parchment.

Another way to crisp the crust is to prebake it for 3 minutes after you've put on the olive oil and before you put on the sauce. (Thanks to Andrea Weigl of *The News & Observer* for this tip.)

Whisk Pizza Dough

If you keep a bowl of this pizza dough in the refrigerator, you will always be minutes away from homemade pizza and garlic flatbread. It keeps for up to two weeks in the refrigerator. When you've used up one batch of dough, just start another one in the same bowl. The bits of dough from the previous batch will give the new batch a slight sourdough tang.

Because you make it up at least a day ahead, this dough needs only half the yeast as some other recipes, even though it uses a goodly amount of healthy whole wheat flour. No kneading, bread machine, mixer, or food processor required.

Active time: 8 minutes
Total time: 1 hour and 8 minutes, plus
rising at least overnight
Makes 2 large pizzas, 3 medium
pizzas, or 6 flatbreads

2 cups white whole wheat flour
    (240 grams)
2¼ teaspoons rapid-rise yeast
1 tablespoon plus 1½ teaspoons salt
    (1½ tablespoons)
1¾ cups warm water (100 to 115°F)
4½ cups all-purpose flour (540 grams)
¼ cup olive oil (60 grams)
1 cup warm water (100 to 115°F)

1. In a big bowl combine the white whole wheat flour and yeast. Give it a quick stir to distribute yeast and then add salt and 1¾ cups of warm water. Stir to dampen flour and then with a whisk or big spoon stir briskly for 1 minute to develop the gluten.

2. Add all-purpose flour, olive oil, and other 1 cup of warm water. Stir mixture until all flour is damp.

3. Cover the bowl with a plate or a piece of waxed paper. Let dough rise for 1 or 2 hours.

4. Refrigerate dough overnight or for up to 2 weeks.

Pizza Sauce

Pizza topped with veggies calls for a full-flavored sauce. Here's one you can make in minutes. If you have fresh basil, sprinkle it on top of the baked pizza instead of hiding it in the sauce.

Active time: 5 minutes
Total time: 10 minutes
Makes enough for 1 ½ recipes of pizza dough. Sauce recipe is easily halved or doubled.

One 28-ounce can crushed tomatoes
   with basil
2 garlic cloves
2 tablespoons olive oil
¼ teaspoon chipotle or cayenne
½ teaspoon oregano

1. Mince garlic and open tomato can. Heat olive oil in a medium pot over medium heat. When oil is hot, add garlic and chipotle. Stir twice.

2. Add tomatoes and oregano. Bring to a boil and then reduce heat and simmer for 5 minutes or until ready to use. Refrigerate or freeze extra.

Pizza Toppings by Season

Freshly grated Parmesan goes a long way. Just one ounce makes a good-sized mound of cheese and adds enough flavor to make your pizza *magnifico*. For a good topping at a great price, watch for sales on pregrated Italian or even Mexican cheese mixes. Replace the mozzarella and Parmesan with the same weight of mixed cheeses.

3 tablespoons olive oil, infused with garlic if using
12 ounces mozzarella, grated
1 ounce Parmesan, grated

Seasonal vegetables

Spring
2 garlic cloves, minced
2 cups mustard greens
4 cups water
½ teaspoon salt
2 cups spring onions, cut into ¼-inch rounds

Summer
1 onion, sliced thinly
1 bell pepper, sliced thinly
2 tablespoons basil leaves, optional

Fall and winter
2 garlic cloves, minced
8 cups water
½ teaspoon salt
2 cups collards or kale
1 onion, sliced thinly

1. **To prepare mustard, collards, or kale**, bring water and salt to a boil in a medium pot over high heat. Rinse and separate leaves from stems (page 42), saving stems for another use. Slice leaves thin, add to water, and cover. When water boils, turn heat off and let pot sit undisturbed for 7 minutes. Drain greens and squeeze dry. Unless you enjoy bitter food, don't save water for your broth jar.

2. **To infuse olive oil with garlic**, put garlic in a small, microwave-safe container with oil and then heat in microwave on high until bubbling and fragrant, about 40 seconds.

Garlic Flatbread

If you keep a bowl of this dough in your refrigerator, you can have hot bread on the table in about 50 minutes, which is mostly the time needed to preheat the oven. The dough is also used for pizza crust and keeps for up to two weeks in the refrigerator.

Garlic flatbread has to be the easiest way to wow your friends and family with your cooking skills. Make the dough ahead of time and then roll it out as guests arrive. Have it ready to eat by the time they've taken off their coats and gotten something to drink. It will make your house smell terrific and delight everyone with its salty, garlicky crunch.

 Active time: 15 minutes
Total time: 50 minutes plus at least an overnight rise for the dough
Makes 6 flatbreads, serving about 4 each

Whisk Pizza Dough (page185)

Topping for each flatbread
  1 tablespoon olive oil
  1 garlic clove, minced
  salt to taste (coarse, kosher-style salt is especially good but optional)

1. Make dough and let rise at least overnight in the refrigerator. Use ⅙ of the recipe to make each flatbread. Preheat oven to 450°F. Divide, stretch, and roll the dough as you would for pizza (page 184).

2. Put garlic with olive oil a small microwave-safe container or small pan on the stove. Heat oil until garlic is fragrant, about 30 seconds on high in the microwave or about a minute over medium heat on the stove. With a brush or your fingers, spread garlic and olive oil over dough and sprinkle with salt.

3. Slide a rimless cookie sheet or pizza peel under dough and parchment paper. Open oven door, slide out the rack with the pizza stone or cookie sheet on it. Grab the back edge of the parchment paper and slide it with dough onto the hot stone or cookie sheet. Quickly slide the rack back in and close the door. Bake for about 8 minutes, until crust is golden and puffy.

4. Tear bread into pieces and serve hot or warm. Any extra bread will keep for two or three days wrapped in plastic at room temperature. Warm any extra bread in a toaster oven or regular oven before serving.

Speedy Grilled Pizza

Here's a pizza you can take from flour and yeast to sizzling goodness on a plate in less than an hour. The first pizza will be ready in about 40 minutes. That's faster than the delivery guy can make it to my house, and it doesn't require the day-ahead planning of Whisk Pizza Dough (page 185). What's more, Speedy Grilled Pizza is perfectly crisp, smoky, cheesy, and loaded with healthy ingredients.

You'll need a stand mixer or bread machine, a gas grill, and a flat grill topper (like a cookie sheet with holes), but if you don't have these, you can still have great pizza . . . it just may take longer. See Notes below.

Active time: 45 minutes
Total time: 50 minutes
Makes two 12-inch pizzas with 6 slices each

Dough
2¼ cups all-purpose flour (270 grams), plus extra for rolling out dough
1 cup white whole wheat flour (120 grams)
2¼ teaspoons rapid-rise yeast (1 packet)
2 tablespoons olive oil
2¼ teaspoons salt
1¼ cups warm water (about 110°F)

Topping
1 onion
1 bell pepper
2 teaspoons olive oil
8 ounces grated Italian mix cheese (mozzarella and Parmesan)
2 tablespoons basil ribbons, optional

Sauce
14 ounces pureed tomatoes (half a 28-ounce can)
1 tablespoon olive oil
1 garlic clove, minced or pressed
1 teaspoon oregano
¼ teaspoon cayenne, optional

1. Put all dough ingredients into a bread machine or the mixing bowl for a stand mixer. Knead for 8 minutes using the dough cycle on a bread machine or medium-low speed on a mixer fitted with the dough hook.

2. Turn the grill on to medium and put the grill topper on the grill to preheat.

3. Slice onion and bell pepper into thin, bite-sized pieces. Put on aluminum foil, drizzle with oil, and wrap foil to make a packet. Put packet on grill topper, close grill, and cook about 7 minutes, until tender.

4. Put sauce ingredients in a microwave-safe bowl, stir to mix, cover, and microwave on medium-high until hot, about 2 minutes.

5. Turn grilling vegetables over. Get out two pieces of parchment paper at least 14 inches square. Put one piece on counter and flour lightly. Get out rolling pin. When kneading is finished, divide dough in half. Put one half on parchment paper, sprinkle with flour, and top with another sheet of parchment paper. Roll dough out into a circle about 12 inches wide and smaller than your grill topper.

6. Remove vegetables from grill. Arrange sauce and pizza toppings near the grill along with a big spoon and fork. Slide the parchment paper and rolled-out dough

onto a cookie sheet and take to the grill. Pick up edge of dough, lift it off the parchment paper, and quickly flop it onto the grill topper. You may need to weigh down the parchment paper or ask someone to hold it. Cover grill and let dough cook for about 5 minutes, until crisp and slightly browned on the bottom.

7. Meanwhile, roll out remaining dough, reusing the parchment paper. When bottom of dough on the grill is stiff and shows grill marks, flip it over to cook other side. Immediately top crust with sauce, cheese, and vegetables. Cover grill and let pizza cook until bottom is crispy and browned and cheese is melted. Slide off grill onto a rimless cookie sheet or a rimmed cookie sheet turned upside down. Repeat to make second pizza.

8. Slice pizza, top with basil ribbons if using, and serve hot. Refrigerate any extra.

Notes

Use hot pizza sauce and pregrilled vegetables so the toppings cook before the bottom burns. Go fairly lightly on the toppings so you can get pizzas off the grill in one piece.

If you don't have a stand mixer or bread machine, knead dough by hand for about 8 minutes.

If you have a charcoal grill, start the fire in advance. I've read that a good charcoal grill temperature would be one that allows you to hold your hand over the coals for about 3 seconds, but no more, at a height of 4 inches.

If you don't have a grill, bake pizza in your oven (see page 184). You'll still be able to satisfy a pizza craving in about an hour.

You can make just one pizza and refrigerate the remaining dough for up to 2 weeks. Before using, let dough come to room temperature for about an hour.

22

Something from Nothing

How can you tell a *Wildly Affordable Organic* kitchen? Look for a broth jar in the refrigerator and a Stoup container in the freezer.

Use those tricks and recipes in this chapter to use perfectly delightful food that many people throw away. Even asparagus is affordable if you use it all!

Broth Jar

Don't pour flavor and nutrition down the drain. Instead, when you drain pasta or boiled vegetables, pour hot water first into any tomato cans or other pots used while making the meal. Let cool and then pour into the broth jar that you keep in the refrigerator. Voilà! Free vegetable broth. You'll never pay 10 cents or more an ounce for store-bought, organic vegetable broth again.

Use broth to boil more pasta or vegetables. Or use it instead of water to make rice, oatmeal, couscous, or soup. Just remember to cut back on salt when cooking with broth instead of water. Enjoy a cup of hot pasta or potato water on a cold day like others drink bouillon. At least every four days, use up or dump broth, wash the jar, and start over.

Bean-Broth Gravy

Make this quick gravy with the rich and tasty broth you made while cooking dried beans. Don't pour it down the drain! This recipe stretches a tablespoon of butter or oil into 4 servings.

Use broth from Cuban Black Beans or kidney beans for a dark gravy. For light gravy, use broth from black-eyed peas or chickpeas. Serve gravy over potatoes, rice, or day-old corn bread.

 Active time: 5 minutes
Total time: 5 minutes
Makes 4 servings, 2 generous
    tablespoons each

1 tablespoon butter or corn oil
1 garlic clove, minced, optional
1 tablespoon white whole wheat or all-
   purpose flour
½ cup broth from cooking beans

1. Melt butter in a small pot over medium heat. If using, stir garlic into butter. Whisk in flour and cook until smooth and bubbling, about 30 seconds. For a darker gravy, cook flour until it begins to brown, about a minute.

2. Whisk in bean broth. Bring to a boil over high heat and then reduce heat to medium-low so gravy barely boils. Cook until gravy thickens, about one minute, whisking occasionally to keep from burning.

3. Use immediately or keep warm until ready to serve. Refrigerate any extra or add to Stoup container (page 198).

Double Asparagus Pasta

This recipe gets to the heart of the *Wildly Affordable Organic* philosophy. Savor asparagus if you love it, but buy it in season, when it tastes best and costs least. Then squeeze every drop of goodness out of it. Make an "asparagus tea" by steeping the woody ends of asparagus in hot milk instead of throwing them away. Have a laugh as you transform a rough ingredient into a delicate dish.

Use the woody asparagus stems from Magic Quiche with Asparagus (page 166) or Skillet Asparagus (page 205) to make this creamy spring pasta dish. Serve on hot angel-hair pasta for a dish that's good enough for company and thrifty enough for a tight budget.

 Active time: 15 minutes
Total time: 15 minutes
Makes 4 servings

2 cups milk, 2% or whole
1 pound asparagus
woody asparagus ends left over from
    another recipe
4 tablespoons butter (½ stick)
2 tablespoons all-purpose flour
¼ teaspoon salt or to taste
1 ounce Parmesan, grated
1 pound high-protein angel-hair pasta,
    freshly cooked and hot

1. Heat milk in a large skillet over medium heat, stirring occasionally.

2. Meanwhile, trim about ¼ inch from stalk bottoms to get rid of any dirty or damaged parts. Gently flex each stem so that it breaks just above woody part, usually ¼ to ⅓ up the stalk. Cut woody ends lengthwise and put into milk, including any ends from another recipe.

3. Just as milk begins to boil, pour milk and asparagus into a heat-proof container to make "asparagus tea."

4. Melt butter in skillet and then add tender asparagus tips. Cook until just bright green and then spoon out asparagus ends onto a plate, leaving most of the butter in the skillet. Add flour to skillet, stir to mix with butter, and cook for about 1 minute, until mixture starts to bubble. Pour milk through slotted spoon or strainer into skillet, leaving asparagus ends behind.

5. Whisk sauce until creamy and somewhat thick. Add tender asparagus tips and cook until warm, about 1 minute.

6. Mix sauce with hot angel-hair pasta. Top with grated Parmesan. Serve at once.

Note

You can use other pasta shapes, but angel-hair pasta cooks quickly and has a delicate texture that works well with this fast sauce.

Halloween Pumpkin Puree

I used to think that decorative Halloween pumpkins were not fit to eat. Although they won't stand up to center stage in a pie like a Cinderella or Long Island Cheese pumpkin, they are good in soups, pumpkin bread, and muffins. Roast the seeds with spices and salt for a great snack or garnish (page 196).

For Halloween, get three smaller pumpkins instead of one giant one. The small ones have thinner skins and are much easier to wash and to cut up. Having more than one pumpkin is also fun because you can carve them so they seem to interact. See my favorite pumpkin trio, "Squeezing the Middle Class," online at cookforgood.com/wao. Unfortunately, it's more timely now than ever.

Active time: about 30 minutes
Total time: about 1 hour
Times and yield depend on the size of
the pumpkin (see Notes) and do not
include any jack-o'-lantern artistry.

1 pumpkin
2 cups water

1. Wash pumpkin with mild detergent before carving it so you don't spread any pesticides or bacteria from the skin to the inside.

2. Scrape out seeds and stringy fibers as you would for carving, but keep seeds to roast. Refrigerate any pieces cut out, such as those for the mouth and eyes. Compost remaining goop.

3. Carve pumpkin and display. I set mine on upside-down plant containers so that they are off the ground and a little away from any creepy crawlies. This also helps the smaller pumpkins look bigger.

4. The next day, throw away the candle used to light pumpkin and scrape out any dripped wax or burnt parts. Cut pumpkin into roughly 3 x 3-inch pieces and put in a big pot with water. Cover pot, bring water to a boil over high heat, and then reduce heat so you can hear water barely boiling. Steam pumpkin until fork tender, about 30 minutes.

5. Drain pumpkin and let cool enough to handle. Cut off skin with paring knife. Process in a food processor fitted with a cutting blade or in a blender until smooth.

6. Use in recipes for breads and soups right away, such as Jack O' Lantern Soup (page 195). Refrigerate or freeze extra.

Notes

The pumpkin I bought for $5 yielded 9 cups of pumpkin puree and 1½ cups of roasted seeds. The pumpkin was about the size of a basketball and weighed 11½ pounds.

If you have the oven going anyway, roast the pumpkin instead of boiling it. Rub cut pieces with oil and cook for about 40 minutes at 400°F, until fork tender.

The shopping lists and price calculations assume you are buying canned pumpkin instead of making your own puree. Making the puree is a fair amount of work, but it lets you enjoy the equivalent of fresh winter squash for essentially no cost.

Jack O' Lantern Soup

Use the pumpkin puree (page 194) from cooking your jack-o'-lantern to make this soup. The onion, butter, and hot pepper create a savory soup that will surprise and delight those who have only had pumpkin sweetened in pies.

 Active time: 7 minutes, starting with pumpkin puree
Total time: 10 minutes
Makes 4 servings, 1 cup each

1 tablespoon butter or corn oil
½ onion
4 cups pureed pumpkin
½ teaspoon salt
¼ teaspoon chipotle or cayenne
about 20 roasted pumpkin seeds or
    1 tablespoon chopped parsley,
    optional

1. Melt butter in a medium pot over medium heat. Chop onion, put in pot, and cook until soft, about 5 minutes, stirring occasionally.

2. Add pumpkin, salt, and chipotle to pot, stirring to mix. Cook until warmed through, about 3 minutes. Taste and adjust seasonings.

3. Serve hot, topped with roasted pumpkin seeds or chopped parsley, if desired. Refrigerate or freeze any extra.

Note

To use canned pumpkin instead of puree: use 2 cups pumpkin and 2 cups chickpea broth or water. The fall shopping list and price calculations assume you use canned pumpkin.

Roasted Pumpkin Seeds

Pumpkin seeds make a filling, crunchy snack. Save them when carving a Halloween pumpkin or before sending a Thanksgiving pumpkin to the compost pile.

 Active time: 5 minutes
Total time: 15 minutes
Makes 12 servings, 2 tablespoons each

1 cup raw pumpkin seeds
1 tablespoon butter, melted, or corn oil
¾ teaspoon cumin
½ teaspoon salt
¼ teaspoon chipotle
¼ teaspoon turmeric

1. Pull pumpkin seeds away from stringy fibers when scraping out pumpkin. Don't worry about getting every scrap of fiber. At this point, seeds can be refrigerated for up to four days before roasting.

2. Preheat oven to 300°F. Line a rimmed cookie sheet with parchment paper, heap seeds on top, and toss with butter and then spices until seeds are evenly coated.

3. Roast seeds for about 45 minutes, stirring every 10 minutes, until dry and just starting to brown. Remove from oven and let cool before eating. Store seeds at room temperature in a tightly closed jar for up to a year.

Notes
Pumpkin seeds are very high in fiber. Limit yourself to small servings or be haunted by digestive distress.

Butter makes pumpkin seeds as addictive as buttered popcorn. Oil lets the spice flavor shine.

Spanish Rice

Different every time and always delicious, this thrifty recipe uses broth saved from making pasta and sauce. You automatically get the flavors of tomato, oregano, garlic, and basil. Delicious with Mexican dishes such as burritos or with most bean recipes.

 Active time: 10 minutes
Total time: about 30 minutes for white rice or 60 minutes for brown rice
Makes 8 servings, ½ cup each

4 cups broth collected when draining pasta or rinsing out sauce pans (page 191)
2 teaspoons olive oil
1 onion
salt to taste
pinch oregano, optional
few dashes hot sauce, optional
2 cups long-grain brown or white rice

1. Save broth in jar when making pasta with a tomato or pesto sauce. Cover and refrigerate until needed, for up to four days.

2. Heat olive oil in a medium pot over medium heat. Chop onion and cook in oil until soft, about 5 minutes, stirring occasionally.

3. Measure broth and, if needed, add water to get 4 cups of liquid. Add to pot and taste. Add salt, oregano, and hot sauce to taste, then cover and bring to a boil over high heat. Rinse rice unless package says not to rinse. Add rice to boiling broth and finish cooking using basic rice recipe (page 203).

Stoup

Want to enjoy what is nearly a free meal? Make some Stoup. Stoup is stew-soup made from good extra food collected in a container you keep in the freezer throughout the week or month. Mine often turns out like minestrone, but it's fun to see how Stoup manages to be different every time. Nudge it in various ethnic directions by adding spices.

 Active time: 2 to 15 minutes
Total time: 15 minutes to 1 hour
Makes at least 4 servings

Leftovers frozen throughout the week
    or month
Produce that needs to be used before it
    spoils
Cheese scraps for garnish, optional
Yogurt for garnish, optional

If needed
    One-half 28-ounce can diced tomatoes
    2 cups shredded cabbage
    1 onion, chopped
    1 garlic clove, minced
    2 cups cooked beans, split peas, or lentils
    ¼ teaspoon cayenne
    liquid from broth jar or saved from
        cooking beans

1. Keep large freezer container (mine holds 2 quarts) for any sort of leftovers that would be good in a stew, such as a few tablespoons tomato sauce, a half-cup of beans, onion half, spicy relish from the Indian takeout, extra rice, or bread crumbs. If you eat meat, add any edible scraps. Add any potatoes when cooking Stoup; they get mushy if frozen.

2. The night before you make Stoup, move the container to the refrigerator to thaw. The next day dump contents in a big pot and heat to boiling over medium heat. Add any vegetables that are nearing the end of their deliciousness, including potatoes, chopped to bite-size pieces. If you don't like bitter food, boil collards or kale separately and drain before adding to Stoup. The mix should have about ½ cup of beans per serving. If it doesn't, add cooked beans to ensure the Stoup has enough protein.

3. Taste Stoup after vegetables have cooked down, about 20 minutes. Sometimes it's delicious just as it is. Add other ingredients if needed. When it tastes good, remove any bits in there for flavoring only, such as parsley stems or bay leaves.

4. Serve hot, topped with grated cheese scraps or a spoon of yogurt if desired. Refrigerate any extra; do not refreeze.

Notes

What not to add. Liquid from canned beans will make your Stoup taste metallic; just pour that stuff down the drain. Save cheese for garnish; don't cook it with the Stoup. Don't add hotdogs, marshmallows, or anything with mayonnaise or else your Stoup will become unspeakably horrible. Other edible meat scraps are okay if you have them, but not hotdogs!

For the sake of tracking the probable costs of making Stoup, the *Wildly Affordable Organic* shopping lists and price calculations assume you'll add all the "if needed" items to make 4 servings of Stoup. Save money by saving extra food when you cook instead of adding these items.

Don't add more to the pot than needed to make it taste good and last 3 meals at most or else it will get so boring you're likely to compost the rest.

Vichyssoise Encore

Some say that vichyssoise, a cold potato-leek soup made with cream, was first made famous by chef Louis Diat at the Ritz-Carlton. This recipe for Vichyssoise Encore puts a thrifty twist on the classic. Make it after you've made a big batch of pesto, using the basil stems and Parmesan rind as flavorings. (Now you see where the "encore" comes from.) Stir in some homemade yogurt and you have a luxurious, cool summer treat.

Active time: 10 minutes
Total time: 40 minutes
Makes 4 servings, 1 cup each

2 cups water
handful of basil stems
2 potatoes
1 onion
½ teaspoon salt or to taste
Parmesan rind, optional
½ cup plain yogurt
basil ribbons or chives, optional

1. Bring water to boil in a medium pot over high heat. Trim basil stems to remove brown ends. Cut stems once or twice if needed so they fit in the pot while still being large enough to remove easily later, and then add to pot. Peel potatoes if not organic or if you want a whiter soup, then chop and put in pot. Chop onion and add to pot with salt and Parmesan rind, if using.

2. When water boils, reduce heat to low so soup barely bubbles. Cook, covered, for about 15 minutes until potatoes and onions are tender.

3. Remove from heat and let cool, then remove basil stems and cheese rind. Make soup smooth by processing it a few pulses in the food processor with the cutting blade, by putting it through a food mill, or simply by mashing it with a potato masher. You can choose between a very smooth, elegant soup or a fairly rough, peasant-style soup. Taste and add salt as needed.

4. To serve, put in bowls and top each with 2 tablespoons of plain yogurt. Swirl in yogurt to make a nice pattern. Garnish with basil ribbons or chives if desired.

Notes

For a faster, comfort-food version, serve soup hot.

Before packing soup into a thermos for lunch, stir yogurt into soup.

Potato peels will color the soup, making it a bit tan but more nutritious.

23

Vegetables and Side Dishes

Eat fruits and vegetables as close to their natural states as you can. You'll save time and money and often get the most nutrition. Enjoy raw carrots, peppers, and cucumbers. Serve broccoli "trees" raw or steamed. See Cook Clean (page 42) for information on rinsing and peeling produce.

These recipes show you how to combine fruits, vegetables, grains, and spices to add variety to your meals with little extra work or expense.

Green Salad

You may snort to see a recipe for green salad, but I include this here so that you will know what is meant by "green salad" on the menu plan and what ingredients from the grocery list are used to create it. If you've only had slightly (or very!) wilted salad from a bag or salad bar, then making your own fresh salad can be a revelation.

All snorting aside, a cool, fresh salad makes a lively contrast to hot-and-heavy bean or pasta dishes.

 Active time: 5 minutes
Total time: 5 minutes
Makes 4 servings, about 1 ¼ cups each

4 cups lettuce
2 carrots, peeled and grated
¼ cup Vinaigrette (page 201)

1. Rinse lettuce leaves thoroughly and then dry using a salad spinner or by rolling up in a clean kitchen towel. Tear lettuce leaves into bite-size pieces.

2. To serve, top the lettuce with grated carrot, either in a big salad bowl or on individual bowls or plates. Top with Vinaigrette, about 2 tablespoons per serving.

Notes
This recipe is for a very basic salad, but of course you can add to it based on what you

have available: spring onions, cucumbers, or fresh tomatoes. When you add a handful of chopped apple, raisins, and walnuts, suddenly it's a special-occasion dish. Add cold, drained beans to make a main-dish **Green and Bean Salad**.

Tossing a salad makes carrots and other heavy ingredients go straight to the bottom of the bowl. Instead, arrange ingredients in a bowl or on a plate.

Vinaigrette

Make this dressing in a flash and use it as a salad dressing, on cooked broccoli or green beans, or as a marinade.

 Active time: 6 minutes
Total time: 6 minutes
Makes 12 servings, 1 tablespoon each

1 garlic clove, minced
3 tablespoons apple-cider vinegar
½ cup plus 1 tablespoon olive oil
½ teaspoon salt
⅛ teaspoon smooth mustard, optional
pepper and more salt, to taste

1. Put all ingredients in a dressing jar. Cover and shake briskly to blend.
2. Shake jar again just before serving, taste, and adjust seasonings. Waiting to taste gives the garlic time to make its flavor known. Refrigerate extra and bring to room temperature before serving.

Notes

To make **Greek Dressing**, use 1 minced garlic clove, 2 tablespoons lemon juice, 2 tablespoons olive oil, ⅛ teaspoon mustard, and ¼ teaspoon salt or to taste. Make like Vinaigrette.

A dressing jar must have a tight-fitting lid, but otherwise it can be anything from a recycled glass jar to a canning jar to a fancy jar marked with recommended proportions of oil and vinegar.

Mustard helps keep the dressing from separating and adds complexity to the taste. Although any type of smooth mustard will do, Dijon is classic.

Apple cider vinegar is on the *Wildly Affordable Organic* shopping list because it provides the best taste at the lowest cost. For variety, splurge on red-wine vinegar or good balsamic vinegar. White vinegar is too bland for dressing.

Classic Cabbage Slaw

Enjoy cabbage slaw when the weather is too hot or cold for lettuce. It's inexpensive and stays crisp for a few days in the refrigerator, so make a big bowl of Classic Cabbage Slaw whenever you are in a money or time crunch.

Active time: 5 minutes
Total time: 5 minutes
Makes 4 servings, ¾ cup each

2 tablespoons mayonnaise
1 tablespoon apple cider vinegar
2 cups grated cabbage
1 carrot, grated
¼ cup diced purple onion, optional
salt and pepper to taste

1. Blend mayonnaise and vinegar in a medium bowl until smooth. Add cabbage, carrot, and purple onion to the dressing and toss to coat. Taste and then add salt and pepper as desired.

2. Serve immediately or cover and refrigerate for up to three days.

Zlaw (Zucchini Slaw)

Use zucchini and red cabbage to make this fast summer slaw. Zlaw goes well with black-bean burgers (page 137). Mixing summer squash with red cabbage creates a colorful side dish. Adding mustard to the dressing adds zing. And what would zlaw be without zing?

Active time: 5 minutes
Total time: 5 minutes
Makes 4 servings, ¾ cup each

2 tablespoons mayonnaise
2 teaspoons apple-cider vinegar
1 teaspoon mustard
2 cups coarsely grated zucchini
1 cup coarsely grated red cabbage
salt and pepper to taste
basil ribbons, optional

1. Blend mayonnaise, vinegar, and mustard in a medium bowl. Add grated vegetables and stir to combine. Taste and adjust seasonings. Top with a few basil ribbons, if using.

2. Serve immediately or cover and refrigerate for a few hours. Zlaw is best eaten the same day it is made, before zucchini makes it watery.

Notes

Any smooth mustard works well here, from Dijon to ballpark. Coarse mustard with seeds does not spread well through the dressing.

For extra color, use a mix of zucchini and yellow squash.

Rice

For clean, fluffy rice, rinse well to remove dirt and starch. Use 2 cups water for every 1 cup rice, plus a half teaspoon salt if desired. It you have time, soak it for up to 12 hours to reduce cooking time. As with beans, even a brief soak helps.

Rice cookers take all the watching out of making rice and keep it warm until you are ready to eat. Just put ingredients in the rice cooker, turn it on, and serve when the cooker says it's done.

To cook rice on the stove, put water and rice in a medium pot, cover, and bring to a boil. Turn heat down to low and then set a timer for 45 minutes for brown rice or 15 minutes for white rice. When the timer goes off, turn off heat but let rice sit covered on the still-warm burner for at least 5 more minutes.

Fluff and serve. Rice keeps refrigerated for up to 4 days and freezes well.

Nutty Rice Salad

Turn kitchen staples into a company-worthy side dish that also keeps well in a lunch box. Serve it with beans or eggs.

 Active time: 5 minutes
Total time: 30 to 60 minutes
Makes 4 servings

2 cups hot cooked rice
1 cup walnuts (110 grams)
2 carrots
1 cup raisins (160 grams)

1. While rice cooks, chop walnuts and toast under a broiler or in a small pan on medium-high heat until fragrant, about 2 minutes. Peel and grate carrots.

2. When rice is done, put walnuts, carrots, and raisins on top of rice and cover pot again. Let sit about 5 minutes to soften raisins and slightly steam carrots.

3. Toss rice mixture with a fork to fluff up the rice and mix in walnuts, raisins, and carrots.

4. Serve warm or at room temperature. Refrigerate any extra. Best eaten within two days.

Note

The Afghan dish Qaboli Palao inspired this recipe. Afghan and Persian cuisine often uses dried fruit in savory dishes.

Glazed Carrots

These carrots are a snap to make. I've had people who say they hate carrots come back for seconds. Try them with Cuban Black Beans (page 140).

 Active time: 3 minutes
Total time: 7 minutes
Makes 4 servings

> 2 carrots, cut in ¼-inch wide half-
>   moons
> 1 teaspoon butter or corn oil
> 2 teaspoons brown sugar
> ½ teaspoon cinnamon

Put carrots, butter, brown sugar, and cinnamon into a microwave-safe bowl and cover. Microwave on medium-high heat for 2 minutes and then stir to coat carrots with flavorings. Replace cover and microwave on medium-high for another minute or so, until carrots are tender. Stir and serve hot.

Green Beans and Marinated Green Beans

Boil green beans on the stove in broth from your broth jar and then return the enriched broth to the jar. Although many vegetables steam to perfection in a microwave, nuking green beans makes them spongy. Cut your cooking and cleaning time by preparing enough for two or more meals.

Rinse 4 cups green beans, cut off tips, and cut into bite-size pieces. Put in a medium pot and add enough broth or water to cover. If using water, add ½ teaspoon salt. Cover and bring to a boil over high heat. Reduce heat and simmer until crisp tender, about 4 minutes.

While beans cook, make Vinaigrette (page 201) if you don't already have some ready. Just as beans become tender, drain into broth jar. Stir ¼ cup Vinaigrette into beans. Serve some beans hot. Refrigerate the rest, allowing them to marinate. Marinated beans are good cold or reheated. Serves 8.

Skillet Asparagus

You don't have to peel, bundle, or boil to enjoy this springtime treat. Instead, highlight the beautiful color and fresh taste of asparagus by cooking it very quickly in a skillet as you would for an Asian stir fry. Don't waste a bite: save the woody ends of the stems to make Double Asparagus Pasta (page 193).

Active time: 7 minutes
Total time: 7 minutes
Makes 4 servings, ½ cup each

1 garlic clove
2 cups asparagus pieces, about
    10 ounces
2 teaspoons olive oil
1 teaspoon lemon juice
salt to taste
lemon zest, optional

1. Mince garlic and set aside. Trim about ¼ inch from stalk bottoms to get rid of any dirty or damaged parts. Gently flex each stem so that it breaks just above woody part, usually ¼ to ⅓ up the stalk. Cut tender stalks diagonally into bite-size pieces about 1 ½ inches long.

2. Heat oil in a medium skillet over medium heat. Add garlic and stir once. Add bite-size asparagus pieces. Cook for 2 or 3 minutes, until asparagus is bright green and crunchy-tender. Remove from skillet so asparagus does not overcook.

3. Sprinkle with salt and lemon juice. Top with a little lemon zest for color if you want. Serve warm or at room temperature. Refrigerate any extra.

Notes

To zest lemon, use a fine grater or a knife to remove the peel's thin yellow outside. The white pith below is bitter.

This recipe comes from Karen Johnson, the first great home cook I ever met. She was a former New Orleans debutant who had moved to the North Carolina coast to raise goats and vegetables while her husband studied marine biology.

Tasty Tahini Greens

Once I realized that tahini was the new bacon, I was able to rework some classic Southern dishes with splatter-free, faster, and healthier results. This recipe tastes like soul food, but swapping fatback for tahini means no cholesterol, much less saturated fat and sodium, and more copper, manganese, calcium, and iron.

Many traditional recipes throw away stems of the greens, which just need a little extra cooking to make them tender. The stems add bulk, which helps keep your big bag of greens from cooking down into nothing.

Collards are my first choice for this dish. They get sweeter once they've been "touched by frost," as they say here, so enjoy them all winter.

 Active time: 20 minutes
Total time: 45 minutes
Makes about 8 servings, ½ cup each

1 tablespoon olive oil
1 onion
1¼ pounds collards, kale, or mustard
   (8 cups chopped)
2 cups water
1 tablespoon tahini
1 teaspoon salt
⅛ teaspoon chipotle or cayenne
½ teaspoon sugar, optional

1. Heat oil in a large pot over medium-low heat. Chop onion and put in the pot, stirring occasionally to prevent burning.

2. Rinse and chop greens (page 42), cutting stems into ¼-inch pieces and leaves into ribbons about ¼-inch across. Add stems to onions as you go.

3. Add water, tahini, salt, chipotle, and sugar, if using, to onion mixture and stir to combine. Turn heat to high and then add leaves. When water boils, turn heat to medium-low and cover pot. Boil greens gently until tender for 15 to 20 minutes, stirring every 3 or 4 minutes to coat leaves with broth as they wilt. Taste and adjust seasonings.

4. Serve hot with hot sauce or vinegar if desired. Refrigerate or freeze any extra.

Grilled Summer Squash Two Ways

Summer squash is cheap, easy to grow, and good for you. But many recipes for yellow squash or zucchini are watery, bland, or have loads of butter or cheese. The trick to making squash a favorite summer vegetable? Grill it! The dry heat gets rid of the extra water and the smoky, grilled flavor makes squash downright interesting. Eat it hot one day and cool as a salad the next.

 Active time: 5 minutes
Total time: 12 minutes
Makes 8 servings

4 summer squash (yellow squash,
**   zucchini, or a mix)**
1 garlic clove
2 teaspoons plus 1 tablespoon olive oil
1½ teaspoons lemon juice
⅛ teaspoon mustard
salt and pepper to taste

1. Start grill. Cut stem ends off squash and then cut squash in half lengthwise.

2. Cut garlic lengthwise four times so you have 8 freshly cut sides. Rub garlic on cut side of squash. Save garlic for dressing. Drizzle squash with about 2 teaspoons of olive oil and rub to coat all over with oil.

3. Put squash on grill skin-side down. Cover and cook for 4 to 5 minutes until skin shows grill marks and squash gives a little when poked with a fork.

4. Meanwhile, make dressing. Mince garlic. In a small jar or glass, shake or whisk together minced garlic, remaining olive oil, lemon juice, and mustard. Taste and add salt and pepper as desired.

5. Turn squash over and grill for another 3 to 5 minutes until grill marks show on cut side and you can easily push a fork into squash. Remove from the grill and cut into bite-size pieces.

6. Serve half hot or at room temperature. Pour dressing over remaining squash and refrigerate, serving cold or at room temperature within two to three days.

Notes

Mix in chopped tomatoes or basil for another twist on the same recipe. If you add cold, cooked black beans or chickpeas, you've got lunch.

Top pizza with grilled summer squash.

If you don't have a grill, cut squash into bite-size pieces after rubbing it with garlic and before coating with oil. Bake at 425°F for about 20 minutes.

Roasted Vegetables

Roasting brings out the natural sweetness in vegetables and fruit. Mix and match vegetables and top with warm hummus for a main dish, then serve extra the next day as a side dish.

Active time: 10 minutes
Total time: 35 minutes
Serves 4 as a main dish or 8 as a side

2 potatoes
2 carrots
2 onions
4 garlic cloves
2 tablespoons olive oil
1 teaspoon kosher or table salt

Spring addition
1 cup green beans

Fall and winter additions
2 sweet potatoes
1 bell pepper

1. Preheat oven to 450°F. Use a nonstick, rimmed cookie sheet or line a cookie sheet with parchment paper.

2. Cut vegetables into bite-size chunks, peeling as needed, and pile on cookie sheet. Drizzle with oil and toss to coat. Arrange pieces in single layer and then sprinkle with salt. Roast for about 25 minutes, stirring halfway through until vegetables start to brown and are tender. Serve hot or at room temperature.

Oven Fries

Quench your longing for french fries with these crispy, lower-fat treats. Pick big Russet potatoes to save time cutting and turning or Yukon Gold potatoes for their buttery flavor. Organic red-skinned potatoes are prettiest.

Preheat oven to 450°F. Cut 4 potatoes in half lengthwise. Cut halves into even slabs ¼-inch wide, heap on a rimmed cookie sheet, and toss with 2 teaspoons olive oil. Arrange in single layer and then roast for 20 minutes. Quickly flip each potato slab over using a thin spatula or two forks and then roast for 10 or 15 more minutes until browned and crispy. Serve hot with ketchup if desired.

 Active time: 8 minutes
Total time: 40 minutes
Makes 4 servings

Roasted Apples

Roast apples while preheating the oven for bread for a sweet side dish or dessert. Roasted apples are fancy enough for a holiday dinner and welcomed by guests who have trouble chewing, ranging from teens with braces to honored elders.

Cut four apples into quarters, core, and slice each quarter into two or three pieces. Melt 2 teaspoons butter with 1 teaspoon brown sugar in a small, microwave-safe dish on high for about 20 seconds. Stir and drizzle over apples, toss, and arrange apples cut-side down on a cookie sheet. Roast undisturbed at 400°F to 475°F for about 20 minutes until golden, puffed, and fork tender.

 Active time: 8 minutes
Total time: 30 minutes
Makes 4 servings

Bright Popcorn

Even with all organic ingredients, a big bowl of this whole-grain snack costs only 35 cents per serving, about a dime less than microwave popcorn, and it provides 4 grams of protein. Its bright golden glow comes from the super-spice turmeric.

This recipe uses an electric wok, which lets you set the temperature exactly, leaves the fewest unpopped kernels, and is easy to clean. But you can also use these flavorings with corn popped in a pan on the stove or in a plain paper bag in the microwave. Skip the garlic if microwaving.

 Active time: 8 minutes
Total time: 8 minutes
Makes 4 servings, about 3 ½ cups each

1 garlic clove, optional
3 tablespoons olive oil
½ cup popcorn
1 teaspoon ground cumin
½ teaspoon turmeric
½ teaspoon salt
¼ to ½ teaspoon chipotle

1. Mince garlic, if using. Put oil and three kernels of popcorn in an electric wok. Cover wok and set the temperature to about 380°F.
2. While waiting for test kernels to pop, mix spices and salt in a small bowl. As soon as the test kernels pop, use a big spoon to remove them from the wok. Put garlic in oil and stir once. Add the rest of the popcorn and cover the wok. Shake the wok frequently as popcorn begins to pop. After the first big burst of popping, crack lid away from you so steam can escape. Continue shaking the wok to prevent burning as long as you hear steady popping.
3. Turn heat off, remove lid, and sprinkle spice mixture over popcorn. Serve hot or at room temperature. To keep for several days, let cool completely and store in a tightly sealed container.

Notes

If blueberries and broccoli are super-foods, then turmeric is a super-spice. The curcumin in turmeric is reported to prevent or reduce a wide range of diseases, including arthritis, cancer, and Alzheimer's disease.[1] As both an anti-inflammatory and an antioxidant, turmeric may slow the aging process.[2] Buy turmeric instead of premixed curry powder, which often has a relatively low amount of this healthy spice.

How can an electric wok be wildly affordable? If you pop your own corn once a week instead of using the microwave kind, you'll save over $20 a year. And you'll have a multiuse appliance that is great for stir fries and scrambles. If you don't have access to a full kitchen, an electric wok and rice cooker can make the difference between cooking many great meals at home and the curse of fast food.

Don't break a tooth on an unpopped kernel. If you are serving rapid eaters or easily distracted people, then serve popcorn in bowls, leaving unpopped kernels behind.

Desserts

One of the oddest comments I get is "Dessert! How can you call it a healthy diet if you have dessert every day?"

How could I not include dessert in menus for a joyous life? Dessert provides a sense of completeness at the end of the meal. It satisfies our sweet tooth and signals to our animal natures that there is plenty to eat—enough for a treat.

One day dessert might be two oatmeal-raisin cookies made with whole wheat flour, whole-grain oats, and raisins. Another day it might be a cupcake made with whole wheat flour, carrots, oil instead of butter, and just glazed with ginger instead of loaded with frosting. The summer recipes use lots of fruit.

These healthy, thrifty desserts include vegetables, fruit, and my favorite source of antioxidants: chocolate. They use whole grains such as oats and white whole wheat flour. High-protein desserts with nuts, eggs, milk, or yogurt round out a soup or salad meal.

The desserts offer a taste of sweetness but not an overload. In fact, they use surprisingly little sugar or honey. In 2003 the average American consumed 142 pounds of sugar and sweeteners a year.[1] If you follow the *Wildly Affordable Organic* plan to the letter, you'll eat just **28 pounds of sweeteners a year**, plus a little more if eating sweetened peanut butter. You won't eat any high-fructose corn syrup—just sugar and honey.

So go wild. Have a cupcake!

Chocolate Pudding

This creamy pudding will satisfy your chocolate craving nutritiously and deliciously. It's got the calcium and protein of milk but little fat because it uses 2% milk and no butter. It's terrific either warm or cold.

 Active time: 20 minutes
Makes 4 servings, a generous ½ cup each

⅔ cup sugar (112 grams)
¼ cup cocoa (18 grams)
3 tablespoons cornstarch (24 grams)
¼ teaspoon salt (2 grams)
2¼ cups milk, 2%
1 teaspoon vanilla

1. Measure dry ingredients into a medium pot. Whisk to combine, getting rid of the lumps. Add 1 cup of milk. Whisk mixture until smooth.

2. Add remaining milk and heat mixture over medium heat, whisking occasionally at first and then more frequently to prevent burning. When it starts to boil, whisk constantly for 1 minute.

3. Remove from heat and stir in vanilla just until blended. Pour into four custard cups or small bowls.

4. Let cool for at least 10 minutes before serving warm or at room temperature, or cover and refrigerate to serve cold later.

Notes

If you are doing a big *Wildly Affordable Organic* cooking day, cook the pudding in the same pot you used to heat milk for yogurt. Just measure the dry ingredients into a small bowl, whisk to combine and get rid of lumps, and then pour into the pot.

Instead of using four small bowls, you can pour hot pudding into one larger bowl.

Pour hot pudding into individual plastic containers and freeze. Pack a frozen pudding in a bag lunch to provide a sweet treat and to keep other ingredients cold.

Vanilla Pudding

Fragrant and smooth, vanilla pudding is delicious on its own, whether warm or cold. Serve it as a warm sauce for fruit or cold with fruit on top. Follow the directions for Chocolate Pudding, but in step 2 whisk egg into remaining milk before adding to pot.

 Active time: 20 minutes
Makes 4 servings, a generous ½ cup each

½ cup sugar (100 grams)
3 tablespoons cornstarch (24 grams)
⅛ teaspoon salt (1 gram)
2¼ cups milk, 2%
1 egg
1 teaspoon vanilla

Oatmeal-Raisin Cookies

This is a variation on a recipe I learned in the first cooking class I ever took. It was in the '70s in the nearby college town, and the focus of the class was to "take your food back from The Man." My notes say, "Add mixed raisins or chocolate or anything." The cookies and the idea are still good.

 Active time: 30 minutes
Total time: 45 minutes baking 3 cookie sheets at a time
Makes 18 servings of 2 cookies each

10 tablespoons butter at room temperature (1 ¼ sticks)
1 ¼ cup white whole wheat or all-purpose flour (150 grams)
¾ teaspoon baking soda
½ teaspoon salt
1 teaspoon cinnamon
¼ teaspoon nutmeg
1¼ cups packed brown sugar (275 grams)
2 eggs
1 teaspoon vanilla
2 cups oats (160 grams)
1 cup raisins (160 grams) or mix of dried fruit, chocolate chips, and nuts

1. Position oven racks in the center of the oven. Preheat oven to 350°F.

2. If butter is cold, cut it into roughly tablespoon-size pieces so it will soften quickly and then put it in a mixing bowl. Put flour, baking soda, salt, cinnamon, and nutmeg in a medium bowl and then stir to mix.

3. Add brown sugar to butter and beat on medium speed until fluffy, about 1 minute. Stir in eggs. Add flour mixture and beat until smooth. Stir in vanilla. Stir in oats and raisins.

4. Drop cookie dough by the tablespoon onto ungreased cookie sheets. Bake for 14 to 16 minutes, until tops of cookies start to turn golden and edges look a bit crisp. If cooking more than one sheet of cookies at a time, remove the top sheet from the oven first, letting each remaining sheet be on top for a moment. As soon as you take a cookie sheet from the oven, move cookies to wire racks using a thin spatula. Otherwise, cookies will harden and be difficult to remove.

5. Eat some warm. Then cool completely and store in a covered container at room temperature or freeze.

Notes

If you don't have nutmeg, use 1¼ teaspoons cinnamon.

Line the cookie sheet with parchment paper to speed cleanup. If you are making pizza the same day, reuse the parchment paper for that.

Peanut Butter Cookies

Homey and crispy, these peanut butter cookies will give you a protein boost while putting a smile on your face. The optional cardamom creates a completely different, somewhat mysterious cookie that adults and children will love, but it's great both ways.

Unlike many recipes, this one uses all peanut butter instead of half peanut butter and half butter. It also uses less sugar than most, at the request of my panel of taste-testers. As a result, it's a healthier, thriftier recipe that is also better for the planet.

 Active time: 30 minutes
Total time: 40 minutes
Makes 16 servings, 3 cookies each

½ cup packed brown sugar (110 grams)
⅓ cup sugar (66 grams)
2 tablespoons white whole wheat or
    all-purpose flour (15 grams)
1 teaspoon baking powder
¼ teaspoon salt
1 teaspoon cardamom, optional
1 cup peanut butter (258 grams)
1 egg

1. Preheat oven to 350°F. Put dry ingredients in a large bowl and whisk to blend. Put peanut butter and egg in a medium bowl and stir until blended. Add peanut butter mixture to dry ingredients, stirring just until thoroughly mixed. Overmixing makes cookies flat.

2. Lightly flour a large cutting board or section of counter. Divide dough into 4 equal parts. One at a time, roll each part into a 1 x 12-inch log. Cut log into 12 even discs. This is easy to do by cutting in half, then each half in half, then each quarter in thirds.

3. Roll each disc between your palms just enough to form a ball and then put on cookie sheet. Space cookies about 2 inches apart. Flatten each ball with a fork, making a cross-hatch pattern by pressing the fork tines twice across each cookie at a 90° angle. If you have room on your cookie sheet, roll and cut another log, adding cookies as space allows. I usually bake all 4 dozen cookies using three cookies sheets.

4. Bake for 10 to 12 minutes until lightly browned. Let cool on cookie sheet for about 2 minutes. Slide a thin spatula under cookies to move to a wire rack. While one batch of cookies bakes, prepare the next batch.

5. Serve some at once. Let the rest cool completely and then store in a covered container at room temperature or wrap well and freeze.

Notes

Rolling dough into logs saves about 5 minutes, compared to dipping by teaspoons from the bowl. It also lets you control exactly how many cookies you make, which will help you manage your portions and your budget.

If you find that your fork sticks to the cookies when you flatten them, try holding the flattened cookies in place with a finger or a table knife while you slide the fork off.

Optionally, use parchment paper to line the cookie sheets for easy cleanup.

Cocoa Cookies

These drop cookies are simplicity itself to make, but they get their complex taste from the honey. Whip up a batch while you are preheating the oven for bread or whenever you need to take cookies to a PTA event or your book club.

 Active time: 20 minutes
Total time: 30 minutes
Makes 12 servings, 3 cookies each.
Doubles well.

1 cup white whole wheat flour
   (120 grams)
6 tablespoons cocoa (30 grams)
½ teaspoon baking soda
scant ¼ teaspoon salt
6 tablespoons butter, at room
   temperature (¾ stick)
14 tablespoons sugar (175 grams)
   (1 cup minus 2 tablespoons)
1 egg
2 tablespoons honey
1 teaspoon vanilla

1. Preheat oven to 350°F.

2. Whisk flour, cocoa, baking soda, and salt in a medium bowl to blend.

3. Cream butter and sugar in a mixing bowl on medium speed until mixture is fluffy. Blend in egg, honey, and vanilla. Stir flour mixture into butter mixture.

4. Drop cookie dough by the teaspoon onto an ungreased cookie sheet, lined with parchment paper if desired. Bake for 8 to 10 minutes. Cool cookies on baking sheet for a minute or two until firm enough to lift with a spatula. They will be very soft right out of the oven. Transfer to a wire rack to cool completely.

5. Serve at room temperature. Store in a cookie jar or other sealed container for up to 4 days or freeze.

Notes

If you're out of honey, use two more tablespoons of sugar.

Lining your cookie sheets with parchment paper will make these cookies easier to lift after baking and make cleanup easier. You can also get the next batch of cookies ready while a batch is baking.

Ice Cream

Use local fruit and milk to make the best, healthiest ice cream imaginable. Go as organic as you can, starting with organic milk. I used to make ice cream only when we had company because I didn't realize you could store homemade ice cream. But now I freeze any extra in single-serving containers and then thaw for about twenty minutes before serving. Fresh is best, but frozen and slightly thawed ice cream is still much better than store-bought, especially ripe-fruit flavors.

Freeze whole recipes of blended ice cream base without milk and extracts for up to a year in quart-size freezer bags. Thaw in the refrigerator overnight and then continue with the recipe.

I love my Donvier hand-crank ice cream maker. Here's how it works. Freeze the Chillfast cylinder at least a full day before making ice cream. Mix up ice cream base and assemble the maker. Pour ice cream base into the bowl and turn the handle on top of it every few minutes. Between turns, eat dinner, dance around the house, or read a book. It's easy to clean too.

Although I avoid special equipment in the *Wildly Affordable Organic* kitchen, an ice cream maker is a good investment. Look for one at yard sales or thrift shops for $10 or less. They make great presents too. We got ours as a wedding present over twenty years ago and it's still going strong.

Strawberry Ice Cream

Make this strawberry ice cream and you'll feel glad to be alive. The intense strawberry flavor and gorgeous deep pink color embody Spring itself. This healthy dessert is easy enough for a weeknight and fancy enough for a dinner party or special occasion.

 Active time: 20 minutes, plus about 40 minutes of occasional attention, depending on your ice cream maker
Total time: 1 hour
Makes 8 servings, ½ cup each

3 cups sliced strawberries or 3 heaping cups whole berries (500 grams)
1⅔ cups sugar (330 grams)
2½ cups whole milk
½ teaspoon vanilla

1. If needed, put the bowl of your ice cream maker in the freezer a day in advance or whatever the manufacturer recommends.

2. Clean strawberries and remove leaves and any bad spots. If you are using a blender, you may want to slice the berries one or two times to make blending easier.

3. Put strawberries, sugar, and milk in blender or food processor fitted with the cutting blade. Process until smooth. Add vanilla and process very briefly to blend. Taste to check for sweetness and add a bit more sugar if needed. If you started with warm berries, refrigerate the mixture until cold. It will keep for up to a day, which makes this a great dinner-party recipe.

4. Pour strawberry mixture into ice cream maker and process according to the manufacturer's directions.

5. Serve at once. Freeze any remaining ice cream in single-serving containers. Thaw frozen servings for about 20 minutes before eating.

Peach Ice Cream Supreme

One summer several years ago, I vowed to figure out how to make peach ice cream so good that it just couldn't get any better. So good that it would stop conversation at a lively dinner party for a few minutes. How good? So good that you will dream about it on a cold, dark night in February.

After weeks of variations, I discovered the secret ingredient: orange-pineapple-banana juice. Just a half-cup of that juice in a container of ice cream showcases the essential tropical nature of the peach. It makes the ice cream complex and interesting without taking the spotlight off the main attraction: ultimately ripe peaches. If I could make only one dessert all summer, this would be it. I also freeze bags of ice cream base to brighten my winter.

 Active time: 20 minutes, plus about 40 minutes of occasional attention
Total time: about 1 hour
Makes 8 servings, ½ cup each

3 tablespoons lemon juice
    (juice from 1½ lemons)
2¼ cups peach pulp and juice
    (450 grams)
½ cup orange-pineapple-banana juice,
    optional, but it makes it "supreme"
1¾ cups sugar (350 grams)
pinch of salt
½ teaspoon vanilla
¼ teaspoon almond extract
2½ cups whole milk

1. Do what it takes to get your ice cream maker ready. I put my Donvier cylinder into the freezer at least 24 hours in advance.

2. Put lemon juice in blender or a food processor fitted with the cutting blade (see Notes). Peel peaches, pit, and cut into biggish chunks (see page 42 for how to peel peaches). Add enough peaches to the blender to make about 2½ cups peach puree when blended with lemon juice.

3. Top off peach puree with orange-pineapple-banana juice, if using, so puree totals 3 cups. Otherwise, add enough peaches to reach 3 cups.

4. Add sugar and then blend to mix. At this point, you can freeze ice cream base for use later.

5. Stir in the vanilla and almond extracts plus as much of the milk as your blender will hold. Put mixture into ice cream maker and stir in any remaining milk. Follow the directions for your freezer to make the ice cream. For the Donvier, I stir it every minute or so for about 20 minutes and then put it into the freezer to finish hardening for about an hour.

6. Serve within 2 or 3 hours. To keep longer, freeze as individual servings in freezer-safe containers and thaw for 20 minutes or so before eating. It may keep longer than two weeks, but I don't know!

Notes

Use very ripe peaches, preferably ice cream peaches from the farmers' market (page 35).

A blender with measurement markings is the perfect tool for this recipe. If you are using a food processor instead, process peaches until smooth and measure until you get about 2½ cups of pureed peaches and lemon juice.

If you don't have pineapple-orange-banana juice, just use an extra half-cup of peaches. The ice cream will still be wonderful.

If you don't have almond extract, use an extra ¼ teaspoon of vanilla.

Feel-Good Peach Cobbler

I created this recipe after running the numbers on my usual cobbler recipe. The new recipe is considerably lighter and more thrifty, using nearly two-thirds less sugar and 80 percent less butter than the original. It also replaces an egg with yogurt. This cobbler even uses more fruit!

Cutting the biscuit topping into star shapes makes it pretty enough for a special meal while making it easy to serve. Feel-Good Peach Cobbler can sweeten a brunch buffet or star as the finale for Sunday dinner. You'll have enough topping left to make 4 biscuits for breakfast.

 Active time: 30 minutes
Total time: 1 hour and 5 minutes
Makes 12 servings, 1 biscuit each plus the fruit under and around it

butter or shortening for pan
9 cups peeled, chopped peaches,
   about 15 peaches (1550 g)
1 cup sugar (200 grams)
2 tablespoons cornstarch (20 g)
1 teaspoon vanilla

Biscuit topping
2 cups all-purpose flour (240 grams),
   plus more for kneading
2 tablespoons sugar
1 tablespoon baking powder
4 tablespoons cold butter (½ stick)
¾ cup plain yogurt (6 ounces or
   170 grams)

1. **Prepare the fruit base.** Preheat oven to 400°F. Butter or grease a 13 x 9 x 2-inch baking pan. Peel and chop peaches into half-inch pieces, putting them in the pan as you go (see page 42 for how to peel peaches).

2. Stir 1 cup sugar and corn starch in a small bowl to blend. Sprinkle sugar mixture and vanilla over fruit. Mix by lifting fruit gently with a large spoon. Cover and bake for 20 minutes until fruit releases its juices.

3. **Prepare the biscuit topping.** Put flour, 1 tablespoon sugar, and baking powder in food processor with cutting blade attachment. Pulse 2 or 3 times to combine ingredients. Cut butter into 4 pieces and put in processor. Pulse until flour mixture looks like coarse sand, about 8 to 10 pulses. Add yogurt and process until dough forms a ball, about 10 seconds. Do not overprocess or else topping will be tough.

4. Flour a clean countertop or cutting board. Put dough on floured surface, sprinkle with flour, and gently pat out until about 1 inch thick. Cut dough into 12 biscuits about 2 inches wide using a cookie cutter or an upside-down glass. If dough sticks, flour edge of cutter. After cutting the first set of shapes, gently gather up dough scraps and pat out again. Cut remaining shapes. If you still have extra dough, see Notes below.

5. **Top and bake.** When fruit is hot and juicy, remove pan from oven. Stir fruit. Arrange biscuits on top of fruit. Brush biscuits with water just until moist and then sprinkle with remaining tablespoon of sugar. Bake for about 35 minutes until biscuits are golden brown and fruit bubbles in center of the pan.

6. Serve hot or at room temperature. Keeps at room temperature for about 2 hours. Cover and refrigerate any extra.

The fruit base keeps the biscuit topping moist, so this dessert keeps well for 2 or 3 days. Reheat servings a few at time in the microwave if desired.

Notes

Have extra dough? My star-shaped cookie cutter leaves me with enough extra dough to make 4 biscuits for breakfast the next day. Just gently pat the last set of dough scraps into a circle. Cut cross-wise into 4 pieces. Put on a small, ungreased pan and bake with cobbler for about 15 minutes. You can also refrigerate dough and bake the next day. Baked biscuits are best right out of the oven, but they will keep for up to a day in a sealed container at room temperature.

The secret to a light biscuit topping is keeping the dough cold and handling it as little as possible. Use cold butter and yogurt. Run the food processor just enough to get the job done, otherwise it will heat up the dough. I've tried using various amounts of white whole wheat flour, but even a half-cup moves the topping from a delicious dessert to a tough and wheaty health food.

Baked Pears with Cinnamon Yogurt Sauce

I make this company-worthy dessert when teaching my 20 Minutes a Day class to foodies. It's full of sophisticated contrasts and looks gorgeous. Bake pears to get the right texture; microwaving won't make the pears silky.

 Active time: 10 minutes
Total time: 55 minutes
Makes 4 generous servings

4 small pears
2 tablespoons packed brown sugar
½ cup water
1 tablespoon lemon juice
¼ teaspoon cinnamon
½ cup Cinnamon Yogurt Sauce
   (page 129)

1. Preheat oven to 350°F. Rinse pears, cut in half lengthwise, and scoop out core. Put cut-side down in a 9 x 13-inch baking dish.

2. Mix remaining ingredients except sauce and pour over pears. Cover and bake for 45 minutes until pears are fork tender.

3. To serve, put 2 pear halves on a small plate and top each with a spoonful of sauce. They are best warm but good cold. Refrigerate any extra.

Chocolate Pumpkin Snack Cake

This recipe takes me back to a cake-mix fad while I was growing up: snack cakes. The idea was that Mom whipped up unfrosted cakes for the kids to eat after school. Because it's not frosted, you can tuck a piece of Chocolate Pumpkin Snack Cake into a lunch box or picnic basket.

Unlike a mix, this healthy recipe uses whole wheat flour and pumpkin puree made from a Halloween pumpkin. The result is light and tender, with a good cocoa flavor and just a faint hint of spiciness from the pumpkin.

 Active time: 15 minutes
Total time: about an hour
Makes 8 servings

1 cup white whole wheat flour
   (120 grams)
⅓ cup cocoa (30 grams)
½ teaspoon salt
½ teaspoon baking soda
8 tablespoons butter, room
   temperature (1 stick)
butter or shortening for pan
1 cup sugar (200 grams)
2 eggs
⅔ cup pumpkin puree (page 194) or
   canned
   plain pumpkin (140 grams)

1. Preheat oven to 350°F. Whisk dry ingredients in a small bowl to blend.

2. Put butter and sugar in a mixing bowl and then cream together on medium speed for about 1 minute. Use butter wrapper to butter or grease an 8 x 8-inch pan. Add eggs to butter mixture and beat until light in color. Mix in pumpkin and then mix in dry ingredients.

3. Spread batter in pan. Bake for 45 to 50 minutes, until a tester inserted into cake's center comes out clean.

4. Let cool for at least 10 minutes. Store any extra covered at room temperature or wrapped well and frozen.

Note

Pumpkins grown to be jack-o'-lanterns are not grown for taste, so often the puree from them is mild and somewhat watery. But pumpkin puree works fine in this snack cake, creating a tender texture and adding nutrition without overwhelming the cocoa.

Chocolate Upside-Down Cake

Sometimes I've just got to have chocolate. This quick, one-bowl cake satisfies that craving and puts a smile on my face with its magic frosting. While the cake bakes, a gooey hot layer of chocolate forms on the bottom of the pan. As you serve each piece, make sure to scrape the bottom of the pan and then flip the piece onto the plate. Voilà! You'll have a tender cake that seems to have frosted itself.

Active time: 15 minutes
Total time: 45 minutes
Makes 8 servings

1 cup white whole wheat or all-purpose
    flour (120 grams)
¾ cup sugar (150 grams)
3 tablespoons cocoa (15 grams)
2 teaspoons baking powder
½ teaspoon salt
2 tablespoons butter
½ cup milk
1 teaspoon vanilla
¾ cup hot water
¾ cup brown sugar (160 grams)

1. Preheat oven to 350°F. Grease or butter a 7 x 11 x 2-inch baking pan.
2. Whisk flour, white sugar, 2 tablespoons cocoa, baking powder, and salt in a medium bowl to blend.
3. Melt butter in microwave or on stove. Add butter, milk, and vanilla to flour mixture. Stir briefly, just until combined and smooth. Pour batter into pan.

4. Heat water in microwave or on stove until hot to the touch but not boiling, the same temperature as hot tap water. Meanwhile, put brown sugar and remaining tablespoon of cocoa in batter bowl. When water is hot, add it to bowl and stir. Pour this mixture into pan over batter. Do not stir.
5. Bake for 30 minutes and then remove from oven and let firm up for about 5 minutes. Cut into servings and then slide a spatula under each piece and flip onto the serving plate. Cover any extra after it has cooled. It will keep at room temperature for about 3 days. To serve cooled cake, flip each piece and microwave just until cake is just warm and top is gooey again.

Notes

Add a scoop of ice cream to make this cake into a casual company-level dessert. It's one of our family holiday traditions to have Chocolate Upside-Down Cake served with peppermint ice cream in December every year.

The original recipe calls for all-purpose flour. I sometimes use white whole wheat flour, which produces a slightly denser cake with a faint bready taste. It's still delicious and has the nutrition of regular whole wheat flour.

Thanks to my dear mother-in-law, Catherine Watson, for allowing me to share this recipe and for making it for us all so many times.

Ginger-Glazed Carrot Cake

This one-layer cake, glazed with ginger, also can be made as 12 cupcakes. It's lighter and more tropical than the traditional two-layer carrot cake with cream cheese frosting and travels better in a lunch bag too. Double the recipe to make 2 layers, 24 cupcakes, or an 11 x 17-inch sheet cake.

Active time: 20 minutes
Total time: about 1 hour
Makes one layer or 12 cupcakes

butter or shortening plus flour for pan
1½ cups shredded carrots, about
    2½ carrots (180 grams)
1 cup white whole wheat or all-purpose
    flour (120 grams)
1 cup sugar (200 grams)
1 teaspoon cinnamon
½ teaspoon salt
1 teaspoon baking soda
½ cup corn oil (112 grams)
2 eggs
½ teaspoon vanilla

Glaze
2 teaspoons ginger
2 tablespoons butter
1 tablespoon sugar

1. Preheat oven to 350°F. Butter and flour a 9-inch cake pan or a 12-cup muffin pan.

2. Peel and grate carrots and set aside. Put flour, 1 cup of sugar, cinnamon, salt, and baking soda in a large bowl and whisk to combine. Stir in oil and then eggs one at a time. Stir in vanilla and finally carrots.

3. Pour batter into cake pan and bake for 30 minutes or scoop into muffin pan and bake 25 minutes. Cake is done when top springs back to the touch and a tester stuck into cake's center comes out clean. Let cool in the pan on a wire rack for 10 minutes.

4. Make glaze while cake cools. Peel and grate or mince ginger. Put butter, ginger, and remaining sugar in a small microwave-safe bowl and microwave on medium until butter is melted and ginger is fragrant, about 1 minute.

5. Remove cake or cupcakes from pan and spread with glaze while cake and glaze are still warm. Serve at once or cool completely, then refrigerate or freeze.

Note
When I grate carrots by hand, I use the large holes on my grater, which gives the cake a rougher but still good texture. For special occasions, I use the smaller holes on my box grater or food processor to make a more delicate cake.

Strawberry Shortcake

My mother-in-law made the best strawberry shortcake I've ever had. Crushing the strawberries releases their juice and fragrance, and the tender cake absorbs the liquid. It's a lovely dessert too, one you can be proud to serve on special occasions.

You can make the cake, prepare the strawberry sauce, and whip the cream the day before, then assemble just before serving.

Active time: 25 minutes
Total time: 25 minutes
Makes 12 servings

1 recipe Hot-Milk cake
2 pounds fresh strawberries, a little
   less than 3 pints (900 grams)
½ cup sugar or to taste (100 grams)
1 cup whipping cream
1 to 2 tablespoons of sugar
½ teaspoon of vanilla, optional

1. Make cake and then make strawberry sauce. Remove tops and any bad spots from strawberries. Crush or puree about half in a blender or food processor with the cutting blade. Slice the rest, reserving 12 slices for garnish, and stir in with crushed strawberries. Taste and add sugar as needed.

2. Put whipping cream, sugar, and vanilla, if using, into a chilled mixer or food processor bowl. Beat on high until soft peaks form.

3. Cut cake into 12 pieces. For each serving, cut cake square in half cross-wise. Put bottom of cake on serving plate or bowl. Top with strawberry sauce. Put top of cake on strawberry sauce. Add more strawberry sauce and a spoonful of whipped cream. Garnish with reserved strawberry slice. Refrigerate any extra strawberry sauce or whipped cream and use within 2 or 3 days.

Notes

I used to whip cream every time I needed it until I found that whipped cream stays fluffy for days if refrigerated.

Strawberry sauce freezes well. Make a double batch and freeze one to enjoy next winter.

Thanks to my mother-in-law, Catherine Watson, for making this most delicious recipe for years and for her permission to share it here.

Hot-Milk Cake

This light cake is essential for Strawberry Shortcake, (page 224), but it is also delicious with other juicy fruit or just by itself. Kids love to help make it because the batter changes dramatically as you mix it.

Active time: 10 minutes
Total time: 30 minutes
Makes 12 servings

½ cup milk
1 tablespoon butter
butter or shortening and flour for the
    pan
2 large eggs
1 cup sugar (200 grams)
1 cup all-purpose flour or white whole
    wheat flour (120 grams)
1 teaspoon baking powder
⅛ teaspoon salt

1. Preheat oven to 375°F. Heat milk until it begins to steam and then add butter to hot milk. Butter will melt. (I microwave milk in a Pyrex measuring cup for about a minute and a half on high.) Grease and flour an 8-inch square pan or a 12-cup muffin pan.

2. Put eggs in mixing bowl and beat on medium-high until they turn light and thick, about 1 minute. Add sugar and beat about 2 ½ minutes more. Sift flour, baking powder, and salt together.

3. Fold sifted ingredients into egg mixture. Fold in hot milk and butter. Work quickly to keep cake fluffy; adding flour and milk mixtures should take no more than a minute.

4. Pour into pan. Bake for 20 to 25 minutes. Cake is done when a tester inserted into center comes out clean. Let cool thoroughly in pan before cutting.

Notes

My mother-in-law's original recipe calls for all-purpose flour, which I sometimes use for special occasions. White whole wheat flour produces a slightly denser, slightly darker cake with more nutrition.

Let this cake show off organic eggs or ones from pastured chickens.

Blueberry Pie

Intense, beautiful, with a flaky exterior and a deep blue, sweet filling, blueberry pie is a country-music star of a dessert. Blueberries are the easiest fruit to prepare, only needing a quick rinse and stem check. Even when you make Sneaky-Wheat Butter Pie Crust, this blueberry pie is fast enough to make on a weeknight. It's fabulous enough for a dinner party or family reunion too.

Despite its glamour, this pie is also good for you. It uses white whole wheat flour in place of all-purpose flour. Blueberries themselves are a super-food, with studies showing they reverse age-related brain problems.[2]

For filling only:

Active time: 15 minutes
Total time: 15 minutes

For complete pie, including cooling:

Active time: 30 minutes
Total time: 1 hour and 52 minutes
*   if freezing dough and 2 hours*
*   and 12 minutes if refrigerating it*
Makes 12 servings

1 recipe Sneaky-Wheat Butter Pie
    Crust
4 cups blueberries (1 quart or
    600 grams)
½ cup sugar (100 grams)
⅓ cup white whole wheat or all-purpose
    flour (40 grams)
½ teaspoon cinnamon
1 tablespoon lemon juice
2 tablespoons butter

1. Make pie crust. While dough chills before being rolled out, pick over and rinse blueberries, removing stems and shriveled or damaged berries. Put in large bowl.

2. Stir together sugar, flour, and cinnamon in a medium bowl. Drain any water from the blueberry bowl and then add sugar mixture to berries, stirring to coat.

3. Roll out bottom of pie crust and put in 9-inch pie plate. Add berries and then sprinkle with lemon juice and dot with pieces of butter. Roll out top crust and cover pie as directed by the pie crust recipe. Preheat oven to 425°F.

4. Chill pie by freezing for 10 minutes or refrigerating for 30 minutes. When chilled, cover crust edges of pie with strips of aluminum foil to prevent overbrowning. Bake for 40 to 47 minutes, removing foil after 30 minutes. Pie is done when crust is golden brown and berries just begin to bubble through slits in crust.

5. Cool for 15 minutes before serving. Serve warm or at room temperature. Keeps covered at room temperature for 3 days.

Note

Crust will be flakiest the day the pie is made. Cool thoroughly before covering or else the crust will become soggy.

Sneaky-Wheat Butter Pie Crust

Fear not making pie crust if you have a food processor and some parchment paper! Even using only a pastry blender, an empty wine bottle as a rolling pin, and a well-floured counter top, you can make a very good pie crust in about 15 minutes. The results taste better than the boxed crusts you'll find in supermarket coolers and are miles better than the ones in aluminum pans.

Sneaky-Wheat Butter Pie Crust has all good ingredients, including a healthy dose of white whole wheat flour. The surprising result is a richer tasting, flakier crust. It's another case where the healthier option is more delicious. Use for Blueberry Pie.

 Active time: 15 minutes
Total time: 35 minutes to 1 hour and 15 minutes, depending on whether freezing or refrigerating dough
Makes 2 crusts, enough for 1 double-crust blueberry pie or 2 single-crust pumpkin pies or quiches

about 6 tablespoons ice water
1 ¾ cups unbleached all-purpose flour (210 grams), plus more for rolling
¾ cups white whole wheat flour (90 grams)
1 teaspoon sugar, optional, though recommended for sweet fillings
½ teaspoon salt
1 cup cold butter (2 sticks)

1. Make ice water by putting a few ice cubes in a cup of water. Put dry ingredients in a food processor fitted with a metal blade. Pulse once or twice to stir. Cut each stick of butter into 8 roughly even pieces and add to flour mixture. Pulse until mixture resembles coarse sand. Add 5 tablespoons of ice water and process until mixture forms a ball, for 10 to 15 seconds. If it is crumbly and dry, add remaining water.

2. Set out two small containers or two pieces of waxed paper or plastic wrap to hold dough while cooling. (Waxed paper will be fine if you will be using the dough within an hour.) Remove dough from the food processor, divide in half, and pat each into a disk about 6 inches across and ¾ inch high. Put in a container or wrap to keep from drying out or picking up smells, then freeze for 10 minutes or refrigerate for at least 30 minutes. At this point you can refrigerate dough up to four days or freeze it for up to a month.

3. While dough cools, clean countertop thoroughly or set out two sheets of parchment paper. Flour one sheet of parchment or countertop. When dough is chilled, set one disk on floured surface and dust with more flour. If using parchment paper, cover with other sheet. Roll dough out in a circle that is about 2 inches larger than your pie plate, working from the center out and rotating dough.

4. If using parchment, remove the top sheet. Center the pie plate upside down on dough, slide your hand between the parchment and the counter, and flip the plate over so dough is on top. Gently remove the parchment. Otherwise, roll one end of dough circle on the rolling pin until leading edge nearly wraps to touch rest of crust. Use the rolling pin to lift up crust and gently center over the pie plate.

5. Press dough into the pie plate, getting rid of any air pockets and making sure

dough touches the plate where the bottom and side meet. Trim dough so it is about a quarter inch wider than the plate rim.

6. Fill crust according to filling recipe. If making filling will take more than 10 minutes and dough disk for top crust is in the freezer, move it to the refrigerator. If making single-crust pie, bake as directed by the filling recipe.

7. For double-crust pie, sprinkle more flour on the parchment paper or counter, take other disk out of refrigerator or freezer, and roll out second crust. Use rolling pin to lift top crust and center on pie, as described in step 4. Trim dough where edge is more than an inch wider than plate rim. Using your thumb and first two fingers, turn top crust under bottom crust, and squeeze gently to seal, going all the way around the rim. I usually do a rough pass to seal and a second pass to make an attractive pattern.

8. Use a sharp knife to cut 5 or 6 slits in crust so steam can escape. Bake as directed by the filling recipe. Use dough scraps to make Grandmother's Knuckles.

Notes

Cold butter makes flaky layers while warm butter melts into flour and makes a tougher crust.

If dough is too stiff to roll, let it warm up a little. If it's too soft, scrape it up and refrigerate or freeze again. If it is sticky, add a little flour.

Time saver: make one pie crust for now and one for the freezer. It will keep for up to a month.

Grandmother's Knuckles

Gather up any extra pie dough and squeeze in your fist to create a log of dough that is the reverse of your hand, about 3 inches long and an inch wide. If you have a lot of extra dough or two mouths to feed, first divide dough in half.

Put shaped dough into a small container or plastic bag with a little sugar and cinnamon and then shake to coat. Bake on an ungreased small pan with pie until it turns golden brown in spots. Cool for a few minutes and enjoy.

Part V
Resources

Recommended Reading

Cookbooks

How to Cook Everything Vegetarian: Simple Meatless Recipes for Great Food by Mark Bittman. This would be my desert-island cookbook, the one I would take if I could have only one. Bittman's introductions to various foods and techniques will cause you to look at even onions and stir-fries with fresh understanding. His brief, crystal-clear directions and humor make the book seem light, and his variations on most recipes make this 996-page book even more comprehensive than its shear heft would indicate.

Madhur Jaffrey's World Vegetarian: More than 650 Meatless Recipes from Around the World. You won't find trendy or fussy food here burdened with faux meat or garish garnishes. Instead, you'll find the international equivalent of the church ladies' cookbooks. This is how mamas cook around the globe.

The Bread Bible by Rose Levy Beranbaum. Most "bibles" aren't worth the name, but Beranbaum delivers in this highly detailed, precise, and clear masterpiece. She explains techniques that others never mention, such as why to scald milk before using it in a yeast dough. Learn to make amazing bread with more time and sometimes more expensive ingredients than my recipes ask for.

The Best Recipe by the editors of *Cooks' Illustrated* magazine. These crazy people try dozens of variations to improve recipes and then tell you about them, step-by-step. The resulting recipes are very good, but even more valuable is the model for refining your own recipes until you think they are the best.

Food Politics and Philosophy

Animal, Vegetable, Miracle: A Year of Food Life by Barbara Kingsolver. If you're thinking about becoming more of a locavore and want to know what it's like at the extreme end, look no further. This page-turner of a memoir delivers with an intimate description of her family's year of growing, raising, and eating only local food. Share the joy of raising chickens, making cheese, and even witnessing heirloom turkey sex!

Food, Inc.: How Industrial Food Is Making Us Sicker, Fatter, and Poorer—And What You Can Do about It: A Participant Guide. Not the gory tour of the abattoir that I feared, this uplifting guide covers current issues in our food systems and what you can do to improve them.

Food Matters: A Guide to Conscious Eating with More Than 75 Recipes by Mark Bittman. If you want to learn more about how food choices can make a difference, read this book. Bittman also covers the forces at work against you, including Big Ag and even our own USDA. The recipes are a little high-end and meaty for me, but he did teach me how to make my own microwave popcorn.

How Hungry Is America? by Joel Berg. Here's a no-holds-barred look at who has been hungry in America, who is hungry now, and why. Berg shows that we're better off now than we were a century ago, but we're worse off than we were in the 1970s. He makes a convincing case for government solutions to hunger instead of a patchwork of volunteer efforts, no matter how well-meaning they may be.

The Omnivore's Dilemma: A Natural History of Four Meals by Michael Pollan. Pollan asked the simple question that triggered a wave of food books and activism: what *should* omnivores eat, since they *can* eat everything? *Dilemma* reads like an adventure novel with a scientist hero, with Pollan embedded in food systems from the industrial to the primitive.

Other Irresistible Reads

On Food and Cooking: The Science and Lore of the Kitchen by Harold McGee. I keep this book with the dictionary on the top shelf of my reading table. I pull it out whenever I get stuck with a recipe or want spend an amusing moment learning about food chemistry and history.

Cooking Green: Reducing Your Carbon Footprint in the Kitchen by Kate Heyhoe. This guide is bursting with easy ways to reduce your "cookprint," including tips on choosing which appliances to use and how to coast your way to savings.

Thank You for Smoking by Christopher Buckley. What is a comic novel about the tobacco industry doing in the company of all these food books? *Thank You for Smoking* is a devastatingly funny evisceration of a tobacco lobbyist and the other self-proclaimed Merchants of Death that he pals around with: the lobbyists for the firearms and alcohol industries. Reading this book will not only make you laugh so hard you'll cry, it will also help you decode Big Ag's defense of industrial agriculture.

Recipes by Oven Temperature

300°F
Roasted Pumpkin Seeds

350°F
Chocolate Pumpkin Snack Cake
Chocolate Upside-Down Cake
Cocoa Cookies
Ginger-Glazed Carrot Cake
Good Whisk Bread
Magic Quiche with Asparagus
Oatmeal-Raisin Cookies
Peanut Butter Cookies
Pumpkin Bread
Two-for-One Apple-Streusel
    Coffee Cake
Whisk Sandwich Bread

375°F
Good Burger Buns
Harvest Lasagna
Hot-Milk Cake
Whisk Burger Buns

400°F
Corn Bread
Feel-Good Peach Cobbler
Sweet Raisin Flatbread or
    Breakfast Focaccia
Swiss Chard Frittata

425°F
Blueberry Pie
Proud Black-Bean Burgers

450°F
Garlic Flatbread
Oven Fries
Pizza
Roasted Apples (flexible: roast
    from 400° to 475°F)
Roasted Vegetables

Vegan-Friendly Recipes

Most of these recipes use no animal products. For the ones that do, substitute corn oil for butter, beet or vegan sugar for honey, and skip the cheese.

Babe's Split Pea Soup
Basic Beans and Peas: Cooking Dried
    Legumes
Bean and Tomato Stew
Bean Burritos
Bean Salad with Fresh Corn, Peppers,
    and Tomatoes
Bean-Broth Gravy
Black Beans in Baked Winter Squash
    with Persian Tomato Sauce
Broth Jar
Chickpea Stew on Couscous
Cuban Black Beans and Black Bean Soup
Enchilada Sauce
Fresh and Easy Salsa
Garlic Flatbread
Garlic Toast
Glazed Carrots
Good Tomato Sauce
Good Whisk Bread
Greek Potato Salad
Green Beans and Marinated Green Beans
Green Salad
Grilled Summer Squash Two Ways
Halloween Pumpkin Puree
Hoppin' John
Hummus
Jack O' Lantern Soup
Lentil Stew with Spring Onions

Noodles in Spicy Peanut Sauce with
    Seasonal Vegetables
Noodles Cooked in Very Little Water
Nutty Rice Salad
Oatmeal for Breakfast Six Ways
Parsley Pesto
Persian Tomato Sauce
Pizza Sauce
Pizza: Putting It All Together
Red Bean Chili
Refried Beans
Rice
Soft Tacos with Refried Beans
Southern Summer Pesto
Southwestern Bean Stew: Heirloom Beans
    with Tomatoes and Roasted Corn
Spanish Rice
Spicy Black-Eyed Peas
Stoup
Tasty Tahini Greens
Tomato Sauce with Bell Peppers and
    Onions
Tomato Sauce with Robust Greens and
    Onions
Tomato Sauce with Spring Onions
Tomato Sauce with Summer Squash
Tortilla Stacks
Whisk Burger Buns
Whisk Pizza Dough

Acknowledgments

Thanks to Jill Nussinow, Registered Dietitian and author of *The Veggie Queen*, for her nutritional guidance.

Thanks to Nancy Olson and the crew at Quail Ridge Books & Music for advice and encouragement; Elizabeth Beal and Nancy Halberstadt at Whole Foods Market for launching my cooking classes; to Erin Kauffman at the Durham Farmers' Market for hosting my first market demo; and to Robyn Mooring and Christine and Bill Ramsey for producing the first Cook for Good videos. Thanks to Andrea Weigl at the *News and Observer* for writing the first article about Cook for Good and to my energetic agent, Lisa DiMona, for discovering me and shepherding this book into print. Thanks to my editor, Katie McHugh, and everyone at Da Capo Lifelong; Lori Hobkirk at the Book Factory; copy editor Josephine Mariea; and Cynthia Young at Sagecraft for their creativity, insight, and attention to detail. Thanks to Jan Leitschuh for suggesting the wildly great title.

Thanks to my market pal Laura Boyes for designing my apron and to Barbara Barron for sharing her home ec-spertise.

Thanks to my newsletter subscribers, class participants, and visitors to my demos, who helped tune the *Wildly Affordable Organic* recipes and way of living. And thanks to all the farmers, co-op and market managers, grocers, and all involved in creating a sustainable food system for making the world such a delicious place.

NOTES

Introduction

1. All prices in WAO were gathered in the appropriate season in 2010 in or near Raleigh, North Carolina.

2. "Food and Nutrition Services," North Carolina Division of Social Services, http://www.ncdhhs.gov/dss/foodstamp/index.htm.

3. "Official USDA Food Plans: Cost of Food at Home at Four Levels, U.S. Average, August 2010," United States Department of Agriculture, http://www.cnpp.usda.gov/Publications/Food Plans/2010/CostofFoodAug10.pdf. Food plan referenced is for a family of four with two adults aged nineteen to fifty and two children aged from six to eight and nine to eleven years.

Chapter 1

1. Michael Pollan, "You Are What You Grow," *The New York Times*, April 22, 2007, http://www.nytimes.com/2007/04/22/magazine/22wwlnlede.t.html.

2. Kelly McCormack, "Food Stamp Diet," The Hill, May 23, 2007, http://thehill.com/capital-living/23926-food-stamp-diet.

Chapter 2

1. Jeanne Yacoubou, "Is Your Sugar Vegan?" *Vegetarian Journal* no. 4, 2007, 15–19, http://www.vrg.org/journal/vj2007issue4/VJ4_2007-Sugar.pdf.

2. Rose Levy Beranbaum, *The Bread Bible* (New York: W. W. Norton & Company, 2003), 550–551.

3. Tara Parker-Pope, "Eating Brown Rice to Cut Diabetes Risk," *The New York Times*, June 15, 2010, http://well.blogs.nytimes.com/2010/06/15/eating-brown-rice-to-cut-diabetes-risk/.

4. Marion Nestle, "The Salmonella-in-Eggs Situation Gets Worse," Food Politics, August 20, 2010, http://www.foodpolitics.com/2010/08/the-salmonella-in-eggs-situation-gets-worse/.

5. "Milk: America's Health Problem," Cancer Prevention Coalition, http://www.preventcancer.com/consumers/general/milk.htm.

6. "Organic Food: Eating with a Clean Conscience," Beyond Pesticides, http://www.beyondpesticides.org/organicfood/conscience/index.htm?cat=2.

7. Anna M. Balinova, Rositsa I. Mladenova, and Deyana D. Shtereva, "Effects of Processing on Pesticide Residues in Peaches Intended for Baby Food, *Food Additives and Contaminants* 23, no. 9, pt. A (September 2006): 895–901, http://www.fstadirect.com/GetRecord.aspx?AN=2006-12-Jd4550.

8. John P. Reganold et al., "Fruit and Soil Quantity of Organic and Conventional Strawberry Agroecosystems," *PloS ONE*, September 1, 2010, http://www.plosone.org/article/info%3Adoi%2F10.1371%2Fjournal.pone.0012346.

9. Andrew Schneider, "Don't Let Claims on Honey Labels Dupe You," *Seattle Post-Intelligencer*, http://www.seattlepi.com/local/394198_honey31.asp.

10. "Organic Honey Standards in Canada," Central Beekeepers Alliance, August 16, 2008, http://cba.stonehavenlife.com/2008/08/organic-honey-standards-in-canada/#forage.

11. Andrew Schneider, "Honey Laundering: A Sticky Trail of Intrigue and Crime," *Seattle Post-Intelligencer*, December 30, 2008, http://www.seattlepi.com/local/394053_honey30.asp.

12. "Bronson Announces First Regulation in the Nation Banning Additives in Honey," Florida Department of Agriculture and Consumer Services, July 13, 2009, http://www.doacs.state.fl.us/press/2009/07132009.html.

Chapter 4

1. Chris L. Jenkins, "Rising Prices Hit Home for Food Stamp Recipients," *The Washington Post*, May 27, 2008, http://www.washingtonpost.com/wp-dyn/content/article/2008/05/26/AR2008052601821.html.

2. David Pimentel and Marcia H. Pimentel, *Food Energy, and Society*, 3d ed. (Boca Raton, FL: CRC Press, 2008), 249–252.

3. Cat Warren, "Thirsty? Dirty? Sorry!," *The Independent Weekly*, January 30 2008, http://www.indyweek.com/indyweek/thirsty-dirty-sorry/Content?oid=1206210.

4. "Fact Sheet on Questions about Bottled Water and Fluoride," Centers for Disease Control and Prevention, updated December 9, 2009, http://www.cdc.gov/FLUORIDATION/fact_sheets/bottled_water.htm.

5. Rob Stein, "A Regular Soda a Day Boosts Weight Gain," *The Washington Post*, August 25, 2004, A01, http://www.washingtonpost.com/wp-dyn/articles/A29434-2004Aug24.html.

6. Julie Steenhuysen, "No Safe Haven: Diet Sodas Linked with Health Risks," Reuters, July 23, 2007, http://www.reuters.com/article/idUSN2339241420070723.

7. Mary Rothschild, "Study Says BPA Exposure, Risk Higher than Assumed," Food Safety News, September 23, 2010, http://www.foodsafetynews.com/2010/09/study-says-bpa-exposure-worse-than-previous-estimates/.

Chapter 5

1. Allison Aubrey, "What Does It Take to Clean Fresh Food?" National Public Radio, September 20, 2007, http://www.npr.org/templates/story/story.php?storyId=14540742.

2. Tara Parker-Pope, "Unlocking the Benefits of Garlic," *The New York Times*, October 15, 2007, http://well.blogs.nytimes.com/2007/10/15/unlocking-the-benefits-of-garlic/.

3. Anahad O'Connor, "The Claim: Never Drink Hot Water from the Tap," *The New York Times*, January 29, 2008, http://www.nytimes.com/2008/01/29/health/29real.html.

4. Rose Levy Beranbaum, *The Cake Bible* (New York: William Morrow and Company, 1988), 438.

5. Elizabeth Bomze, "Digital Scales," *Cook's Illustrated*, September/October 2008, 23.

Chapter 6

1. "Obesity and Overweight," Centers for Disease Control and Prevention, updated June 18, 2010, http://www.cdc.gov/nchs/fastats/overwt.htm. This figure is for noninstitutionalized adults aged twenty years old and older.

2. "Health: OECD Says Governments Must Fight Fat," Organisation for Economic Co-Operation and Development, September 23, 2010, http://www.oecd.org/document/35/0,3343,en_21571361_44315115_46064099_1_1_1_1,00.html.

3. "Learn More!" Small Plate Movement, http://smallplatemovement.org/learn_more.htm.

4. Hunger and Poverty Statistics, Feeding America, http://feedingamerica.org/faces-of-hunger/hunger-101/hunger-and-poverty-statistics.aspx.

5. Brian Wansink, *Mindless Eating: Why We Eat More Than We Think* (New York: Bantam Dell, 2006), 70–76.

6. Anthony Bourdain, *Kitchen Confidential: Adventures in the Culinary Underbelly* (New York: Ecco Press, 2000), 83.

Chapter 7

1. Jura Koncius, "Nickel Tax on Disposable Bags Prompts People to Turn to Reusable Bags," *The Washington Post*, February 4, 2010, http://www.washingtonpost.com/wp-dyn/content/article/2010/02/02/AR2010020202855.html.

2. Charles P. Gerba, David Williams, and Ryan G. Sinclair, "Assessment of the Potential for Cross Contamination of Food Products by Reusable Shopping Bags," The University of Arizona UA News, http://uanews.org/pdfs/GerbaWilliamsSinclair_BagContamination.pdf.

Chapter 10

1. "Dietary Guidelines for Americans 2005," U.S. Department of Health and Human Services, http://www.cnpp.usda.gov/Publications/DietaryGuidelines/2005/2005DGPolicyDocument.pdf.

2. World Health Organization, *Diet, Nutrition and the Prevention of Chronic Diseases*, WHO Technical Series 916, section 5.7.3, http://www.fao.org/DOCREP/005/AC911E/ac911e00.htm.

3. T. Colin Campbell and Thomas M. Campbell II, *The China Study: The Most Comprehensive Study of Nutrition Ever Conducted and the Startling Implications for Diet, Weight Loss, and Long-term Health* (Dallas: BenBella Books, 2006), 205.

4. Jane Brody, "A New You: Jane E. Brody on Nutrition," *The New York Times*, January 29, 2008, http://science.blogs.nytimes.com/2008/01/28/a-new-you-jane-e-brody-on-nutrition/?apage=2.

Chapter 16

1. U.S. Department of Agriculture, *USDA National Nutrient Database*, http://www.nal.usda.gov/fnic/foodcomp/search/. Bean broth protein value from liquid from stewed kidney beans.

2. Jane E. Brody, *Good Food Book: Living the High-Carbohydrate Way* (New York: W. W. Norton & Company, 1985), 59–63.

3. Harold McGee, *On Food and Cooking: The Science and Lore of the Kitchen* (New York: Scribner, 2004), 48.

Chapter 17

1. USDA National Nutrient Database, http://www.nal.usda.gov/fnic/foodcomp/search/. Bean broth protein value is from liquid from stewed kidney beans.

2. Office of Dietary Supplements, "Dietary Supplement Fact Sheet: Folate," National Institutes of Health, updated April 15, 2009, http://ods.od.nih.gov/factsheets/folate.asp.

3. Steve Sando, "Viva Frijoles!" Rancho Gordo, http://www.ranchogordo.com/html/rg_cook_advanced_beans.htm.

4. Jan Havlicek and Pavlina Lenochova, "The Effect of Meat Consumption on Body Odor Attractiveness," Chemical Senses 31, no. 8 (2006): 747–52, http://chemse.oxfordjournals.org/content/31/8/747.short.

5. National Center for Complementary and Alternative Medicine, "Herbs at a Glance: Soy," National Institutes of Health, http://nccam.nih.gov/health/soy/.

6. "Is This the Most Dangerous Food for Men?: Soy's Negative Effects," *Men's Health*, http://www.menshealth.com/men/nutrition/food-for-fitness/soys-negative-effects/article/0ad3803313651210VgnVCM10000013281eac/2.

7. Harold McGee, *On Food and Cooking: The Science and Lore of the Kitchen* (New York: Scribner, 2004), 488–489.

8. "Bad Bug Book—Phytohaemagglutinin," U.S. Food and Drug Administration, updated May 4, 2009, http://www.fda.gov/Food/FoodSafety/FoodborneIllness/FoodborneIllnessFoodborne PathogensNaturalToxins/BadBugBook/ucm071092.htm.

Chapter 20

1. Harold McGee, "How Much Water Does Pasta Really Need?" *New York Times*, February 24, 2009, http://www.nytimes.com/2009/02/25/dining/25curi.html.

Chapter 23

1. J. P., "Curcumin Research," Healthy Fellow: Your Natural Health Critic, July 28, 2009, http://www.healthyfellow.com/303/curcumin-research/.

2. S. Salvioli, E. Sikora, E. L. Cooper, and C. Franceschi, "Curcumin in Cell Death Processes: A Challenge for CAM of Age-Related Pathologies," *Evidence-based Complementary and Alternative Medicine, Oxford Journals* 4, no. 2 (April 2007): 181–190, http://ecam.oxfordjournals.org/cgi/content/full/4/2/181.

Chapter 24

1. U.S. Department of Agriculture, "U.S. Food Consumption Up 16 Percent Since 1970," *Amber Waves: The Economics of Food, Farming, Natural Resources, and Rural America,* November 2005, http://www.ers.usda.gov/AmberWaves/November05/Findings/usfoodconsumption.htm.

2. U.S. Department of Agriculture, "Nutrition and Brain Function: Food for the Aging Mind," *Agricultural Research Magazine* 55, no. 7 (August 27, 2007), http://www.ars.usda.gov/is/ar/archive/aug07/aging0807.htm.

Index

Note: The letter t after a page number indicates a table.